Voices from Pulpit and Pew

A MEMOIR FROM RETIREMENT

BRUCE J. JOHNSON

WESTBOW
PRESS®
A DIVISION OF THOMAS NELSON
& ZONDERVAN

WestBow Press books may be ordered through booksellers or by contacting:

WestBow Press
A Division of Thomas Nelson & Zondervan
1663 Liberty Drive
Bloomington, IN 47403
www.westbowpress.com
844-714-3454

Scripture quotations are taken from the New Revised Standard Version Bible, copyright 1989, Division of Christian Education of the National Council of the Churches of Christ in the United States of America. Used by permission. All rights reserved.

ISBN: 979-8-3850-0357-0 (sc)
ISBN: 979-8-3850-0358-7 (e)

Library of Congress Control Number: 2023913723

Print information available on the last page.

WestBow Press rev. date: 8/25/2023

Dedication

To Lois, my dearest wife and trusted partner in life and ministry, without whom my long and meaningful ministry would not have been possible.

CONTENTS

Appendixes

ACKNOWLEDGMENTS

Members and friends of the First Congregational Church of Coventry, CT., staff and the community of Coventry whose voices have inspired mine and whose hearts, so trustingly and charitably open to me, taught me significant things about life and death, friendship and faith, sacrifice, and service.

Reverend Dr. Elizabeth Kennard-a trusted and talented colleague and friend whose initial review and thorough edit of my manuscript encouraged me to persevere in completing this book.

Reverend David Taylor is a much admired and notably successful colleague upon whose collegiality and ministerial insights I have relied on while staying true to this project's mission.

Mr. Larry Mickel, a friend, educator, and lifelong churchman, has been generous with his time and a well-developed skill of wordsmithing. I am grateful for the many ways he has affirmed my instincts and insights and what might be called 'best practice' for ministry.

Mr. David Olzewski has for several years been my 'go-to' computer consultant, sometimes even taking over my computer to ease my anxiety and lessen my frustration and to help me complete essential tasks.

Mr. and Mrs. James and Karen Bement are active and trusted members of the church and good friends. They were integral to the administrative and ministerial duties of the First Church. Recently, they helped to collect and communicate the images in the book, and Jim actively corrected my computer missteps.

Mr. Scott Rhoades, a celebrated local artist and longtime member of First Church, provided his most recent pen and ink rendering of the church for the cover of this book.

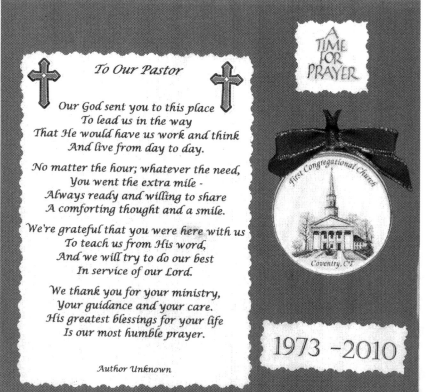

A TIME FOR PRAYER

To Our Pastor

Our God sent you to this place
To lead us in the way
That He would have us work and think
And live from day to day.

No matter the hour; whatever the need,
You went the extra mile -
Always ready and willing to share
A comforting thought and a smile.

We're grateful that you were here with us
To teach us from His word,
And we will try to do our best
In service of our Lord.

We thank you for your ministry,
Your guidance and your care.
His greatest blessings for your life
Is our most humble prayer.

Author Unknown

First Congregational Church

Coventry, CT

1973 –2010

INTRODUCTION

On April 29, a cheerful Sunday morning in the spring of 1973, I preached a sermon for the position of Pastor/Teacher of the First Congregational Church of Coventry, Connecticut. I must have done an acceptable job because I was subsequently called to the position. Now, almost fifty years later, it is still fun to answer inquiries about my career with the response: "First Church, my first and only church." What seems most remarkable, at least in terms of my perceptions and feelings about our covenant, is that what was true for me then about the integrity and authenticity of my call to Christian ministry and the pastorate at First Church is equally and enduringly true today. I felt called and blessed then. I feel called and blessed today, even after thirteen years of retirement.

When I was presented to the membership of First Church, the Pulpit Supply Committee printed a brochure recommending me as their candidate. As an introduction, I wrote for that brochure a few words about my understanding of Christian ministry. I'd like to quote what I wrote:

> *The heart of all Christian ministry rests in the words of Jesus when He said: 'No one has greater love than this, to lay down one's life for one's friends.'*
>
> *(John 15:13, NRSV)*

I still believe that observation about ministry. When I wrote those words, however, I am sure that I was thinking more in terms of the laying down and opening of my life for the congregation than theirs for me. What I have learned over these five decades of experience and reflection, though, is that the essence of my experience in Coventry had more to do with the latter than the former. Once called as pastor/teacher, I now sense that I was, in fact, more the pastor/pupil. The irony of these decades is that while I was called to be the pastor/teacher, to preach the gospel and teach the faith, in fact, the congregation assumed those functions as often, if not more often, than I did. Congregants gave themselves generously and taught me about faith, forgiveness, justice, hope, and love. We became the friends Jesus had envisioned, exchanging stories of what we knew and didn't know, what helped and what hurt, and what love looked and felt like in life. Along with me, they both talked about faith and lived it. They gifted me the privilege of taking part in their religious stories, teaching me nearly all I know about ministry. I am profoundly grateful for their sacrifices, generosity, and affection. This memoir is born of that gratitude and represents my effort to preserve in writing not only something of a historical account of our years together but to recognize and record the voices that have spoken over these years from pulpit and pew with such authenticity and effectiveness about our Christian faith and ministry.

Several years ago, the Reverend Thomas Adil, one of six members of our parish who were ordained into Christian ministry during my tenure as pastor, introduced me to a quote from the philosopher, Pascal:

> *The heart has its reasons, of which reason knows nothing…*
> *We know the truth not only by reason, but by the heart.*[1]

One of the joyful discoveries I made during the planning and completion of this project is that although at certain times in our lives the heart may have its reasons that reason does not know, in time and as gifts of grace, the heart eventually reveals those reasons and reason understands better.

In his book, *The 8ᵗʰ Habit: From Effectiveness to Greatness*, Stephen R. Covey cited a plaque that hangs on the wall at a roadside store in rural North Carolina:

> *The brain said, 'I'm the smartest organ in the body.'*
> *The heart said, 'Who told you?'*[2]

---

[1] Blaise Pascal, Pensées.

[2] Stephen R. Covey, *The 8ᵗʰ Habit: From Effectiveness to Greatness* (Free Press, New York, 2004) p. 51.

The heart tells and teaches us everything. I learned this fundamental truth at First Church. Today, I understand better what has truly been ordained and covenanted about my pastoral relationship with this congregation and its relationship with me. This memoir is about what I think and feel after four decades of service and one decade of retirement. I hope I can speak effectively from the heart about what I learned, sharing the plans and possibilities God had in mind for us on that cheerful Sunday morning in 1973. To do otherwise would, I'm sure, feel like a betrayal of our unique covenant. George E. Valliant, the author of a celebrated book on aging titled *Aging Well,* rightly made the following observation:

The heart speaks with so much more vitality than the head. [3]

This book reveals the belief that my head has gained a better understanding of ministry from the hearts of those who spoke with such vitality over the years from our pulpit and pews.

---

[3]   George E. Vaillant, *Aging Well: Surprising Guideposts to a Happier Life* (Little Brown and Company, Boston, 2002) p. 15.

CHAPTER I

The First Congregational Church of Coventry

"Where Dreams and Visions Become Reality"

A BRIEF HISTORY[4]
(1712-2010)

The First Church of Coventry was established when a group of early Christian homesteaders arrived in the northeast corner of the state during Queen Anne's reign (1702-14). Jonathan Edwards was a promising prodigy in an East Windsor, Connecticut parsonage. In 1701, Yale College was founded in New Haven, while the city of Hartford was only a small settlement on the banks of the Connecticut River. The state was in its seventy-eighth year and governed by the Hooker Constitution.

The people who settled in Coventry were of that same sturdy stock that settled Massachusetts and the rest of Connecticut. They came mainly from Northampton, Massachusetts, and Hartford, but there were also families from Reading and Lancaster, Massachusetts, and from Stonington, Killingworth, and Windham, Connecticut. In his much relied upon history of the First Congregational Church of Coventry, Henry E. Robinson notes that the town was established in May 1706 by the General Court, but it was

---

4   Much of the information included here comes from a brochure that was printed for the 250th anniversary of the church, 1962. It was titled; "A Brief History."

not until 1711 that it received its name of Coventry. A petition to the General Court asking for permission to lay a tax upon the land for the support of a minister was submitted and granted in 1712.[5] The church secured lands overlooking the lake, where now we enjoy the town's Green. Here they constructed their first meetinghouse in 1716 and a congregation worshipped there until 1869. Historians dispute how many meetinghouses were near the Green, but records suggest one was enlarged in 1736 and replaced in 1766. Fire destroyed this building in 1897 and today, only a marker remains.

In the early days, church and town were virtually one. In fact, only church members could vote in town elections, and they held town meetings in the church meetinghouse. We find in the church records that the town voted thirty-five pounds in 1715 toward the building of the first meetinghouse. A few months later, the town appropriated forty-five pounds for the same purpose. They voted money for glazing the windows in 1716. Yankee thrift and a pay as you go policy postponed further work until 1719 when twenty pounds was voted to finish the balcony. Church attendance was mandatory, and the building proved too small. In 1736, the meetinghouse was enlarged by adding seven feet on each end of the building. The completion of the galleries happened in 1738.

In 1745, the people in the northern part of town, finding difficulty in making the long trip "through the wilderness" to the First Church Meeting House for worship, received permission from the General Court to establish the Second Church and Parish. Shortly thereafter, Andover organized as a separate church and parish, drawing its members from both Coventry parishes.

The exceptional ability of the pastors and their long pastorates marked the first century of the church. It was the age of the homespun, the homemade, and the handmade. Everyone in the community went to church. There they got their news and spiritual food and sense of purpose. Law compelled all to keep Sunday, and the halfway covenant was the practice of the church. [6] Most of the day on Sunday was spent at the meetinghouse, and we read of several families who built "Sabbath houses" near the meetinghouse, in which

---

[5]   Henry E. Robinson, A History of the First Congregational Church of Coventry, South Coventry, Connecticut (Hartford: Hartford Seminary Foundation, 1939) pp. 5-6.

[6]   For an excellent discussion of the Half-Way Covenant, enjoy reading *The New England Soul* by Dr. Harry Stout, a Coventry resident, and a University of Connecticut professor. (pp. 58-61.)

they could rest, eat, and keep warm between services. This was also a trying time for the church. During this period, the foundations of society were laid. The Meeting House had to be built, maintained, and enlarged, while people constructed homes for themselves and went about daily duty of providing for their families. There were periods of revival and periods of spiritual depression. One church member, Nathan Hale, became nationally and historically famous for patriotic martyrdom. Another, Jesse Root, became a man of renown as jurist, chief justice of Connecticut, congressional representative, and a distinguished member of the Constitutional Convention of 1818.

During the second century of the First Church's existence, there were significant changes in both the people's way of life and the church's life. The Industrial Revolution brought many industries into Coventry, with mills springing up along the brook in the village. The adoption of the new State Constitution in 1813 brought an end to church as a state supported institution. Both attendance at worship and support of the church became voluntary. Much shorter pastorates, fluctuating membership and interest, and a division in the church marked this period.

By 1842, the old building on the hill needed major repairs. One group in the church wished to repair the old meetinghouse, whereas another, a larger group, desired to erect a new building in the new center of town along the mill stream. The result was a split between one group, which kept their worship services in the old meetinghouse, and another group, which moved to the village and became The Village Church. This structure, our present meetinghouse, was erected at a cost of $10,491 and was dedicated on June 28, 1849. The architectural authenticity of the building has been preserved, with the exception being a flat metal ceiling installed in 1899, when the church was redecorated, thus covering the original plaster dome ceiling. The top of the dome ceiling is still visible under the rafters and may be seen by climbing the stairs to the bell tower.

The bell bears the following inscription:

First Bell Cast AD. 1848
Destroyed by Fire AD. 1903

PROV. VIII, IV, UNTO YOU, O MEN, I CALL;
AND MY VOICE IS TO THE SONS OF MAN.

First Congregational Church
South Coventry, CT.

The two Congregational churches in South Coventry struggled to survive for a long time until they achieved church union on January 6, 1869. A mutual council voted for the union, and the newly formed church started with 138 members. Members adopted the original name, the First Church of Coventry. Sadly, the old meetinghouse on the hill sat unused for almost thirty years and was destroyed by fire on June 1,1897.

The first record of a parsonage is from 1870 to 1875, when the Ladies' Society purchased land on Wall Street and built a parsonage. This home continued to be the parsonage for the First Church of Coventry and the First Congregational Church of Coventry until it was sold in 1956. A new parsonage, on Nathan Hale Drive, was purchased, and it served as the parsonage until 1978, when the trend among ministers in the United Church of Christ became home ownership. Our minister, the Reverend Dr. Bruce Johnson, and his wife, Lois, purchased a home on Barnsbee Lane in November 1977, and the church sold the Nathan Hale Drive parsonage in 1978. Today, the church does not own a parsonage.

During this same second century of its life, the First Church of Coventry had both periods of revival and periods when the life of the church ebbed very low. Interest in missions grew in New England in this century and the First Church gave generously to them. During this period, the Sunday school also came into being, although it was called Sabbath School until about 1888.

In 1901, the First Church of Coventry became the First Congregational Church of Coventry. During all its preceding years, the church and the two churches during the period of division were combined with the Ecclesiastical Society, which handled all the funds and owned and controlled all church property. In April 1891, the First Congregational Ecclesiastical Society of South Coventry was dissolved. All funds and properties were turned over to the First Congregational Church of Coventry, and from that time on, the church controlled all its own funds and affairs.

The third century of life and ministry at the church has been an extraordinary one. As had been the case before, there have been times of growth and prosperity and times when, but for the faithful service of a few members, the church would have died. Thirteen ministers have served during this period with several serving only two years. A couple of unrelated Johnsons hold the longest pastorates. The Reverend Dr. Charles G. Johnson served for fourteen years, 1921 to 1935. Reverend Dr. Bruce J. Johnson has been the minister for thirty-seven years, 1973-2010. The church grew and developed under his leadership. Property, budget, and membership were the main areas of growth. Over this period, the church purchased a couple of strategic, contiguous pieces of property, enabling the church to expand its ministries and parking lot and build its Center for Christian Education. The budget grew from $25,964 in 1973 to $306,128 in 2004. In June 1973, there were 310 members. In 2005, the church had 669 active members. Finally, in the year of Reverend Johnson's retirement, 2010, the church had 634 active members, and that membership set the annual budget at $288, 985.

Well documented is the fact that the twentieth century brought with it enormous changes throughout society and the world, sweeping changes and broad strokes of human history that have in no small way affected the life and ministry of the church. The effects of war (WWI, WWII, Korea, Vietnam, and most recently, Gulf Wars I and II), automobiles, televisions, computers, space science, travel, the internet, and regrettably, presidential scandals have all had an enormous impact. The church has not functioned in a vacuum, but within the context of a society, nation and world challenged by the ebb and flow of events and experiences, inventions, and lessons learned, and mistakes repeated. Throughout, it has remained steadfast in its trust in the gospel and has spoken to the times and issues from its perspective of faith.

No less dramatic in some ways, however, have been the changes in and around First Church, especially over the last fifty years. First, most immediate to any observer are changes that have taken place in terms of the facilities. These have been years of rising enrollment in the Church School and a deeper commitment to youth ministry. The church purchased several properties and completed construction projects to meet Christian education needs. The Phillips house, on the corner of Main and Mason, was purchased in 1954 and dedicated to Mr. Louis A. Kingsbury as the Kingsbury House. During this time, there were large numbers of students and double sessions, and the Kingsbury House and Quandt Hall were the education center until 1971. However, the church was in dire financial straits, and concerns were raised over the safety of children walking from Sunday school to the church. Amid these adversities and other concerns, a new vision was born. It began with the courageous and skilled renovation of the church hall, which was commonly called 'the vestry' by the members of the church. It was an enormous project to be undertaken by the congregation, but they completed the task. The Auditor's Report for 1971 shows that donations amounted to \$9,347.13 and disbursements were \$9,245.21. The pastor, the Reverend James McBride, guided the congregation, rekindling their spirit and imagination. This led some to dream of owning land near the church. They could see what our physical plant could be, were we to have the opportunity and resources to purchase the properties. Still more members set out to make it happen. What transpired over the next twenty years certainly seems providential. The list of acquisitions is:

> Kenyon property---1969
> Burnham property---1972
> Lang property---1982

Smith property---1984 saw the purchase of the Smith property, and the building on it with four apartments. The building was then moved to the Lang property, which is now home to a housing complex of seven apartment units.

Uplifting event

Dreams and Visions
December 5th, 1985

The crowning achievement of this renewed energy and expansive vision was the construction of our Center for Christian Education (1985-1987), whose painted white clapboards continue to glisten in the sun for all who look to the church as a sign of hope and promise, both for the church and the community. Throughout the building there are memorial plaques that pay tribute to the tireless efforts and extraordinary generosity of members, past and present. On just about every day of the week and especially during the school year, the church serves as a hub of ecclesiastical and educational activity as children from all over the community pass through its doors to attend private and public preschool classes, choir rehearsals, Sunday school classes for all ages and youth group programs.

In 1996, the church voted to replace its thirty-year-old Allen organ with a new state-of-the-art electronic MDS 51-S Allen organ, which cost $39,635. They installed the magnificent instrument in early October 1997, and a dedicatory service was done on January 6, 1998. Richard Grant, the renowned organ recitalist, performed a marvelous recital on May 31, 1998, for the Allen Organ Company.

During the final year of the century, members and friends of the First Church worked through the arduous process of writing a "Mission Statement" for the First Congregational Church of Coventry. Only after many meetings and revisions was an acceptable draft approved at a special meeting of the church membership held on January 23, 2000. The "Mission Statement" of the church reads:

THE mission of the First Congregational Church of Coventry is to worship and serve God through word and deed. In the name of Jesus Christ, we welcome and include all people as sisters and brothers.

WE pledge and dedicate our lives and resources to God, working to transform both church and society into more just and compassionate communities.

WE fulfill this mission by faithfully preaching the gospel, by educating our adults and children and by living out the teachings and example of Jesus Christ.

Yet another vision became reality when, on November 26, 2000, we conducted a Service of Dedication at the conclusion of a yearlong renovation project. The list of renovations is impressive:

- Chancel Cross
  Given in loving memory of Rupert and Bertha Hodgkins
  by Clayton and Carol Hodgkins,
  Gerald, Lydia, Rhonda, and Gerald Hodgkins Jr.
  Ronald, Linda, Heather, Heidi and Lindsey Hodgkins Family
  and Friends

- Brass Chandelier
  Given in loving memory of Ruth E. Spink
  By Mark M. Spink and Family

- Hearing Assistance System
  Given in loving memory of Reverend William and Elizabeth North
  By Frederick, II and the Reverend Carol North and Family
  (Mr. Peter R. Hutt crafted and donated a beautiful holder for all
  in celebration of his marriage to Ms. Marcie D. Chavalier. May
  24, 2003)

- Redecoration of Sanctuary
  Done in Memory of Loved Ones
  By Family and Friends

- A display case in the sanctuary holds a "Book of Remembrance," crafted by Mr. Carl Larson to honor those remembered through donations.

Two years later, at a special meeting of the membership of First Church, which was held on January 26, 2002, attention and resources were turned toward the deteriorating exterior of our church. The project included repainting the exterior of the sanctuary, restoring the pillars and porch, adding a wheelchair accessible ramp, and repairing and repainting the steeple. Tom Wilsted led a capital campaign with a budget and challenge goal for *Building on Generations: Preserving Coventry's Historic First Church.* At its conclusion, the campaign was enormously successful, raising in pledges and gifts $120,000. Today, our beautifully restored structure stands as an inspiration to our community, a sign of hope to the world and a tribute to the vitality and commitment of the congregation. [7]

The historic roots of First Church extend deep into the rich soil of "congregationalism." The United Church of Christ resulted from much prayer, discussion, and hard decisions. [8] This brief paragraph appears in our confirmation curriculum and provides a useful synopsis of the chronology:

> *Informal conversations about the desirability of uniting the Congregational Christian Church and the Evangelical and Reformed Church began on March 18, 1941, in Columbus, Ohio. After many conferences between representatives of the two groups. A Basis of Union was adopted in 1948, the union took place 1957 at Cleveland, now the home of the United Church of Christ central offices, and the constitution was adopted in 1961 at Philadelphia.[9].*

---

[7] As a result of a massive failure of an aged chestnut ridge beam in the sanctuary roof in 2019, the ridge had to be repaired and the roof replaced. In addition, the interior of the worship center had to be brought up to code and redecorated, a very costly project indeed! Members of the church and community gathered to rededicate the sanctuary in June 2023.

[8] Robert T. Fauth, "So You Are a Church Member" (United Church Press, 1964), p. 23-24.

[9] My Confirmation, (United Church Press, Philadelphia, 1963)

Bruce J. Johnson

Members of the First Congregational Church of Coventry met on May 14, 1961, at a special meeting that was called for voting on the merger. The minutes of that meeting offer some interesting reading.

A Special meeting of the church was held Sunday evening May 14, 1961 at 7:30 p. m. for discussing and acting upon the following resolution:

Whereas the General Synod of the United Church of Christ has it that this church on July 7, 1960, approved the document entitled 'Constitution of the United Church of Christ,' and

Whereas the General Synod has requested this church to ratify or approve said document and

Whereas said document provides that a vote of ratification or approval will be regarded also as a vote by this church to become part of the United Church of Christ and

Whereas this church also regards its vote of ratification or approval of the Constitution of the United Church of Christ to be a vote to become part of the United Church of Christ,

It is resolved that The First Congregational Church of Coventry, Inc. approves the Constitution of the United Church of Christ.

And it is further resolved that if the United Church of Christ proposes in any way to amend Section 21 of the said Constitution as an autonomous body, this church, by a majority vote of church members present at a special meeting called for the purpose, may withdraw from the United Church of Christ.[10]

Of the members who were present at the special meeting, twenty-eight voted in favor of adoption. One vote was cast against the merger. All eight absentee ballots were in favor of the union.[11] To this day the members of the First Church are zealously "congregational" as supporters of the United Church of Christ. What I mean by this is that we covet our autonomy while we commit fully to being a "united and uniting" church.

---

[10] Today, Section 21 is Article 5, section 18. The opening lines say: 'The autonomy of the Local Church is inherent and modifiable only by its own action. Nothing in this Constitution and the Bylaws of the United Church of Christ shall destroy or limit the right of each Local Church to operate in the way customary to it…" For full text, consult www.ucc.org.

[11] The Pilgrim Church Register, p. 271.

Today, we are in communion with yet another denomination, The Disciples of Christ, and before too long, they too will be members of the United Church of Christ.

And so, as of this writing, the First Congregational Church of Coventry has measured the 311 years since its founding in 1712 with its rule of faith and its call to commitment and community involvement. Over its lifetime of worship and mission, thirty-six called pastors have occupied its pulpits:

MINISTERS OF THE FIRST CONGREGATIONAL CHURCH OF COVENTRY- 1712 TO PRESENT

THE FIRST CHURCH OF COVENTRY- 1712-1769

Reverend Mr. Joseph Meacham	1712-1752
Reverend Mr. Oliver Noble	1759-1761
Reverend Dr. Joseph Huntington	1763-1794
Reverend Mr. Abiel Abbot	1795-1811
Reverend Mr. Chauncy Booth	1815-1844
Reverend Mr. Henry Blake	1845-1848
Reverend Mr. Charles Hyde	1849-1854
Reverend Mr. Joel A. Arnold	1854-1868
Reverend Mr. E. P. Hyde (Supply)	1862

THE VILLAGE CHURCH OF SOUTH COVENTRY 1848-1869

Reverend Mr. Henry Beach Blake	1850-1855
Reverend Mr. Louis E. Charpiot	1859-1861
Reverend Mr. Samuel Brown (Supply)	1862-1864
Reverend Mr. Alphens Winter	1864-1868

THE FIRST CHURCH COVENTRY 1869-1901

Reverend Mr. John P. Hawley	1869-1875
Reverend Mr. E. B. Huntington (Supply)	1875-1877
Reverend Mr. William D. Morton, (Supply)	1877-1880
Reverend I. W. B. Headley (Supply)	1881-1882

Reverend Dr. Frank Edwin Jenkins	1882-1886
Reverend Mr. A. J. Quick	1887-1892
Reverend Mr. Benjamin Franklin Perkins	1892-1897
Reverend Mr. Sidney Hall Barrett	1897-1899
Reverend Mr. Nestor Light	1900

THE FIRST CONGREGATIONAL CHURCH OF COVENTRY 1901- 2023

Reverend Mr. Nestor Light	1901-1912
Reverend Mr. Walter I. Eaton	1913-1915
Reverend Mr. Harris C. Beebe	1916-1920
Reverend Dr. Charles G. Johnson	1921-1935

(Reverend Dr. Charles G. Johnson became the church's first Pastor Emeritus)

Reverend Mr. Henry E. Robinson	1936-1941
Reverend Mr. James A. Dailey	1941-1943
Reverend Mr. Charles D. Broadbend	1943-1945
Reverend Mr. Hugh S. Barbour	1945-1947
Reverend Mr. Harold E. Parsons	1947-1951
Reverend Mr. Truman D. Ireland	1951-1956
Reverend Mr. James R. MacArthur	1956-1966
Reverend Mr. William E. Belden	1966-1969
Reverend Mr. James A. McBride	1969-1972
Reverend Mr. Robert Heavilin (Supply)	1972-1973
Reverend Dr. Bruce J. Johnson	1973- 2010

(Upon his retirement, the membership elected Mr. Johnson the church's second Pastor Emeritus.)

Reverend Dr. Elizabeth S. Kennard	1989-1993
(Associate Pastor)	
Reverend Sara Jane Munshower	2005- 2006
(Settled Supply)	
Reverend James Silver (Interim)	2010 - 2012
Reverend Dr. Sara Worcester	2012 - 2016

Reverend Stephen C. Washburn (Interim)   2017 - 2018
Reverend Dr. Barry McCarthy (Interim)   2018 - 2019
Reverend David C. Nutt   2019 - present

For over three centuries, the First Congregational Church of Coventry has faithfully and effectively shared the power of God's love revealed through Jesus Christ. It has stood proudly as a sign of promise for continuing prosperity in matters of faith, ministry, and mission. Indeed, because we, as a congregation, can look back on our past with such pride, we can turn as well toward our future with confidence and a renewed spirit of a resolute, and relevant Christian faith.

CHAPTER II

Voices from the Pulpit and Pew

'An Operational Theology for an Incarnational Ministry'

Introduction

Retirement offered me time for reflection, and I have embraced both the time and the process so that I might put to print these thoughts about our years of ministry at the First Congregational Church of Coventry. We were truly blessed over these four decades, and I was honored to be our church's pastor/teacher/student over those years and now, since my retirement in 2010, am likewise honored as its Pastor Emeritus. Throughout this time, we have been "doing ministry" in the name of Jesus Christ, and what a faithful and fruitful ministry it has been! We embraced the challenge of being responsible trustees of the rich traditions of the church and of educating and equipping others for the significant tasks of discipleship and Realm building. Over the last few years, however, I felt the need to reflect on who we have been and who we have become. There was this pesky need to identify and express what we have learned and for what purpose. What appears on these few pages is a compilation of my thoughts, and I hope, insights about both the process and the product.

One of my most trusted mentors through the years was my adviser for the Doctor of Ministry program at Boston University, which I completed successfully in 1989. The now late Reverend Dr. Merle Jordan, PhD. (1931—2018) developed and imparted a unique perspective on church life and ministry, one that influenced me significantly. This perspective identified and defined what he called the distinction between an *"operational theology"* and a *"professed theology."* The latter refers to what a believer might think and say about what we believe, derived more from what we have been told and taught by others than experienced ourselves. The former refers to what Jordan calls the "implicit religious story" of an individual or congregation and what it shows to be the actual truth about what we believe and value. Someone once said that the distinction between these two theologies is that one is of the heart and the other is of the head. This may be overly simplistic but still useful. Jordan clarifies operational theology as the religious stories we live by, including our unconscious material. The critical point of difference here is that an "operational theology" emerges naturally from a belief system based upon experience and an "implicit religious story" that reflects and realizes those beliefs. A "professed theology" is more intellectual and creedal. As I reflect on my tenure as pastor of First Church, I appreciate that I have always been more interested in our *"operational theology"* than our *"professed theology,"* that is, more interested in what I have seen and experienced as being at work in the development and unveiling of our religious story, than any set of creedal formulations that purport to interpret those same stories. I have always been more interested and intrigued by the theological themes that emerge from within the transactions of our lives than those that might apply to them.

I would like to share three illustrations that make clear what I understand an "operational theology" to be.

First, during the early years of our ministry, the Willimantic Chronicle, our local daily newspaper, used to provide space in its Saturday edition for a feature called *Saturday Sermon.* Area ministers, priests and rabbis were invited weekly, and rotating, to write a short homily for publication. I did an Advent sermon on December 15, 1979, and as I now look back, it said a great deal about our operational theology.

"Oh, But It Does Matter"
by the Reverend Bruce Johnson
First Congregational Church of Coventry

In his book, *All the Dammed Angels*, Professor William Muehl of Yale Divinity School tells this insightful short story:[12]

> *One December afternoon many years ago, a group of parents stood in the lobby of a nursery school waiting to claim their children after the last pre-Christmas class session. As the youngsters ran from their lockers, each one carried in his or her hands the 'surprise,' the brightly wrapped package on which he or she had been working diligently for weeks. One small boy, trying to run, put on his coat and wave all at the same time, slipped and fell. The 'surprise' flew out of his grasp, landed on the tile floor, and broke with an obvious ceramic crash.*
>
> *The child's first reaction was one of stunned silence. But in a moment, he set up an inconsolable wail. His father, seeking to comfort him, knelt and murmured, 'Now, it doesn't matter, son. It doesn't matter.' His mother, however, much wiser in such affairs, swept the boy into her arms and said, 'Oh but it matters. It matters a great deal.' And she wept with her son.*

This story is poignantly illustrative of what God is trying to say to us during this season of Advent. Oh, but it does matter to God. It matters a great deal whether we are feeling whole, happy, free, and fulfilled. It does matter to God. It matters a great deal whether we believe in our world's prospects for peace and our potential for goodwill in and among all peoples of the world. It does matter to God; it matters a great deal whether we experience the incarnation of God's love amid the shattered dreams and scattered expectations on which we have tried to work so diligently.

Because it does matter, you and I are invited each year to celebrate and experience anew the rejuvenating and reconciling truth and beauty of Christ's birth. We bring to the moments of the month "the hopes and fears of all the years" praying that they will be met in Him. "We hear the Christmas angels, the great glad tidings tell," and pray that He will come to abide with us, our Lord, Emmanuel.

---

[12] William Muehl, *All the Dammed Angels*, (Philadelphia: Pilgrim Press, 1972) p. 39.

During this season, let us all remember that it does matter to God. It matters a great deal whether we come to know and allow ourselves to be comforted and inspired by the beauty, joy and meaning of Christ's birth.

I believe this theme has been integral to our sense of call and identity, to the quality of our life together and the effectiveness of our mission. At no point throughout all these years have I ever sensed that we thought we didn't matter to God. At the heart of our operational theology and central to our worship, our sacramental life and our daily ministries is this fundamental belief: we matter! Three quotes come to mind. One is from the Reverend William Sloane Coffin, the former Chaplain at Yale University. The second is from scripture; and the third is from Professor Jordan:

> *Of God's love, we can say two things: it is poured out universally for everyone from the Pope to the loneliest wino on the planet; and second, God's love doesn't seek value, it creates value. It is not because we have value that we are loved, but because we are loved that we have value.*[13]

> *For God so loved the world that he gave his only Son, so that everyone who believes in him may not perish but may have eternal life.*
>
> (John 3:16, NRSV)

> *... the Loving Heart of Reality initiates atonement for humankind.*[14]

The second anecdote that conveys an essential theme for our operational theology comes from my Doctor of Ministry Program at the Boston University School of Theology. Although I started my studies in 1979 intending to do a program in Christian ethics, during that first summer, I met Professor Merle Jordan, who, like a few others in my life, proved to exercise enormous influence over the shaping of my pastoral identity and my understanding of ministry. In his book, *Taking on the gods: The Task*

---

[13] William Sloane Coffin, *Credo* (Louisville: Westminster John Knox Press, 2004) p.6.

[14] Jordan, p. 31.

of the Pastoral Counselor, he tells a story that illustrates well what has been important to us. The story goes:

> A familiar story concerns a little girl named Maria. Her mother was a devout, religious woman who was trying to raise Maria with a sense of love and acceptance. She didn't want Maria to be a fearful person. The essence of the mother's teachings to Maria was:
>
> "God loves you; God will guide you; God will protect you. You never need to be afraid."
>
> But one night there was a terrible thunderstorm. Maria was in her bedroom by herself. She had her nose pressed to the windowpane, watching the lightning zigzag through the sky, and listening to the crashing of thunder. 'Mommy, Mommy, I'm scared,' she cried out. Her mother came to the door of Maria's room and said, 'Now, Maria, haven't I taught you that God loves you and protects you and you never have to be afraid of anything?' 'I know, Mommy, I believe all that. But tonight, I need someone with skin on.'[15]

Throughout my tenure as pastor of First Church, we were a congregation that has "worn its skin well," being there 'in person' in times of celebration and sorrow, in times of compatibility and conflict.

The third story is a story told by Rabbi Harold Kushner about "a day at the beach," a day that many of us have shared. I know that I have seen the following scenario unfold many times while on vacation in Ocean City, New Jersey. He writes:

> I was sitting on a beach one summer day, watching two children, a boy and a girl, playing in the sand. They were hard at work building an elaborate sandcastle by the water's edge, with gates and towers and moats and internal passages. (At Ocean City, New Jersey, they have competitions, but they are not built within

---

15   Jordan, p. 129.

range of the waves!) Just when they had nearly finished their project, a big wave came along and knocked it down, reducing it to a heap of wet sand. I expected the children to burst into tears, devastated by what had happened to all their hard work. But they surprised me. Instead, they ran up the shore away from the water, laughing and holding hands, and sat down to build another castle. I realized that they had taught me an important lesson. All the things in our lives, all the complicated structures we spent so much time and energy creating, are built on sand. Only our relationships to other people endure. Eventually, the wave will come along and knock down what we have worked so hard to build up. When that happens, only the person who has somebody's hand to hold will laugh.[16]

Interestingly, while Mary Wilsted was our organist and a member of the church, she organized a caring ministry she called 'Helping Hands and Hearts.' At First Church, there was always a hand to hold and always a heart ready to help. Indeed, faith among the members and friends of the First Church has been genuine and deeply personal. We, like Maria, believed deeply. However, creeds can take one only so far, and provide just so much for a people who walk the beaches of life and build their intricate but fragile lives sometimes within reach of the waves. So, we have also been a congregation that has needed one another as persons with "some skin on," who offer to hold each other's hands and be physical presences in times of celebration and sorrow, in times of confidence and confusion, courage and fear.

We can say this same thing differently, in more theological terms, by saying simply that ours has been an incarnational ministry. The word becomes flesh, not just in Jesus, but in us; not just in terms of Jesus' relationship with us, but equally so in our relationship with each other. God is never more God than when He/She has some "skin on."

This chapter contains stories, sermons, letters, and reflections that show our congregation's operational theology. Those included here are but a selected few from among many. Hopefully, they will say enough and reveal my joyful sense that we know we matter to God and to one another, flaws

---

[16]   Rabbi Harold Kushner, "The Power of Holding Hands." (Reprinted under fair use guidelines)

and all. As a people of faith, we have the courage to have our "skin on" and "hands out" to make incarnate the redeeming presence and love of God.

****

Our Implicit Religious Stories

"A Pimple on Prom Night"

In the early days, before copiers and computers, when our church office was equipped only with an electric typewriter and mimeograph machine, the Coventry Broadcaster, a weekly shopper newspaper that was owned and operated by a member of the church, Marion Schultheiss and her daughter and son-in-law, Lynn and Joseph Duval, did most of the church's printing. The Broadcaster published our weekly bulletins, our monthly Church Call, and our annual reports. It was also the primary newspaper for classified advertisements. If you wanted to sell something, a classified ad in The Broadcaster was usually the way to do it. I was in there often, not placing advertisements but imposing on this commercial venture with church matters.

On one visit, I met a young woman, a contemporary, a wife and mother. Her name was Elizabeth Caine. She was a school psychologist by education and professional training, but she sensed God was drawing her toward the Christian ministry. Not long after that meeting, amid the piles of weekly shoppers, Leslie became involved in the church. Given her intellect, spiritual maturity, and her mastery over the written and spoken word, she surprised no one when she volunteered to do a sermon. As expected, she was skilled in crafting her sermon and was superb in her delivery. I will forever remember the opening paragraph for that sermon, the one bearing the catchy title, *Mirror, Mirror on the Wall.* It was a deeply personal recollection from her high school years about a certain prom night.

> *There are two ways of seeing yourself when you look in the mirror. One we recall too easily from our adolescence. Remember getting dressed up for the big dance? The clothes had to be just right, stylish but not faddish, colorful enough to get you noticed but not loud. And you combed your hair and fussed*

with it forever. The guys made sure they got every single whisker
when they shaved, and the girls put on makeup as if they were
reproducing the Mona Lisa. Finally, when you were all done,
you'd stand back and look in the mirror for the last appraising
look. Do you remember what you saw? Did you see how nice
your hair looked, or how well your clothes went together? Your
mother inevitably said you looked perfect, but as you looked in
the mirror, you saw the truth: you saw the pimple. And that's
the only thing you saw! And you were convinced that all night
long, that was the only thing anyone else would see...[17]

I remember that description of her prom night for two reasons. First, it introduced me to a woman's perspective and how effective it could and would be for homiletics. Second, I was so engaged by its theological truth, gifted from a high school experience. The real challenge in life is to see and value ourselves as God sees and values us, not as we are inclined to do. We see only the pimple that renders us vulnerable before the tribunal of judgment that says we're flawed. We are also convinced that everyone else shares that same assessment. Conversely, God sees only His beloved son or daughter and calls us forth, telling us we are not only fine but, in fact, the finest and fairest. Our pimples have no power to change God's mind or diminish God's love. God forgives our sins, flaws, and blemishes, and wants us to accept and affirm who we are. God wants us to see the whole person and celebrate all that is right and good. God also wants us to attend the prom confidently and have fun!

On that Sabbath, Leslie occupied and spoke from both the pulpit and pew and how blessed the congregation was.

Most of us remain strangers to ourselves, hiding who we are,
and ask other strangers, hiding who they are, to love us.[18]
Leo Buscaglia

---

[17] Elizabeth Caine, "Mirror, Mirror, On the Wall." Sermon delivered on March 21, 1982, at The First Congregational Church of Coventry, Connecticut. (Leslie would soon graduate from Yale Divinity School with a Master of Divinity degree, be ordained at First Church on March 13, 1983, and then earn a Doctor of Ministry degree from the Ecumenical Theological Seminary in Detroit.)

[18] Leo Buscaglia, *Born for Love* (New York: Ballentine Books, 1992), p. 165.

Bruce J. Johnson

****

"Hymns and Hers in the Pew"

*Beautiful music is the art of the prophets that can calm
the agitations of the soul; it is one of the most magnificent
and delightful presents God has given us.*

Martin Luther

A Choir's EYE view of Bruce!

most # frequent view

SEEKING DIVINE HELP

Mysterious reappearing Sign

at 10:25 am

On February 10, 1974, I was installed as the thirty-fourth pastor of the First Congregational Church of Coventry, and of course, I remained so until my retirement in 2010. Over those years, we were fortunate to have had outstanding organists and choir directors, such as Donald Hand, Dr. Frank Cookson, Cheryl Wadsworth, Margo Lazzerini, Mary Wilsted, Christine Collins and Susan Duggan, Bruce Gale, and Fred North II for the last fifteen years. We have had Cherub Choirs, Youth Choirs and Adult Choirs. Our church was blessed by the competency of our organists, who led us in singing both beloved and new hymns and inspired us with instrumental preludes and postludes, and anthems that lifted the soul just when it was needed. Music has been a prominent ministry all on its own, and these voices from our pews, men, women, and children, were and are among the most genuine and grace filled. I still remember vividly the Sunday when the adult choir sang, under the direction of Dr. Frank Cookson: ***By the waters of Babylon, there we sat down and there we wept when we remembered Zion. On the willows, there we hung up our harps. For there, our captors asked us for songs....*** (Psalm 137, NRSV) Many of us wept with those who sang as they remembered Zion.

And I remember the many Sabbaths when the adult choir challenged itself to enhance chorally the joy of an Easter morning or the whispery solemnity of a Christmas Eve. The youth choir put smiles on the faces of parents during Children's Sundays, and Bruce John, with his band of merry assistants Janet Jungden, Jason Altieri, Kim Chambers and George Jacobi, led many little cherubs in singing their hearts out, proclaiming that Jesus loved them and that they loved Jesus! There was so much joy in that sanctuary. Nothing can match the sung testimony of faith, hymns, anthems, and special music, in its power to touch the heart or lift the spirit and bring people together celebrating their sense of community and Christian mission. Oh, how appreciative I have been!

On my final Sunday at First Church, Bruce John, a highly successful and sought-after performer in the area and an active member of the church, sang an original song as a tribute to the essence of our relationship over these decades of ministry. I have always called him lovingly, "Big Man," and he was never bigger than on this day. The title of the song is: *More than a Preacher* [19] His lyrics read:

---

[19]   Reprinted with Permission, Bruce John, 2010

Chorus:
You're more than a preacher, more than a teacher.
You're the congregation's mentor and our best friend.
Even though you retire, you've fanned our faith fire.
Our journey together will never end.

Over twenty-five years ago, when I came to you
My life was as low as it could be.
You led by example, and let me sample
What a life filled with grace Can truly be.

Chorus:

I've always sat by the door, second pew in on the right
In case I had to go back to my worldly ways.

But you kept my attention and never mentioned
Fire and Brimstone, H__ and how I'd have to pay.

Chorus:

You helped bury my sister, my father, and my mother.
You've baptized my children and married me twice.
All the families around me have the same kind of feelings.
Because you've been there for them with love and advice.

Chorus:
You're more than a preacher, more than a teacher.
You're the congregation's mentor and our best friend.
Even though you retire, you've fanned our faith fire.
Our journey together will never end.

For you, O Lord, have made me glad by your work.
at the works of your hands, I sing for joy.
(Psalm 92: 4, NRSV)

****

"Somethin out of Nothin"

"Memories are like a patchwork quilt…
each section is sown together,
to be wrapped around us
for comfort and warmth
in the years to come."

"Our lives are like quilts…
bits and pieces,
joy and sorrow,
stitched with love."
(Anonymous, shared by National Quilters Circle)

I have learned over the years that quilters are special people and their "masterpieces of the heart," as they are called, have been important to the life of First Church on several distinct levels. I have read that the name derives from the Latin, meaning "stuffed sack," which was translated into middle English as **'quilte'** or "wrapped around the body," providing both padding and blanket. We have some wonderful quilters at First Church. Quilting has been their pride and passion. They often gave hand stitched quilts for fundraising, particularly for the church fair. The names of the quilters changed over the years, but not the value and beauty of the work. Mary Carlson and some members of the Friendly Circle, a Ladies' Group of members and friends of the church, Lydia Hodgkins, Laurel Atwood and her 4-H group of parents and kids, Regina Malsbury and friends are but a few I have seen working in our social hall. As best as I can recall, most of the quilts had names. The list includes such names as "The Hope of Hartford," "Love at the Country Fair," "American Medley," "Harvest

Glory," and "Meadow Lily." If we could read between the tiny stitches, what stories they would tell? For many years, Lynn Lukach has created the "timeless treasures of art" for our holiday church fair and for a concern that is up close and personal for her, cancer research.

The Advent season of 1991 brought with it a special gift from Judy Hill for the Johnson boys, Tim, and Peter. That was the year they received a matching set of "Advent Quilts" for their beds, and it has been a tradition ever since to bring them out each Advent. Sown on the top of the quilt are a Christmas tree and candy canes, a dinosaur, a ball and bat for Tim, and a soccer ball for Pete. At the top of the tree is a shining star. We have always valued them for what they are---quilts---but we have also valued them for their symbolic meaning. Lois and I have cherished the idea that wrapped around their bodies is the love God gives in the birth of the Savior beneath a star's white light.

Accompanying the quilts was the following poem that speaks first of quilting but then of life, a philosophy and attitude I discovered and enjoyed in plentiful supply throughout my years in Coventry.

Closing Song
1988 Candace Anderson
"Somethin out of nothin" I heard my grandma say,
As she cut the squares for my new quilt, In her living room that winter's day.
A blue and a red look good on a bed with a print from a worn-out dress.
How she found time for another fine quilt, I never thought to guess,

.

.

.

And in this life of mysteries, the challenges aren't few,
And you know you'll always find somebody who's had it harder than you.
But whether it's a house or a song or a farm or a speech or a job to do,
I think of them, too, and try to do a little "somethin out of nothin" too.

Our life together at First Church was a bit like a quilt, panels of people and experiences, sewn together with the thread of love and stitched with faith. Indeed, one thinks of that wonderful passage from Colossians 3:14-15, (NRSV):

...Above all, clothe yourselves with love, which binds everything together in perfect harmony. And let the peace of Christ rule in your hearts, to which indeed you were called in the one body.

Our interwoven lives and ministries have been all about the 'bits and pieces,' at one time separate but now bound in harmony. They tell a story of good people living by faith in complicated and sometimes conflicted times but who kept the faith and continued to cherish the traditions of hearth and home, of community and church, of God and country. Maybe if we were to look at each person and each life story, we might feel that there's not much there, and yet, God has certainly stitched us together and made 'somethin' of us!

Great things are done by a series of small things brought together. [20]

Vincent van Gogh

****

"Amazing Grace"

The most beloved of all Christian spirituals is the classic "Amazing Grace," written by an English Anglican priest and poet John Newton in 1772 and published in 1779.

We all know the words well:

Amazing Grace, how sweet the sound that saved a wretch like me!
I once was lost but now I am found, was blind but now I see.
'Twas grace that taught my heart to fear and grace my fears relieved.
How precious did that grace appear the hour I first believed.
Through many dangers, toils and snares, I have already come;
'Tis grace has brought me safe and grace will lead me home.
My God has promised good to me, whose word my hope secures;
God will my shield and portion be as long as life endures.

---

[20]   Vincent Van Gogh, Brainy Quote.

On September 29, 1979, I had the privilege of presiding at the wedding ceremony that united two good friends in marriage, Glenden Dunlap and Grace White. Grace comes from a family whose roots reach far back into the history of Coventry. Glen was from Philadelphia. They worked together at the Phoenix Mutual Insurance Company for many years, and after Louise, Glen's wife of forty-four years, died in April 1979, their friendship blossomed into a deep devotion, and their life together was marked by a fulfilling companionship. Glen is the quintessential "man of letters" and someone whom others and I tease about his verbosity. Grace is the essence of her name. Both were active in the church's life, serving as officers and on boards, Grace for most of her life and Glen for the length of his membership.

In 1989, after several years of truly care-full attention given by Glen to Grace while her Alzheimer's disease advanced, Grace needed more care than Glen could provide, so, it was decided that Grace should live at a nursing home in Manchester, Connecticut, called Fenwood. Her care at Fenwood was competent and kind. Glen was faithful in his visits and loving in his interaction with Grace. Mrs. Margo Lazzerini, our Director of Music from 1987 to 1997, began the custom of playing "Amazing Grace" in church on Grace's birthday. This tradition was always very meaningful to me, not just because it helped us remember with fondness someone who had been separated from us but because of what I understood through Glen about the grace that was operational in our theology.

Let me explain what I mean. It is not uncommon these days for caregivers who have placed loved ones in nursing homes to be asked about the cognitive abilities of their loved one, especially where Alzheimer's is the debilitating disease. The most often asked question is something like:

"Does she know you?"

I feel a deep and immediate inner sadness when I hear that family and friends no longer visit because meaningful recognitions or significant communications are absent. In all the discussions I ever had with Glen directly or overheard, there was one repeating theme that carried the message of our operational theology. When asked about how Grace was doing, Glen would always be direct and honest in what he would describe about Grace's progressively failing condition. Invariably, he would be asked the above question, and I never heard him respond with anything other than:

> "It doesn't matter whether she knows me-
> -- what matters is that I know her."

That response captures and expresses what I think is at the center of our congregational understanding of God. What is so amazing about God's grace is that no matter what the measure of recognition we may or may not offer God, what matters is that God knows and loves us fully and unconditionally. I trust this theme was and is emphasized repeatedly, in worship and mission and at meetings.

> *Do not seek for anything, do not perform anything: do not*
> *intend anything.*
> *Accept the fact that you are accepted. If this happens to us,*
> *we experience grace.*
> Paul Tillich, *The Shaking of the Foundations*

****

"Bent-Nail Ernie and Crooked Pipe Frank"

> *But someone will say, 'You have faith and I have works.'*
> *Show me your faith apart from your works and I, by my*
> *works, will show you my faith.*
> (James 2: 18, NRSV)

We had paid the rent for our student apartment at the Yale Divinity School in New Haven, Connecticut, through the month of May 1973. So, it was early in June when Herb Crickmore and Frank Kristoff showed up at our apartment on Canner Street. They drove a rented Ryder truck from neighboring Willimantic to New Haven to help us with our move to Coventry. Loading the truck was a simple task. Our total cache of possessions hardly covered the floor of the truck! We had met Herb on a couple of previous occasions. A real churchman, he sang in the choir, served on various boards, and proudly spoke of his family's lineage and legacy in the life of First Church. His name will come up often as I reflect on these four decades of ministry. Frank's name and face, however, were new. From the very start, Frank cautioned me playfully about expecting to see him in church, a refrain to which I have gladly listened, and frankly, (forgive the pun please); it has been an endearing refrain.

One thing that became apparent quickly was that Frank had a sidekick. His name was Ernie LeDoyt, a lanky and loquacious man, always charming, generous, and gentlemanly in his manner and manners. These partners were the handymen of First Church, two of many men who gave unselfishly of their time and expertise for the improvement and maintenance of our buildings and grounds. Frank and Ernie, though, were in a class by themselves, at least for the early years of my pastorate. I thought that there was no job too large or too small, too easy, or too difficult. Frank and Ernie could, and would, do it. They were helpful and generous to Lois and me, completing improvement projects at the parsonage on Nathan Hale Drive and then, after the sale of the parsonage in 1978, at our own home on Barnsbee Lane. To this day, we still tease Frank about gluing down the Formica countertop over Ernie's square! Watching them work was always pleasurable because they had fun. Although both were the proverbial "jack-of-all-trades," certain specific roles were agreed upon. Ernie handled electrical matters. Frank did most of the plumbing, and together they hammered out the carpentry projects. Unfortunately, even though the Master was no doubt quite an experienced artisan Himself, some of His workers in the field were much less skilled. I am one of them. I enjoyed working alongside Frank and Ernie, settling for a somewhat companioned role but delighted in it, primarily because I got to watch a certain faux pas happen in progress. Frank and Ernie would laugh at themselves and then get on with the business of making things right. At some point, amid all the chatter and clatter that occurred as they worked, they got nicknamed "Bent-Nail Ernie" and "Crooked Pipe Frank."

On June 14, 1985, Ernie LeDoyt died at what I now know to be a very young age, 59, and the truth be known, I still carry with me a profound but always kept private sadness over his death and the large sense of loss we have endured because of it. Yet, for me, these two nicknames and the memories that attach to them preserve some of what has been best and brightest about our operational theology. In the Gospel according to Luke, we are told:

> *After this the Lord appointed seventy others, and sent them*
> *on ahead of him, in pairs to every town and place where he*
> *Himself intended to go.*
>
> (Luke 10:1, NRSV)

Their mission, we are told, was to proclaim that the Kingdom of God is near, even at hand. In the "Bent-Nail Ernies" and the "Crooked Pipe Franks" of church life, the Kingdom of God always seems near, not because of what they say about what they believe or don't believe, but because of what they show to be true for them through good works, their contagious spirit of generosity and the fun they had while working for the church.

The Word does wear skin well, and faith at First Church is most alive not only in the thoughts of people but in their deeds.

****

"The Seekers"

> *Love is as love does.*
> *The principal form that the work of love takes is attention.*[21]
>
> M. Scott Peck

> *Ask and it will be given you; seek and you will find;*
> *knock and the door will be opened for you.*
> *For everyone who asks receives, and everyone who seeks finds,*
> *and for everyone who knocks, the door will be opened.*
>
> (Matthew 7:7-8, NRSV)

Over the years, when thinking about the financial state of my life or even the parish, I have quipped often: "I'm so poor, I can't even pay attention." The quip usually elicits a chuckle or two, probably because we have all felt that poor. As I reflect on our ministry in Coventry and

---

[21]   M. Scott Peck, *The Road Less Traveled* (New York: Simon and Schuster, 1978), p.120.

what I have repeatedly mentioned in this memoir as our "operational theology," it occurs to me that the activity of paying attention has always been an important one. Indeed, in his immensely popular book, *The Road Less Traveled: A New Psychology of Love, Traditional Values and Spiritual Growth,* M. Scott Peck defines the work of love as paying attention.

In no area of our ministry together was paying attention more significant than in my relationship with the older members of our congregation. My deepest sense of satisfaction came from my relationship with the Bible study group known as The Seekers. I said frequently that I felt richly blessed by my Yale Divinity School education and training. One of the key lessons learned about being effective and successful, if those are the right words to use, was that one had to "pay attention" to what is happening in peoples' hearts, relationships, and lives. This is especially true for one's ministry among those our society calls "senior or older citizens," or, as some prefer, "seasoned citizens."

In November 1984, Marie LaMarre Ford did a survey among our older members for a course requirement at St. Joseph's College. Those she questioned identified the need for a Bible study just for them. 'The Seekers,' as Marion Spencer named us, assembled in response to that survey, and we met every Monday from twelve noon to 2 p.m. until my retirement in 2010. The original participants were Margaret Jacobson, Glenden and Grace Dunlap, Elizabeth Couch, Dorothy Chesters, Dottie Wolf. Alice Leach, Adaline Hoff, Marion Spencer, Prall Merriam, Helen Kershner, Ruth Gale, Elizabeth North, Mildred DeCandia, Pauline Little, Adella Colburn, and Roberta Upson, and we should now include the next generation, Kerttu Kersen, Jane Pintavalle, Vernon and Kathleen Sanborn, Anne Hicks, Jim and Jill Hackett, Lucille Morse and Pamela LaMarche! In the beginning, I would drive around town picking up a few. There was Aunt Helen, Ruth Gale, and Adaline Hoff. On a Monday in the late 1980s, I drove into the parking lot of the church with 298 years in the car!

So taken with our name and our identity, Prall Bacon Merriam privately took on the challenge of expressing this identity in verse. The most unpretentious, gentle woman I have ever known, Prall composed this poem in February 1986, and I used it affectionately in funeral and memorial services, celebrating the faith, life, love and good humor of our Seekers.

The Seekers
By *Prall Bacon Merriam, (February 1986)*
(Reprinted with permission)

We are the Seekers
in search of the truth;
We've one thing in common
and it is not youth.

Opinions divergent we
freely express
And time and again from
the topics digress.

Our leader shares with us
his wisdom and learning
And back to the lessons keeps
gently returning.
The books of the Bible
we're learning to know
And our knowledge of scripture
continues to grow.

At lunch time the topics
are many and various
Running the gamut from
deep to hilarious.
And Bruce, too, is gaining
in wisdom and knowledge
on many a subject not
taught him in college.

We celebrate birthdays
share pictures and books,
While Dot pours the coffee
and helps out the cooks.
We find most rewarding
our meetings together
And nothing deters us
but bad health or weather.

Our classes lasted two hours, one hour for lunch, one for bible study. However, most of the real learning took place during lunch when my elders friends conducted several conversations all at once, teaching me stuff I had not learned in college! Some of it was oral history. Some of it was local lore. Still more was simple gossip. Dottie would tell us about her parents' Ice House, which was at the end of the trolley line at the Lakeside Bar and Grill on Coventry Lake, and she sometimes showed us pictures of the saws they used to cut blocks of ice out of the frozen lake. Grace regaled us with stories about the trolley line itself and how it linked Coventry to the big city of Willimantic. She used the trolley line to get to school each morning at Windham High School. North Coventry kids went to Manchester High School. Margaret would then chime in with stories about investigations she conducted in Willimantic as the first Connecticut State Policewoman. In addition, many were stories about growing up in Coventry and attending the one room schoolhouses or sledding on Manning Hill before cars made it too dangerous. Lib Couch was still resentful of the Reverend Charles Johnson for reprimanding her one Sunday afternoon for wearing short shorts in church. Betty North laid claim to being the resident historian for lake activities of years past. There were stories of home remedies and family recipes. 'The Seekers' were children of the Depression. So, hardly a lunch went by without some mention of how that experience shaped their outlook, attitudes, and values. Church was always so important to them. They remembered the Ladies Association with fondness and their efforts to provide bandages for the war effort, or blankets for mission, and even fresh, homemade donuts made each Saturday morning and sold from the church kitchen. They told stories about previous pastors and applauded efforts by the church to convert the old Methodist church building into a youth center. The move from their kitchen table wisdom to that of scripture's insights seemed seamless and natural for them. Indeed, they seemed to understand that each individual life was part of a much bigger story and possessed a significant and implicit religious dimension and truth.

That made us all seekers in search of truth, who, while sharing our stories, paid attention to one another's oldest longings and newest learnings about life and love, about our sacred scriptures and secular scripts, about our families and community, about our heroes, hopes and hurts. Some were serious; others were hilarious, but each was precious and cherished and managed with care. Although there may be much that highlighted our differences and identified what was divergent in our views, "We've one thing in common" and that was our faith in Jesus Christ and our shared commitment to seek the truth and serve it as His disciples. What a joy it was to be counted among "The Seekers!" And for this pastor, he gained so much "in wisdom and knowledge on many a subject not taught him in college."

****

"Nicholas, We Frown on such Behavior."

*Finally, beloved, whatever is true, whatever is honorable,
whatever is just, whatever is pure, whatever is pleasing,
whatever is commendable, if there is any excellence, if there
is anything worthy of praise, think about these things. Keep
on doing the things you have learned and received and heard
and seen in me, do; And the God of peace will be with you.*
(Philippians 4: 8-9, NRSV) Prall's favorite scripture)

I still have on my bedroom bureau a picture of Prall Bacon Merriam. It is a small picture inserted in the corner of a wedding photo. Prall is seated in a wheelchair, regally attired in a lovely floral dress with one of her great-great grandchildren standing at her side. There was no one quite like Prall in all of Coventry, a woman born to privilege and status at an estate on the Hudson River, New York. She was college educated at Vassar and was a woman of letters, but lived in such an understated way. I'm not sure if anyone ever used the front door of their home on Ripley Hill Road. Rather, it was always the side door off the driveway that led directly into the kitchen that bore all the traffic. Upon entering the house, the guest was always welcomed by a bulletin board display highlighting the holiday of the month or the colors of the ever-changing seasons of New England. The kitchen table was as far as most visitors would get, this because conversations just seemed natural over a cup of tea or coffee. In January 1996, Rachel Naomi Remen, MD. published a *New York Times* bestseller, titled *Kitchen Table Wisdom: Stories that Heal*. I have always believed that Prall's kitchen table was a place where wisdom and compassion did their best healing.

Prall loved her little piece of property on Ripley Hill Road, with its flower and vegetable gardens, Christmas trees, the pond out back and nature's creatures everywhere. When the asparagus pushed their noses up through the early spring ground, Prall invited Lois and me to come over to the house for an early cutting. On one such visit, and after a cup of tea, we emerged from the house and headed toward the garden. As we walked to the garden, the family dog, an Irish Setter named Nicholas, raced around, seemingly without purpose or direction, which was okay with Prall, at least

— 37 —

until we reached the asparagus patch. Upon our arrival, however, Nicholas was still racing around bodies and darting through legs and trampling on the tender springtime shoots of asparagus. One might have thought that Prall would be angry, but she wasn't at all. The only thing she said, almost as if under her breath, was,

"Nicholas, we frown on such behavior."

And with those simple words, Nicholas calmed down. It was a most amazing sight. Prall then went on with cutting stalks of asparagus for the new pastor and his very appreciative and entertained wife.

Lois and I recall this episode often and with such amusement. Yet, on a more serious note, I think that Prall's attitude reflects or represents accurately our theological view. We know God frowns on our misbehavior, but whatever judgment God renders, it is offered with mercy and forgiveness. Over these many years, I repeated often, and usually it resonates with our folk, this fundamental belief:

We are forgiven not because we repent,
but we repent because we are forgiven.

So central to our life of faith is the truth expressed by Paul to the church in Rome:

No, in all these things we are more than conquerors through
him who loved us. For I am sure that neither death nor life,
nor angels, nor rulers, nor things present, nor things to come,
nor powers, nor height, nor depth, nor anything else in all
creation, will separate us from the love of God in Christ Jesus
our Lord.

(Romans 8: 37-39, NRSV)

****

The Story of the Supper of the Month

"Turkey Soup for the Church's Soul"

The day will come when, after harnessing space, the winds, the tides, and gravitation, we shall harness for God the energies of love. And on that day, for the second time in the history of the world, we shall have discovered fire.

Teilhard de Chardin[22]

---

[22] Jack Canfield and Mark Victor Hansen, *Chicken Soup for the Soul* (Health Communications, Inc., 1993) p. 1.

Jack Canfield and Mark Victor Hansen are internationally known speakers who have delivered hundreds of keynote speeches, workshops, and training seminars. As part of their popular speaking style, Canfield and Hansen always used inspirational, motivational, and uplifting stories to help their audiences discover, experience, and retain key concepts and approaches. With good reason, therefore, I hold in high regard the quote by Elie Wiesel:

God created man because He loved stories. [23]

After much encouragement from those who felt uplifted and inspired by their talks, Canfield and Hansen published their first collection of stories in 1992 under the title: *Chicken Soup for the Soul*. Since then, and because of the popularity of that book, they have now published an amazing array of *Chicken Soup* books. At my last count, it was fifty-three (53). That's a lot of literary bowls of chicken soup! Consider this impressive list:

Chicken Soup for the Woman's Soul I, II; Chicken Soup for the Mother's Soul I, II; Chicken Soup for the Father's Soul; Chicken Soup for the Teenage Soul I, II, III; Chicken Soup for the Expectant Mother's Soul; Chicken Soup for the Pet Lover's Soul; Chicken Soup for the Horse Lover's Soul; Chicken Soup for the Country Soul; Chicken Soup for the College Soul;
Chicken Soup for the Soul at Work; Chicken Soup for the Nurse's Soul; Chicken Soup for the Golfer's Soul;
Chicken Soup for the Jewish Soul; Chicken Soup for the Christian Soul; Chicken Soup for the Grieving Soul; Chicken Soup for the Surviving Soul; Chicken Soup for the Veteran's Soul; Chicken Soup for the Soul of America.

The quote above from Teilhard de Chardin was the lead quote for their first book and sets the tone for all the rest. It also captures what we experienced over the years at First Church while making quart upon quart of metaphorical turkey soup, all of it simmered in our own kitchen over the fire of our love for the church and its mission in the world. One successful "Supper of the Month" after another provided the ingredients for the telling of this story.

---

[23]   Quoted from the Preface of Wiesel's novel, *The Gates of the Forest*, and his Hasidic parable about the great Rabbi Israel Baal Shem-Tov. First published in 1964.

These suppers were our version of Chicken Soup, and they made not only an extraordinary contribution to keeping and enriching the soul of our church, but did so in such a personal way. What a story the "Supper of the Month" is and what a significant role it played in the life and ministry of First Church!

Mr. Herb Crickmore started it in 1974 as an effort to raise money to pay off a small debt the church had incurred when it purchased some kitchen cabinets in 1971. However, it soon took on a meaning all its own, something far more meaningful than money. Herb was its chair and often the chief cook for twenty-one (21) years. F. Pauline Little was the one who called people to donate desserts or volunteer to wait tables. To my knowledge, no one ever could say 'no' to Pauline. Herb's sister, Ethel Harris, was also in the kitchen, especially when the gravy had to be made. Rose Fowler, Karen Bement and Colleen Gally have followed as chairpersons. Stuart Pratt was a much-trusted chef. Together and with the aid of quite a large staff of volunteers, they served a splendid meal at an affordable price and most important of all, had church members and friends working side by side in a shared commitment to a common purpose, the church. It became a ministry of the church on its own, providing food and fellowship to our single largest group of patrons, the older adults of our community and those of our neighboring towns as well. By the way, I own a copy of Canfield and Hansen's *Chicken Soup for the Golden Soul*, and I prefer our Supper of the Month, whether the meal is roast turkey or pork. Consider for a moment, if you will, these few extraordinary statistics. During three decades of sponsoring the suppers, at my last accounting, we fed approximately 57,669 patrons, not including all the volunteers, and raised $185,037 for the support of our facilities and ministries!

People have asked me countless times if I am the pastor of the church that has the suppers, and I usually responded proudly with "Indeed I am!" We were known for our suppers, but not just because of the quality and quantity of food. People marveled at the level of commitment and enthusiasm shown by members and friends. Karen Bement and Colleen Gally once described the Suppers of the Month in these terms:

As we have said time and again, it is a place where friendships begin and blossom. It is a time of fellowship and service...

(2004 Annual Report, p. 19)

The church was fed and nourished by doing the suppers, and as a result, it seemed easy to be the church in the world. The turkey suppers truly were "Chicken Soup for the Church's Soul." Herb had a signature way of signing off on most of his annual reports. He would say:

Many, many thanks again to all, from the youngest to the young-at-heart. We couldn't have done it without you.

That is the truth! We can do little without each other, side by side; hearts and hands linked. We know it and show it.

****

"*Welcome to Holland*"
(Reprinted with permission)

'The Gift of Cameron Morris Schoenbrod Joy'
April 17, 1997-January 22, 2001

Some people come into our lives and quickly go,
Some people move our souls to dance.
They awaken us to a new understanding with
the passing whisper of their wisdom.

Some people make the sky more beautiful to gaze upon.
They stay in our lives for a while, leave footprints on our hearts
And we are never, ever the same.
(Poster copyright 1995 by Flavia)

A single cobblestone bears the name of Cameron Morris Schoenbrod Joy at the Edgartown Lighthouse Children's Memorial. He died in his parents' arms on January 22, 2001 after living but three years. His name and memory are now literally chiseled in stone, but for his parents, Kevin and Jennifer, grandparents, other family members, doctors, nurses, and caregivers, it's the footprints that he has left on people's hearts that matter the most. Cameron was an extraordinary little boy, born April 17, 1997, eight weeks premature with multiple disabilities and discharged from the hospital on July 4th. With the devotion, education and support of his parents and extended community, he lived an "able" life as an advocate for disability rights. Together they took part in conferences, seminars, and workshops from Maine to Washington, D. C. They are even featured in the Council for Exceptional Children's annual report for 2001. Newspaper accounts of those three years testify to his accomplishments. From his wheelchair, he taught medical residents about compassion and caring for families, and he helped teachers and childcare providers understand inclusion.[24] No one was ever the same after meeting Cameron.

Cameron's family gave me insight into their experience. They shared with me a wonderful reflection on a universal experience, written by Emily Perl Kingsley.

Welcome To Holland
by Emily Perl Kingsley
Copyright©1987 by Emily Perl Kingsley.
All rights reserved.
(Reprinted by permission of the author)

I am often asked to describe the experience of raising a child with a disability - to try to help people who have not shared that unique experience to understand it, to imagine how it would feel. It's like this......

When you're going to have a baby, it's like planning a fabulous vacation trip - to Italy. You buy a bunch of guidebooks and make your wonderful plans. The Coliseum. The Michelangelo David. The gondolas in Venice. You may learn some handy phrases in Italian. It's all very exciting.

After months of eager anticipation, the day finally arrives. You pack your bags and off you go. Several hours later, the plane lands. The flight attendant comes in and says, "Welcome to Holland."

"Holland?!?" you say. "What do you mean Holland?? I signed up for Italy! I'm supposed to be in Italy. All my life I've dreamed of going to Italy."

But there's been a change in the flight plan. They've landed in Holland and there you must stay.

---

[24]   Courtney Challos, Chicago Tribune Obituaries, January 29, 2001.

The important thing is that they haven't taken you to a horrible, disgusting, filthy place, full of pestilence, famine, and disease. It's just a different place.

So you must go out and buy new guide books. And you must learn a whole new language. And you will meet a whole new group of people you would never have met.

It's just a different place. It's slower-paced than Italy, less flashy than Italy. But after you've been there for a while and you catch your breath, you look around…. and you begin to notice that Holland has windmills… and Holland has tulips. Holland even has Rembrandts.

But everyone you know is busy coming and going from Italy… and they're all bragging about what a wonderful time they had there. And for the rest of your life, you will say "Yes, that's where I was supposed to go. That's what I had planned."

And the pain of that will never, ever, ever, ever go away… because the loss of that dream is a very, very significant loss.

But… if you spend your life mourning the fact that you didn't get to Italy, you may never be free to enjoy the very special, the very lovely things … about Holland.

***

Life is full of such trips. John Lennon's aphorism is quoted often because there is a certain homespun wisdom to it:

Life is what happens to you while you are making other plans.[25]

We make plans, harbor hopes and dream dreams and then life happens. Sometimes things simply don't work out as planned for us, our parents and children, our friends and neighbors. I continue to reflect daily on the wisdom of something de Chardin, Dyer and Stephen Covey have said:

> *We are not human beings on a spiritual journey but spiritual beings on a human journey.*[26]

---

[25] John Lennon, Lyrics from song "Beautiful Boy (Darling Boy)" Verse #3.

[26] Stephen Covey, *The 7 Habits of Highly Successful People* (New York: Simon & Schuster, 1989) p. 319.

He might be on to something there. This is how someone like Cameron can speak truth and wisdom to us. Our human journeys are filled with their Hollands, the times and places that are marked by initial disappointment and even despair because they are not what we had in mind or that for which we had planned and prepared but are ready to reveal and bless us with their own unique promise and pleasure. On our human journeys, our planned destinations are not always reached. Sometimes, we cannot accomplish our goals and miss out on the pleasures we expect. Yet, amid the burdens and blessings of where we are, there is beauty to be seen, treasures to be enjoyed, moments to be cherished, and unexpected promises to be fulfilled. I am reminded of something I have said often when referring to Moses and the Exodus, that journey of the Israelites from their slavery and poverty in Egypt to the freedom and prosperity of the Promised Land. In modern-day terms, we talk not so much of the Promised Land, but the Promised Time, that moment, when, in the here and now, we realize that every moment and experience is God-given and always for the blessing of those who have arrived unexpectedly at a certain time and place not of their choosing. It is God's way of saying: "Welcome to Holland!"

> *Everything is gestation and then bringing forth. To let each impression and each germ of a feeling come to completion wholly in the dark, in the inexpressible, the unconscious, beyond the reach of one's own intelligence, and await with deep humility and patience the birth hour of a new clarity: that alone is living the artists' life: in understanding as in creating.*[27]
> *(From LETTERS TO A YOUNG POET by Rainer Maria Rilke, translated by M. D. Herter Norton. Copyright 1934, 1954 by W. W. Norton & Company, Inc. renewed © 1962, 1982 by M. D. Herter Norton. Used by permission of W. W. Norton &Company, Inc.)*

****

[27] Rainer Maria Rilke, *Letters to a Young Poet*(New York: W.W. Norton, 1934) pp. 29-30.

"Thoughts in May 1990"
(Reprinted with permission)

My beloved speaks and says to me:
Arise, my love, my fair one,
and come away.
For now, the winter is past,
The rain is over and gone.

The flowers appear on the earth,
The time of singing has come,
And the voice of the turtledove
Is heard in our land.

(Song of Solomon 2:10-12, NRSV)

When Jane Pintavalle first shared with me her "Thoughts in May, 1990," I was so impressed that I submitted an abbreviated version to the *Upper Room* for publication. Unfortunately, and for some inexplicable reason, the editors of the *Upper Room* chose not to publish it, but I am making the opposite choice. Throughout my ministry here at First Church, I have been in awe of those who have suffered great loss or experienced great adversity and have done so with grace and hope. They are invariably an inspiration to us all, and Jane is certainly that in this written piece. Although Catherine was not a member of our church, she was certainly part of our church family. She died in April 1989 at St. Francis Hospital with family at her bedside after a courageous battle with cancer. She was only thirty (30) years old. One year later, Jane, her mother-in-law, and a Seeker, wrote these thoughts with the soft-spoken gentleness and goodness that are so characteristic of her.

"Thoughts in May 1990"[28]

This spring I was quite surprised at how pretty our yard looked. It was something like the feeling you get when you have been away for a long time and suddenly you are home again, and everything looks good to you.

---

[28]   Reprinted with permission of the author.

Could I have forgotten what spring was like since Cathie died in April a year ago, and we didn't even notice spring---then it rained all summer after that?

I don't mean to say that we have gotten over her death. I don't suppose that we will ever do that, but now the edges of the sadness have dulled, and we notice again how beautiful the maples can look with their pale green leaves in May.

The violets pop up in unexpected places in the grass in clumps of bright purple, blue and white. The little space that I call my kitchen garden is very shady now that we've added a porch, but the violets are thriving there, settling in around the chives and parsley.

Our yard is actually pretty ragged. The grass refuses to grow in spots and the snowplow left some scars where it missed the driveway. The ground moles seem to be having a field day as they tunnel around below the surface of the lawn. I imagine them as looking fat and happy after they ate my tulip bulbs. They left me the yellow and white tulips though. Those were probably not as tasty as the other colors.

But the raggedness doesn't bother me. Spring is here, and it is exciting to see the changes warm weather brings.

The primroses along the driveway have been bright and perky for weeks now in their creamy whites, deep wine, and yellows.

On the side of the backyard where the stonewall parallels the ditch, some miniature daffodils poked through last year's leaves. I raked the leaves away carefully because they were so small. When the daffodils went by, some orange tulips came up. Then I discovered the dark-red trillium that I had transplanted from Prall's yard a couple of years ago and had forgotten. Some adder tongue leaves came up close by, but no blossoms yet. They must have been in the shovel full of soil I dug with the trillium.

Down in back by the wall, the day lily leaves seem to have sprung up overnight and look like they are just waiting to show off their orange blossoms. In front of them stands a ragged row of late daffodils.

One of the last of the old apple trees in our yard split in half and was almost uprooted one windy night last winter. At one time, our property was part of a farm, so we have remnants of stonewalls and apple trees here and there. This particular tree stands in one corner of our backyard with the woods behind it. Every year it produces little green apples that fall to the ground before they are ripe. We never need to rake them up because the deer come in when we are not looking and eat them and leave only their tracks in the soft soil underneath the tree.

A few years ago, Cathie drove out here on a beautiful day in late summer to make raspberry jam with me.

Just as we were putting the last lid on the last jar of jam, we noticed a doe had stepped into the backyard and was obviously enjoying the apples---juice running out of the sides of her mouth.

Cathie got her camera and took a picture. At the sound of the shutter, the doe turned her big radar ears toward us. Then, with one effortless motion, she seemed to float over the wall and disappear into the woods. The picture came out very well, and I treasure it. I treasure the day too. It was one of those special times.

In April this year, Gene and our neighbor cut up the broken parts of the apple tree and cleared away the debris. They decided that they would take the rest of the tree down soon---but now they've changed their minds because it has blossomed again.

Even though the part of the tree that is left tilts at an awkward angle, the long branches of delicate white blossoms look lovely back there, so typical of springtime in the country.

The tree didn't give up just because it was badly broken, and its roots must cling tenuously to the soil to survive.

In another year, when winter is over, we may find that it has lost the battle, and it will be gray and lifeless, but I don't think so. I think it will continue to have blossoms for years, dwindling in numbers probably, but it will add to the beauty of the season as long as it is able. It will blossom and produce little green apples because that is what the plan is.

Also part of the plan is making raspberry jam and seeing deer in the yard and a hundred other things that will remind us of our dear daughter-in-law who died so young. We feel the pain and the joy those memories bring, but I think we are already beginning to put away the anger and the sorrow for what we have lost. Indeed, we are feeling so grateful for the precious time that she was here.

Even the saddest things can become, once we have made peace with them, a source of wisdom and strength for the journey that still lies ahead.[29]

Frederick Buechner

****

---

[29] Frederick Buechner, *Telling Secrets* (San Francisco. Ed. Harper, 1991) p. 33.

"Mildred and Her Teddy Bears"

I loved visiting Mildred. She was oppositional, outspoken, colorful in her language, and unrestrained with her opinions. A trusted source of information about Coventry and First Church, their respective histories, and members, I always left her home more informed than I was when I arrived. She attended church regularly and never missed a meeting of the congregation or the opportunity to say what she thought. By the time I arrived in Coventry, she was becoming less mobile and even disabled. She worked the dessert table for the Suppers of the Month from her chair, or some might say her throne. It did not surprise anyone that Mildred, along with Janice McCauley, would eventually become the strongest and most persuasive advocates for making our sanctuary accessible to the physically challenged. Whenever I visited, I never expected that she would answer the doorbell or the sound of my knock on the door in person. Rather, she would shout her permission to enter the house from her recliner in the living room. Once inside, I would sit in the only empty chair available. Her living room was ordinary for a ranch style home, long and somewhat narrow with a brick fireplace at one end and her recliner at the other. The room was filled with a collection of miscellaneous furniture, including a couch, chairs, doll furniture, and stools. What made the room so unique was Mildred's extensive collection of teddy bears. They were everywhere, occupying every available spot on the mantel over the fireplace, the couch, the chairs, the stools, and the end tables. Miniature teddy bears were perched on the large, framed mirror on the wall and on the shades of both the table and floor lamps. There they were, big and small, old and young, each wearing different outfits, some to match the occasion. Together, they brought Mildred comfort and companionship in her later years. Each had its own biography. The manufacturer provided some, others by the artist who created the teddy bear. And there were some biographies that were created by Mildred based on the few details that connected to the circumstances by which they came to live with Mildred. Most visitors got to listen to the biography of choice.

For many years, although I appreciated her interest and effort in collecting teddy bears, I did not quite understand her attachment to them. To the best of my recollection, I never owned one and remained clueless as to their importance. Then, one day, a professor at Boston University's School of Theology included a book by John McDargh in his assigned reading list. The title was: *Psychoanalytic Object Relations Theory and the Study of Religion: On Faith and the Imaging of God*. That is quite a title! So, imagine my surprise when, in his Preface, he provided the cited report:

> *At one point several years ago, while the ideas presented in this book were still taking shape, a colleague of mine struggling to understand this research challenged me with the question: 'Are you trying to say that God is nothing but a cosmic teddy bear?' 'No' I replied, 'but I am arguing that we cannot understand fully what compels human beings to seek after that which they name 'God' until and unless we understand something about our relationship to our teddy bears.*[30]

Ever since having that epiphany, I have appreciated deeply and even envied the relationship certain parishioners have had with their teddy bears, at least those who confess to sleeping with them still. My research persuaded me that nothing can match the teddy bear's gift of unconditional acceptance, love and reassurance, nothing except the unconditional acceptance, love and reassurance that God shows us in Jesus Christ. Perhaps sometimes, the Word doesn't need skin on, just a teddy bear close at hand! That too is such Good News!

****

"Golf Is No Game"

Golf is the closest game to the game we call life. You get bad breaks from good shots; you get good breaks from bad shots — but you have to play the ball where it lies.

Bobby Jones

---

[30] John McDargh, *Psychoanalytic Object Relations Theory and the Study of Religion: On Faith and the Imaging of God* (University Press of America, 1983) p. xiii.

After the church membership voted to extend a call to me to be pastor of First Church, they invited Lois and me to visit Coventry to learn more about the church and the community. The day ended with a lovely evening of fellowship and a delicious dinner at the Altnaveigh Inn and Restaurant in Mansfield, just off the campus of the University of Connecticut. Before these evening events took place, however, Leonard Gillon, the chair of the committee, gave us a tour of the town, which included, upon our insistence, a visit to local golf courses. We saw the Skungamaug River Golf Course on Folly Lane, owned, and operated by John and Susie Motyka, the Twin Hills Golf Club on Bread and Milk Street, more commonly referred to as Route 31N, and he took us out of town as well to get a look at the Willimantic Country Club, located unsurprisingly on 'Club Road.' Lois and I were, from the start, so pleased that the church implicitly approved of our interest in and commitment to golf as our preferred form of recreation. And, over these fifty years, Lois and I have played a lot of golf. We played regularly at each of the local courses, and for the last thirty-five years, at the Ellington Ridge Country Club in Ellington, CT., both as individuals and as a couple, often referring to the husband/wife tournament as the Divorce Open! More than a few times, our vacations involved golf, and annually, we tried to play in state tournaments as a couple. No one really knows who said: *Golf is a good walk spoiled,* but sometimes it is certainly true.[31] That being acknowledged, it has been for us a source of wonderful enjoyment and has enhanced many friendships over the years, all with the endorsement and active support of the church. Indeed, as one of the celebratory activities sponsored by the church celebrating my retirement, there was a charity golf outing at the Willimantic Country Club, the proceeds of which were given to the Coventry Food and Fuel Bank.

Golf was a way I bonded with friends, and connected with diverse social and business groups. Among those golfing buddies were Norbert St. Martin, Royden Smith, Bruce Campbell, Paul Watson, Dr. James Watson, Dr. Michael Keenan, Carl Larson, Stuart Magdefrau and my beloved best friend, Peter Sturrock. For many years, I served on the Board of Directors of Windham Hospital and with that role, occupied a spot on the committee promoting the Windham Classic, a charity golf tournament that raised money for the hospital. I always enjoyed introducing myself as

---

[31]   Often attributed to Mark Twain, it is highly unlikely that he said it.

a local pastor, implying that my playing partners might want to consider being on their best behavior throughout the round!

The longtime head professional at the Willimantic Country Club, known affectionately as Willie Hunter, used to say of every day: "Aye laddie, it's a great day for a game of golf." He was, of course, one among many who consider golf to be "the greatest game mankind has ever invented." (Arnold Palmer) However, at least on some level, I have always thought that it was not much of a game. Rather, it is serious business. Indeed, the great Hall of Fame player, and commentator, Peter Allis, often referred to as the "Voice of golf," once opined on the essence of golf in the following way:

> *It is not a matter of life and death. It is not that important. But it is a reflection of life, and so the game is an enigma wrapped in a mystery impaled on a conundrum.*[32]

With a definition like that, how could it be a game?

These are my thoughts. First, Christian golfers have two bibles. The first is the recognized sourcebook of our faith, *The Holy Bible.* The second is a book known by any golfer worth his putter as *Harvey Penick's Little Red Book: Lessons and Teachings from a Lifetime in Golf.* Along with the technical tips and tricks he shares to help with the golf swing and prevent the shank, Penick is deeply respected, even revered, for his commitment to provide lessons for living life, lessons learned from golf. A story told by Penick about his daily routine at the Austin Country Club promotes my favorite and most useful lesson. Penick tells it this way: "I once heard a woman ask," 'I wonder how Harvey makes a living? All he does is hang around Austin Country Club.' Choosing not to address the validity or invalidity of the woman's observation, he chooses instead to explain the intent and relevance of what he taught during all that hanging around. He says: "In a roundabout way I have somehow tried to teach each of my students that golf and life are similar. There's nothing guaranteed to be fair in either golf or life and we shouldn't expect it to be different. You

---

[32]   Canfield, Hansen, Aubery and Mark and Chrissy Donnelly, *Chicken Soup for the Golfer's Soul* (Deerfield Beach, Florida: Health Communications, Inc., 1999) p. 338.

must accept your disappointments and triumphs equally."[33] Sounds like serious teaching to me.

Second, the much beloved Arnold Palmer's nickname was "The King" even though he is quoted as saying:

> There is no king of golf. Never has been, never will be. Golf is the most democratic game on earth. It punishes and exalts us all with splendid equal opportunity.[34]

Also attributed to "The King" is the following quip, jokingly shared:

> I have a tip that can take five strokes off anyone's game. It's called an eraser. [35]

Indeed, there are several ways to compare golf courses, such as layout design, course conditions, amount of play, the quality and availability of a nineteenth hole, and my favorite, does the scorecard come with a pencil with or without an eraser! Somehow, we need to get rid of those few failures of the golf swing, don't we? Just kidding!

All kidding aside, however, I think that there is a serious lesson in this game of golf, which is not a game but "an enigma wrapped in mystery and impaled on a conundrum," a serious lesson that has sustained golfers for generations. Most of us believe Penick's guiding principle from his secular scripture: *There's nothing guaranteed to be fair in either golf or life and we shouldn't expect it to be different. You must accept your disappointments and triumphs equally.*

In addition, although "The King" may have been joking at the time about the usefulness of an eraser, our other Bible affirms a truth that lifts from our souls the weight of our disappointments and failures, the faulty swings at life, some hooks, some slices and maybe even from time to time, the dreaded shank or even the whiff. We know real "Royalty," one who erases the stigma of our sin and frees us to live creatively, compassionately, kindly and with honor and hope. The scriptures say it this way:

---

33 Harvey Penick, *Harvey Penick's Little Red Book: Lessons and Teachings from a Lifetime in Golf* (New York: Simon and Shuster, 1992) p. 172.

34 Arnold Palmer, Golf Monthly, December 10, 2021.

35 Arnold Palmer, Source, ESPN.

Let no evil talk come out of your mouths, but only what is useful for building up, as there is need, so that your words may give grace to those who hear. ... put away from you all bitterness and wrath and anger and wrangling and slander, together with malice, and be kind to one another, tenderhearted, forgiving one another, as God in Christ has forgiven you. (Ephesians 4: 29-32, NRSV)

And you thought that I was out playing the game of golf? "Aye laddies and lassies, a great day for the serious business of golf."

****

"No Vermonters in Heaven"

(While engaged in ministry, we are reminded often that dealing with issues of life and death and the pain of grief by proclaiming the Kingdom of heaven is serious business. Our inclination is to maintain that this foundational responsibility is no laughing matter, and it is not. However, Lucille Morse thought differently and playfully, poetically, taught me a truth of enduring note and did so with humor. I am, to this day, profoundly grateful.)

In heaven, all the interesting people are missing.
Friedrich Nietzsche

If there are no dogs in heaven, then when I die, I want to go where they went.

Will Rogers

Lucille Morse is from Lyndonville, Vermont, and like so many others, she and her husband, Russell, came to Connecticut in search of work after WWII. Lucille and I have a special and very playful relationship. My picture was displayed in her living room, along with other family photos. She is a woman who has faced much adversity throughout her life, first in childhood and later as an adult wife and mother. She has persevered and triumphed because of her deep and abiding faith and ever-present good humor. I know of no one else at First Church who is more convinced that salvation has been given to her in Christ and when Jesus calls her home, she will be happy to go. However, she is also someone to whom I have made a promise that when that time comes, I will surely commend her to the heavenly Kingdom, but with one stipulation. With a wink and a chuckle, Lucille has always warned me she couldn't possibly stay in heaven if, upon her arrival, she discovers as true something that has been rumored for generations, that there are no Vermonters in heaven.

"No Vermonters in Heaven"
(Not copyright protected)

I dreamed that I went to the City of Gold,
To Heaven resplendent and fair,
And after I entered that beautiful fold,
By one in authority, then I was told
That not a Vermonter was there.

"Impossible, sir, for from my town
many sought this delectable place,
And each must be here, with harp or a crown,
And a conqueror's palm, and clean linen gown,
Received through unmerited grace."

The angel replied: "All Vermonters come here
When first they depart from the earth,
But after a day, a month, or a year,
They restless and lonesome and homesick appear
And sigh for the land of their birth.

They tell of ravines, wild, secluded, and deep,
And of flower-decked landscapes serene,
Of towering mountains, imposing and steep,
Adown which the torrents exultingly leap,
Through forests perennially green.

They tell of the many and beautiful hills,
Their forests majestic appear,

They tell of its rivers, its lakes, streams and rills,
Where nature the purest water distills
And they soon get dissatisfied here.

We give them the best the Kingdom provides,
They have everything here that they want,
But not a Vermonter in heaven abides;
A very brief period here he resides,
Then hikes his way back to Vermont. [36]

I am not surprised that one of America's most beloved poets, the four-time Pulitzer Prize for Poetry winner, Robert Frost, was from Vermont. Neither would I be surprised to learn that his understanding and appreciation of the Kingdom of heaven would be covertly influential in the lives of other Vermonters, especially Lucille Morse. In his iconic poem, "Birches," Frost wrote the following verse:

I'd like to get away from earth awhile
And then come back to it and begin over.
May no fate willfully misunderstand me
And half grant what I wish and snatch me away
Not to return. Earth's the right place for love:
I don't know where it's likely to go better.
I'd like to go by climbing a birch tree,
And climb black branches up a snow-white trunk
Toward heaven, till the tree could bear no more,
But dipped its top and set me down again.
"That would be good both going and coming back.
One could do worse than be a swinger of birches.[37]

Earth's the right place for love:
I don't know where it's likely to go better.

---

[36] Johnstone, E.F. "No Vermonters in Heaven" (Digital Vermont: A Project of the Vermont Historical Society: Rutland, Vt. Tuttle Co. 191?)

[37] Robert Frost, "Birches" from *The Poetry of Robert Frost,* Edward C. Lathem, editor (New York: Henry Holt and Company, 1969) p. 122.

What a superb observation by this noted Vermonter! And, when believed by anyone, it is no wonder that one might muse that "hiking oneself back to Vermont" rather than staying in heaven might be a viable, even a desirable option. After all, earth is the right place for love, and where is the earth more beautiful?

Therefore, it is certainly not a bad thing to conceive of and talk about the Kingdom of heaven both with anticipation and appreciation, along with a somewhat irreverent sense of humor!

****

Sacraments and Rites

Baptism: "Let the Children Come"

Keep love in your heart. A life without it is like a sunless garden when the flowers are dead. The consciousness of loving and being loved brings a warmth and a richness to life that nothing else can bring.[38]

Oscar Wilde

---

[38]   Oscar Wilde, Quoted in Goodreads

One of my favorite stories is told by Tony Campolo about his good friend, Peter Arnett, the onetime CNN television commentator, and reporter. The story goes:

> *I was in Israel, in a small town on the West Bank, when an explosion went off. Bodies were blown through the air. Everywhere I looked, there were signs of death and destruction. The screams of the wounded seemed to be coming from every direction. A man came running up to me, holding a bloodied little girl in his arms. He pleaded with me and said, "Mister, I can't get her to a hospital! The Israeli troops have sealed off the area. No one can get in or out, but you're press. You can get through. Please, mister! Help me get her to a hospital. Please! If you don't help me, she's going to die."*

> *Arnett put them in the car, got through the sealed area and rushed to the hospital in Jerusalem. The whole time he was hurtling down the road to the city, the man was pleading from the backseat, calling out to him. "Can you go faster, mister? Can you go faster? I'm losing her… I'm losing her!"*

> *When they finally got to the hospital, the girl was rushed to the operating room. Then the two men retreated to the waiting area and sat on the bench.*

> *Peter said that they just sat there in silence, too exhausted to even talk.*

> *After a short while, the doctor came out of the operating room and said to them solemnly, "She's dead."*

> *The man collapsed in tears and as Arnett put his arms around the man to comfort him, he said, "I don't know what to say. I can't imagine what you must be going through. I've never lost a child."*

> *The man looked back at Arnett in a startled manner and said, "Oh, mister! That Palestinian girl was not my daughter. I'm an Israeli settler. That Palestinian is not my child. But mister… there comes a time when each of us must realize that every child, regardless of that child's background, is a daughter or a son. There must come a time when we realize that we are all family."*[39] (Taken from *Let Me Tell You a Story* by Tony Campolo, Copyright 2000 Tony Campolo. Used by permission of HarperCollins Christian Publishing)

I believe that we at First Church realized long ago that we are family and that all children are our sons and daughters. No sacrament or celebration expresses it more perfectly than how we make such a fuss over baptism! During the forty (40) years of my pastorate at First Church, I have presided over close to six hundred baptisms. Understanding the significance of baptism for First Church was to understand something profoundly personal about the operational theology of the congregation. Baptism for the United Church of Christ, Congregational, is one of two sacraments, and we believe that among its many meanings, the most fundamental is: *"Baptism is the outward and visible sign of a inward and invisible reality, the reality of God's unconditional love and forgiveness as made sure and certain in Jesus Christ. In baptism, we celebrate our union with Him and the salvation that comes by faith because of grace."*[40]

One of the heartfelt baptismal traditions at First Church was the writing of a letter to the child who was to be baptized. The best among them was the most personal and were delivered as sermons. The one that follows provides an accurate sense of how meaningfully these letters have contributed to the celebration of the sacrament for the families and the church, and in time, the "guest/guests of honor."

***

---

[39] Tony Campolo, *Let Me Tell You a Story* (Nashville, Word Publishing, 2000), p. 120-121.

[40] Rone Cole-Turner, Your Child's Baptism," UCBHM.

April 26, 1998

Dear Jacob, Mark, Karysa-Jean and Evan:

For each of you, as has been the case on every other occasion when children have come here to be baptized, today is a very special day in your young lives. Your parents brought you to this well-cared for sanctuary of the First Congregational Church in historic Coventry to be baptized into the Christian faith. They are accompanied by many, but not all, of your extended families. ***In your case, Karysa-Jean, I see four,--- that's right, four, --- very proud generations.*** Indeed, I know each of your families and you are very blessed to have wonderful extended families and a rather wide circles of friends, each of whom, I suspect, will no doubt have plenty of advice for you as you grow and mature into adulthood. At one time, each of you was but a hope and a dream. Then, you became a movement in your mother's womb, and with our advanced technology, a picture in their hands and now, a lovely little girl and three handsome boys. Your parents have told me you are terrific. **No surprise!** The rest of us can see the overflowing pride and joy of your parents. We know you must be feeling it too. You are **"dressed to the nines,"** as we sometimes say. Jacob, you are the oldest of the four this morning and believe it or not—you are in a big boy's suit. **Handsome, indeed!**

The spirit of this occasion is very special for everyone and, if you don't mind my saying it, for me. Each of you has been brought here accompanied by your own unique familial story, and I'm feeling very privileged to be a participant in those stories.

Jacob and Mark: This is a bitter/sweet time for your family. It is made sweet by who is here and how happy they are—Gram and Grandpa Bowen, Grandma Brown (Mark- your brothers call her YaYa!), aunts and uncles and others who love you dearly. But someone is missing, and his absence has your mom tearful. Your Grandpa Brown- "Papa," died just a few months ago. When someone we love dies, we hurt a lot and sometimes for a long time. However, God understands and hurts with us. In fact, there is a line from this morning's Psalm 30 that I love. It goes like this:

Weeping may linger for the night, but joy comes with the morning.
(Psalm 30:5, NRSV)

On this, the morning of your baptisms, joy visits us like a much beloved friend. Papa would be so proud and happy today. He understood something about the meaning of baptism. Jacob, he used to love giving you and your brother, Dylan, your baths. He had fun getting you all dressed for school or ready for bed, and when the scrubbing was done and the hair was combed, he used to say to your mom,

Ok! They're as clean as two shiny nickels!

Baptism means something like that—through the waters of baptism we are reminded that we are made as clean as a shiny nickel by God's unconditional love and forgiveness.

Karysa-Jean: Holding you this morning got me in touch with some unfamiliar but quite wonderful feelings. My association with your family goes way back. I presided at the wedding of your great-uncle Forster and great-aunt Thuy. It was their first and only marriage and it was my first, but not the only one! As I say, you have four generations of your family represented here, and yours is not the first baptism I've performed for the family. Indeed, I baptized your mother and then your brother, Earl. (I think it was in March 1992.) I know, you are now saying to yourself—"My

God, how old is this guy?" Let me tell you—not so old that he has forgotten how talkative your brother was on his baptismal day! Thanks for letting me have my say today.

All this, too, tells us something important about baptism: that God's love in Jesus Christ is an enduring love that sustains us from generation to generation. We want you to know and believe that, and to trust in it.

Evan: You are the third of the brothers who will be known as "The Lorentson Bobsled Boys." Like Cody and Alex, you are precious not only to your mom and dad, but to each member of both sides of your family. You live in the house where your parents were married and the back entrance to the house off the deck is like an art gallery. There's some mighty fine finger-painting being done by your brothers! Together, your clan forms a very wide circle of love, and, as with your little friends, Jacob, and Mark, you are being baptized on a day invested with a deep poignancy. Your uncle Gary and cousin Alyssa have come here from Wilton, CT., to share with you the joy of your baptism and to be strengthened by the gift of love that God gives for life's blessings and burdens. Tomorrow, though, they will travel to Yale-New Haven Hospital for a very serious but promising operation. Your aunt Melissa is very sick with two failing kidneys. Your uncle Gary will give her one of his so that she can live. He blushes when the family calls him a hero, but that's what he is. By example, he is showing us what the true meaning of love is all about, both God's love for us and our love for each other.

David Wilkerson said it this way:

Love is not only something you feel. It's something you do. [41]

I think that he's got it right. Your uncle Gary has it right. By the way, your uncle Gary and aunt Melissa are Alex's godparents! Neat, huh?

A few moments ago, you were all baptized. Your parents acknowledged their faith in Christ and promised to raise you with Christian values. In addition, other members of the church, now your family of faith, stood and promised to help them. You can't imagine how we all feel, given this sense of belonging and shared commitment to each other. Perhaps

---

[41]   Wilkerson, David, Goodreads.

someday, when you participate, as we do today, you will know that same glorious feeling.

What makes it so glorious are the truths it affirms. You are a gift from God, created out of love and for love. This means that although you have been entrusted to us, you do not really belong to us alone--**YOU BELONG TO GOD.** The essential relationship in your life must be your relationship with God. Our responsibility is to help you discover, understand, and deepen it so that it enlivens and enriches all other relationships. We will attempt this as members of your family, some bonded by blood, all by faith. The central theme of family life is love and the source of that love is God, and we believe that the best expression of it is in the person and life of Jesus of Nazareth, the risen Christ, to whom you are uniquely connected. As you grow up in the church, you will hear the words "Good News." When you hear them, they will always refer to the "good news about God's love in Jesus Christ." What is both good and newsworthy about God's love is that when you know it, feel it, trust in it, you get to feel whole, healthy, hopeful, and very happy. You get to feel forgiven (**clean as a shiny nickel!**) and safe, secure, free, and filled with peace. Faith brings with it a joy beyond description. Without it, things can be tough. Our prayer for each of you is that you will come to experience and rejoice in this love, and believe me, for a lifetime, will hear God say:

My grace is sufficient for you, for power is made perfect in weakness.
(2 Corinthians 12:9, NRSV)

It is difficult being a kid these days, or an adult either. I've said in sermons on more than one occasion that our society is not child friendly. Recently, a popular magazine reported it costs $1,455,581 to raise a child. That's a lot of money! Maybe that's one reason you and your playmates represent the group most victimized. Family instability, poverty, violence, abuse, and substance abuse are all too common, and television and video games provide a difficult form of entertainment. But let me make a promise to you right here and now. We will do our best on your behalf to keep you safe, to protect your childhood and to prepare you for responsible adult Christian living by teaching you what we know and value most about life, truth, freedom, faith and matters of the heart.

Jacob, Mark, and Kari: Evan's dad — along with being a professional protector of the environment, is an aspiring writer of children's stories and poetry. Before you learn to read, I'm sure that he will be a published author. Among his writings is a delightful rhyme that teaches things about how to live and relate to one another that we all should know. I include it and a couple of additional verses especially written for this occasion. The title of the rhyme is "Don't Tease the Bees, Please."

"Don't Tease the Bees, Please"
by Robert Lorentson (1998)
(Reprinted with permission)

Don't tease the bees please
They don't mean a thing
Cause it's a fact
They'll tease you back
And they can make it sting.

(Teasing)
****

And if you find a porcupine
Who says he needs a squeeze
If he's a stranger
It spells danger
Just say, Go Away Please!

(Avoiding strangers)
****

Never laugh at a giraffe
For being much too tall
Cause from their view
They think that you
Are looking much too small.

(Laughing at someone who's different)
****

It's fair to share with grizzly bear
And sharing is more fun
But if you don't
I hope you won't
Be too afraid to run.

(Sharing)
****

Don't remark to a tiger shark
That you've got him beaten
You shouldn't brag or raise your flag
In case he hasn't eaten

(Gloating)
****

And if you see a chimpanzee
Who's reading from a book
Just count to ten
And look again
Things aren't always how they look

(Look closely before believing)
****

You mustn't smile at a crocodile
When their teeth are showing
It's best to say
Have a nice day!
But it's time I should be going

(Avoiding mean people)
****

Don't try to wipe off zebra stripes
Or paint them on a horse
Being a friend does not depend
On how we look of course.

(Skin differences are okay)
****

Don't lassoo (lasso) a kangaroo (buffalo)
You might just make him jumpy
And what's more
You might get sore
Your road will soon get bumpy

(Consequences of actions)
****

You should never cheat a cheetah
Just because he is so fast
Just try your best
Say, "Be my guest"
If one should run right past

(Cheating- trying your best)
****

And if you see a lion cryin
Looking very sad
Just smile and say
Are you Ok?
It often makes them glad

(Concern for others)
****

And it's not cool to fool a mule
Whenever he is slow
Because his speed
Might mean he needs
Some special help to go.

(Helping others)
****

If you should bunk with a skunk
And your nose is reeling

Be sure that you
Don't shout PU
It might just hurt his feelings

(Hurting someone's feelings)
****

Don't try to lie to a rhinoceri
It puts them out of joint
It's just not wise
To tell them lies
I'm sure you get their point!

(Lying)
****

SO
****

All God's creatures
Kids to preachers
Flourish with His love
Baptizing you the way we do
Says ***"I LOVE YOU"*** from above

So don't forget
When you get wet
With baptismal water
God sends His love from up above
to every son and daughter.[42]
****

Jacob, Mark, Karysa-Jean and Evan: Be well, be happy and remember always that God loves you and so do we!

---

[42]   Reprinted with permission of author. Bob Lorentson is, in fact, a published author as an environmental scientist. The title of his book is: *Hold the Apocalypse-Pass Me a Scientist Please and Other Humorous Essays from an Optimist in Dreamland.*

Yours in Christ:

Bruce J. Johnson, Pastor

****

"And the Almond Tree Blossomed"

(Confirmation at First Church)

*I said to the almond tree, 'Sister, speak to me of God,'
and the almond tree blossomed.*
Niko Kazantzakis' *Report to Greco* [43]

Only recently did I read the above quote and find it the essence of what we expected from our ministry to the youth of our parish. Our calling was to enable them to speak of God through how they blossomed as persons and as Christians, and here at First Church, this calling was second to none.

Confirmation and youth ministry have been significant for the First Church over the past decades. Indeed, this was a period in our nation's history that was tough on kids. Along with what we might call the normal challenges of growing up, much attention was given to alarming issues such as children having children, drug and alcohol abuse, teen smoking, gang, gun and youth violence. Over this time, Sunday school opened

---

[43]   Cited from *Callings: Finding and Following an Authentic Life* by Gregg Levoy, (New York: Harmony Books), p.326.

and completed the teaching of their curricula. In 1973, we had about 30-40 children in the Sunday school, which held their classes in the duplex house commonly called the Church Lane House and was located directly behind church. Today, our Sunday school is housed in our new Center for Christian Education and registers about 160 children. Our youth programs as well were run uninterrupted and were blessed by the able and caring leadership of both volunteers, and for eighteen years, the able staff guidance of Jim and Mary Ellen Hetrick and since then, Ruth Waugh and Fred North. Confirmation classes varied in size from one (Kevin Crickmore, class of 1981 to one of our largest, the class of 2002, a class of 16.)

Our kids, from the youngest to the oldest, were great because I think that we, as parents and a congregation, did well at keeping them safe, growing their self-esteem, inculcating in them a responsible and compassionate value system, and nurturing them in their Christian faith.

The march of confirmation classes has been extraordinary. They have each, with sibling following sibling, embarked upon their "Journey of Discovery"[44] with some trepidation, but in the end, they completed their walk of faith through our community and were blessed with the precious sense of a genuine confirmation. For each class I tried to convey the essence of confirmation:

Confirmation is:
* Personally recognizing and accepting the claim of God on one's own life--- God's self-revelation taking place in Jesus Christ.
* Actively, consciously, and responsibly entering the life of the people of God, the community of Christian pilgrims.
* Being sent out to help identify and participate in God's work in the world.[45]

Second, especially in recent years, we tried to include in the liturgy of the Rite of Confirmation and then the "Owning of the Covenant" the sense that there is a symbolic transference of the tradition of the church to

---

[44] Taken from "Confirming our Faith: A Confirmation Resource for the United Church of Christ." (New York: United Church Press) p. 4.
[45] "Confirming our Faith," p. 16.

another generation. Liturgy and symbols can be powerful expressions of what is "operational" in the life and witness of a congregation, and I think that what we did and said on Confirmation Sunday was a case in point. Perhaps the text of that ceremony would be instructive.

The Transference of the Tradition and Faith

Symbols:

Baptismal Certificates:
Parents: When you were infants, we had you baptized. On the occasion of your baptism, we promised to nurture you in the Christian faith and to love you in such a way that you will one day feel free enough and strong enough to choose for yourself to be Christian. Today we rejoice in your decision and commitment and, as a symbol of your assuming the responsibility of your faith, we present your baptismal certificate to you.
Confirmands: We thank you for honoring our baptismal vows and today, joyfully accept and confirm our baptisms.

Scripture: (Trustee) This Bible is the sourcebook of our faith and is the record of our inspiring Judeo-Christian tradition. It is and always will be uniquely authoritative in the life of this congregation. In the best spirit of the United Church of Christ, we believe that there is yet more light and truth to be revealed by it. Those who have preceded you have loved it and followed its teachings. Now we entrust it to you.
Confirmands: We accept this Bible as our sourcebook of faith and promise to love it and live by its teachings and truths.

History: (Historian) This History of the First Congregational Church of Coventry is the written record of how those who have preceded you endeavored to be faithful to their calling as Christians and to their covenant as members of this church. It reveals a proud tradition of worship and service. Although it has a first chapter, there is no last, only the latest. We now entrust it to you.
Confirmands: We accept this history with reverence and promise to author not the last but only the latest chapter of our history.

Candle: (Diaconate) Jesus once said: "I am the light of the world; the person who follows me will not walk in darkness but will have the light of life." Then, on another occasion, He said to His followers, "You are the light of the world." Indeed, those who possess the light become the light and the hope of the world. This candle that burns so brightly does so symbolically as the light of God's love in Jesus Christ. In lighting the candle you now hold, we entrust it and its meaning to you. Love it. Live it. Be it.

Confirmands: We accept Him as the light that enlightens and enlivens us. We promise to keep it burning so that those who worship and serve Christ with us, as well as those who will follow, will discover the power and privilege of being the children of God.

Blessing: (Pastor) Beloved, we greet you with joy. We pledge to you our friendship in the Lord and will give you our support in prayer and service that you may continue to grow in the knowledge and love of God, be witnesses of Jesus Christ, our risen Lord and active participants in the mission and ministry of this church. As a sign of our pledge, we extend to you the right hand of Christian faith and community.

There is a passage from a book that was a gift to me from our former director of music, Margo Lazzerini. It is titled: *Stories of the Spirit, Stories of the Heart: Parables of the Spiritual Path from Around the World,* and, to my mind, this paragraph captures what I think is the essence of the deeply personal confirmation journey.

Others teach us the fundamentals needed for beginning any authentic spiritual venture: integrity, compassion, and attention. But we ourselves must discover how to bring these into blossom. The map is not the journey.

One Hassidic rabbi named Zashu told his students, "When I die, God will not ask me, was I like Moses or was I like Joshua in my life. He will ask me, was I like Zashu."

To see with clarity and to respect what is here and now in our lives, to fulfill and offer our own inner gifts-- this is our spiritual path. To let our lives be a deep expression of heartfelt values, to know what awakens us and nurture it-- this is our way.[46]

Through confirmation, we taught and learned to speak of God by blossoming as Christian men and women who see with clarity and purpose that following Christ is the best "way of life" for us.

****

Marriage

"A Renewal of Vows on a Diamond Anniversary"

...and He said, 'For this reason a man shall leave his father and mother and the woman her home and be joined, and the two shall become one flesh. So they are no longer two but one flesh. What, therefore, God has joined together, let not man put asunder.

Matthew 19: 5-6

Those who have never known the deep intimacy and hence the companionship of happy mutual love have missed the best thing that life has to give.

Bertrand Russell

Thirteen days after 'Black Tuesday,' the day of the great stock market crash of October 29, 1929, Walter and Viola Thorp were married at the historic church of Jonathan Trumbull, the First Congregational Church of Lebanon, Connecticut. Marriage is a sign of hope for a dark and despairing world. This was especially true in their case. I am reminded of a saying from the Jewish teacher and leader of Hasidism, Ba'al Shem Tov:

From every human being there rises a light that reaches straight to heaven, and when two souls that are destined to

---

[46] Christina Feldman and Jack Kornfield, editors. *Stories of the Spirit, Stories of the Heart* (San Francisco: Harper-Collins, 1991) p. 301.

> *be together find each other, the streams of light flow together*
> *and a single brighter light goes forth from that united being.*

Walter and Viola's single bright light has been shining since November 11, 1929. Yes, do the math, that's seventy-five years.

Eight years before they were married, the United States Congress passed legislation approving the establishment of the Tomb of the Unknown Soldier in Arlington National Cemetery. November 11th was chosen for the date of the ceremony dedicating that site and, concurrently, November 11th was established as a legal holiday to honor all those who took part in World War I. As we all know, in 1938 it was called Armistice Day and then on June 1, 1954, President Eisenhower signed legislation changing the name to Veterans Day. Every year since, along with a grateful nation that honors its soldiers, Walter and Viola also reaffirmed the vows that united them in marriage and had them promise to love, honor, cherish and obey each other for a lifetime. Walter was twenty-three and Viola was sixteen.

So, November 11th is their wedding anniversary, and on Thursday, November 11, 2004, they will celebrate their seventy-fifth anniversary. We call it their Diamond Anniversary. As of this writing, Water is ninety-eight years old and Viola, well, being such a lady, I suppose it might not be appropriate to mention in print. They have lived long, happy, and productive lives. They have been active members of First Church for fifty-four years, having joined in July 1954. During my time as pastor of First Church, I have married 550 couples, not one as young as Viola was, and I can't imagine any being so blessed to reach their seventy-fifth wedding anniversary. For all their marriage, Walter and Viola were, sadly, avid Boston Red Sox fans. Walter remembers the year the Red Sox won the World Series, 1918, and has said often and with a laugh that he hopes they will do it again in his lifetime. Well, ironically, here in the diamond year of their marriage, they got to see them do it again. Amazing!

When I reflect on Walter and Viola and their marriage and what I have learned from them, two special quotes come to mind.

First, because they have had four children, fourteen grandchildren, fifteen great grandchildren and two great, great grandchildren, I am reminded of something that the late Henri J. M. Nouwen and Walter J. Gaffney wrote in their neat book, titled *Aging: The Fulfillment of Life.*

Entering into the world, we are what we are given, and for many years thereafter, parents and grandparents. Brothers and sisters, friends and lovers keep giving to us, some more, some less, some hesitantly, some generously. When we can finally stand on our own feet, speak our own words and express our own unique self in work and love, we realize how much has been given to us. But while reaching the height of our cycle, and saying with a great sense of confidence, 'I really am,' we sense to fulfill our lives we are now called to become parents and grandparents, brothers and sisters, teachers, friends, and lovers ourselves, and to give to others, so that when we leave this world, we can be what we have given.

Aging is the gradual fulfillment of the life cycle in which receiving matures in giving and living makes dying worthwhile. [47]

Second, over the years, I enjoyed reading and hearing various types of readings for the wedding ceremonies I performed. The following selection, with its basic truth, was and remains one of my favorites.

The Art of A Good Marriage
(shortened version-eight lines)
Wilfred Arlan Peterson

A good marriage must be created.
In marriage the little things are the big things...
It is never being too old to hold hands,
It is remembering to say "I love you" at least once a day,

.

.

It is having the capacity to forgive and forget,
It is giving each other an atmosphere in which each can grow,

---

[47] Henri J. M. Nouwen, Walter J. Gaffney, *Aging: The Fulfillment of Life* (Darton, Longman and Todd, Ltd. And Doubleday and Company, Inc., Garden City, New York, 1966) p. 3.

> *It is a common search for the good and the beautiful,*
> *It is not only marrying the right person, it is being the right*
> *partner.*

Walter and Viola were special people who were right for each other. Their marriage began at the start of the Great Depression when they were very young. Today, they are, according to the calendar, quite old, but watching them renew their vows while seated in wheelchairs and holding hands and with a circle of familial love around them, one couldn't help but be impressed with how young and playful they still are with their affection and sincerity. They have said, "I love you" thousands upon thousands of times. They have probably forgiven and forgotten as many times as they have said, "I love you." They lived during a century of extraordinary challenge and change, times of scarcity and times of abundance, periods of war and peace, but they have not aged, really. Why not? My best answer to that question is quite simple. They stood together and faced the world, never relinquishing their common search for the good and the beautiful, no matter what the circumstances.

Life is all about living and giving from the heart, and God has made us in such a way that aging with grace and staying young are the same thing. We must stay open to the world's messages of beauty, courage, kindness, compassion, and love. They also require that we understand that receiving can only mean something worthwhile when it matures in giving.

On this Diamond Anniversary Day, I am reminded of the television advertisement for the sale of diamonds. DeBeers is the sponsor. The jingle goes:

A diamond is forever.

Well, today, we remember what scripture tells us: *love never ends,* and what Walter and Viola made so interesting: "marriage is forever, too."

CHAPTER III

Voices in the Passage[48]

It is a fearful thing to love
what Death can touch.[49]

INTRODUCTION

As I reflect on our ecclesiastical identity and purpose in the community of Coventry, I am proud to confirm that no aspect of Christian ministry has meant more than that shared with the dying and the grieving. It has been such a privilege to be a companion with the dying and an even greater privilege to have been called upon to preside at services that celebrate life, acknowledge death, and help people grieve in their own way. Without exception, I felt pastorally affirmed when people remarked they "enjoyed" a funeral service. In some ways, I considered it the highest of callings to give voice to the prophet, poet, and pastor, to the husband or wife, a father or mother, a brother or sister, a family member or friend on behalf

---

[48]   Title is borrowed from Cynthia D. Gentile's book of poetry, *Voices in the Passage.* (South Windsor, CT, Brewster Bay Press, 1984)

[49]   This quote comes from a lovely collection of poetry by Cynthia D. Gentile, Glenden Dunlap's daughter, titled *Voices in the Passage.* It is a line cited by Josephine Jacobsen from an old New Hampshire gravestone and has been the one quote that I have cited most often throughout my ministry. The original author was the Spanish Jewish poet Yehuda Halevi (1075-1141), often referred to as one of the greatest Hebrew poets.

of hurting and sometimes fearful hearts who are forced to experience the swirl of emotions around the passing of a loved one. I cherished this role and its attending privileges and responsibilities above all others in the ministry. In the "passage," we have shared this "call" and prioritized it during these many years.

Since coming to First Church in 1973, I have performed over 700 funerals and memorial services. Repeatedly, I witnessed and felt the pain of loss in people's hearts. Rainer Maria Rilke, the poet, expressed the emotional prayer of everyone:

> *O Lord, give each of us his own death,*
> *the dying, that issues forth out of life*
> *in which he had love, meaning and despair.*[50]

Would that it could have been this way for all those who were members of our family, our community and church over these four/five decades. However, it was not. Too few got to choose their own death. The 1996 Nobel Prize for Literature winner, Wislawa Szymborska, paints a vivid image of death having the right of way. This is how Szymborska says it:

Seen from Above

> *The dead beetle lies on the path through the field.*
> *Three pairs of legs folded neatly on its belly.*
> *Instead of death's confusion, tidiness and order.*
> *The horror of this sight is moderate,*
> *its scope is strictly local, from the wheat grass to the mint.*
> *The grief is quarantined.*
> *The sky is blue.*
>
> *To preserve our peace of mind, animals die more shallowly:*
> *they aren't deceased, they're dead.*
> *They leave behind, we'd like to think,*
> *less feeling and less world,*

---

[50] Sherwin B. Nuland, *How We Die: Reflections on Life's Final Chapter* (New York: Alfred A. Knopf, Inc., 1993) p. 264.

departing, we suppose, from a stage less tragic.
Their meek souls never haunt us in the dark,
they know their place,
they show respect.

And so the dead beetle on the path
lies unmourned and shining in the sun.
One glance at it will do for meditation---
clearly nothing much has happened to it.
Important matters are reserved for us,
for our life and our death, a death
that always claims the right of way.[51]

Because we matter, important matters are reserved for us, our lives, our loved ones, our deaths, but death usually claims its right way without waiting for permission. And because of this poignant reality, I not only felt "called" but "authorized" to invest time and training, truth, and the blessings of experience in giving voice to and for the grieving.

The strongest connection I felt with the history and life of our congregation was through those who died and for whom I did services. They were young, and they were aging and old. Their deaths were tragic and triumphant. Each provided an occasion for us to cry together and laugh together. I encouraged the telling of stories, the sharing of memories, the display of memorabilia and family photos. We confirmed our faith and celebrated the ties that bind and bless our hearts in Christian love, as the beloved hymn says. At these painful and poignant moments, I felt such genuine affection for all. Some say what is most personal is also most universal. That bit of wisdom proved to be true. In being very personal in my remembrances and reflections about members and friends of the parish, we spoke about valued and honored parts and pieces of ourselves and our own unique story. This chapter is about some of the life tributes I and others have written. The focus may be upon the names and life stories of specific individuals, but what is being shared really applies to us all. I believe we learn so much about life and how to live it amid our

---

[51] Szymborska, Wislawa, *View with a Grain of Sand: Selected Poems* (New York: Harcourt Brace and Company, 1993) p.103.

acknowledgment and acceptance of death, even if it harshly claimed its right of way.

****

"Suffer the Little Children"

The deaths of infants and children were and still are the toughest. A few years ago, Judy Hill, one of our best pie bakers and quilters, shared with me a wonderful book by Diane M. Komp, MD, titled *A Window to Heaven: When Children See Life in Death*.[52] Dr. Komp is the Professor Emeritus of Pediatrics at the Yale School of Medicine and a doctor who revisited her faith through her patients. She spoke of her practice and her patients when she quoted Charles Dickens. The quote is tender, poignant, and powerful.

> *To my patients: 'I love thee*
> *little people; and it is not a*
> *slight thing when they, who are so*
> *fresh from God, love us.'*
> Charles Dickens, *The Old Curiosity Shop.*

There is something about an infant's death or a child's life and death that touch us at the softest of places in our soul and challenges our faith in ways that no other death can. I remember these *little people* by name. There was Frank Bassett, Heather Marie Kristoff, Brie Megan Kelly, Benjamin Richard Touloujian, Robert Francis Plaster, Robert T. Meek, III., Parrish A. Thompson, Carrie Elynn Shaw, Mark Whittiker, Ryan Christopher Hutchins, Sarah Anne Zurmuhlen, David Cameron Wedderspoon Jr., the twins, Ryan and Reese Miller, Garth Christopher Smith, Jr., Brian Craig Mannick, Christopher James Tourtellotte, Noah John Brescia, Felicia Marie Marley, Damien Marchand, Cameron Morris Schoenbrod Joy, Angel J. Colburn and Kellan Blair Keenan.

---

[52]   Diane Komp, *A Window to Heaven: When Children See Life in Death* (Grand Rapids, Michigan: Zondervan Publishing House, 1992). p. 5.

I feel grateful that we said and did things years ago that are only now receiving increased attention and inclusion in new liturgies.[53] Somehow, we knew from the start that we could and should find the rightful voices for these very premature passings.

Our respect for life and God's covenant of love has been our priority throughout these decades. For this reason, the words of Jeremiah rang truest, not just for him, but for us and our children.

> *Before I formed you in the womb, I knew you,*
> *and before you were born, I consecrated you.*
> *(Jeremiah 1:5, NRSV)*

These little ones, so fresh from God, are named and loved and their deaths created a profound sense of loss for their parents and the community, but we knew 'a priori' that God had consecrated them. In a society that some say has trivialized the trauma of infertility and diminished the significance of stillborn or infant death, we sought to affirm and address the needs of those who had experienced such a loss and with it, all the hopes and dreams, plans, possibilities, and promises. Indeed, when Jesus walked among the people on that hillside overlooking the Galilee and delivered his "Consider the Lilies of the Field" sermon and talked about beauty and worth, we can't imagine His not being mindful of those "so fresh from God." And so, without fail, we tried our best to replicate that same divine regard for life throughout our ministry and church life.

****

---

[53] This reality has only recently been called "Silent Sorrow" by Rev. Millicent Feske who is about to publish a new book titled: *For Want of a Child: A Pastoral Response to Infertility*. In addition, in the fall of 1998, served on the "Pregnancy Loss and Prevention Steering Committee for the Windham Memorial Hospital in an effort to develop "a series of lectures concerning pregnancy loss and grieving and in developing a support program for women who have sustained either ectopic pregnancy, miscarriage, abortion, stillborn, neonatal death or SIDS death."

Bruce J. Johnson

"A Little Child Shall Lead Them"

When the prophet Isaiah spoke so poetically about the future hope and peace of Israel, he used these beautiful words:

> *The wolf shall live with the lamb,*
> *and the leopard shall lie down with the kid,*
> *and the calf and the lion and the fatling together,*
> *and a little child shall lead them..*
>
> *(Isaiah 11:6, NRSV)*

The children of our parish brought us to a place where hope abounds, and we experienced peace as a genuine gift of grace. Children's stories and youth choirs in worship, crowded Sunday school classes and Pilgrim Fellowships in mission were signs of promise throughout these four decades. Yet, as I reflect on my years here, I am again reminded that our faith proved most alive in times of death, especially the tragic deaths of some of our teenagers and young adults. These, too, had names, and parents and grandparents. They have life stories and implicit religious dramas, which when told, helped to grow the faith of those who celebrated their lives and mourned their deaths.

I am reminded of Cheryl Ann Chobot, Curt K. Wittig, Bradford J. Bristol, Patricia C. Kristoff,(Patricia was Heather's mother and Peter's wife. She died in a car accident four months after her three-month-old daughter Heather died), Wayne K. Little, Peter M. Duprey, Richard F Coughlin, Jr., Arthur C. Willimans, Michelle Dawn McKinney, Cynthia Elizabeth Figueroa, David C. Heon, Steven A. Mills, William H. Welliver, Craig P. LeDoyt, Donna Lynn Jacobson, Brian Thompson, William E. Phelan, Evie Marie Cowart, Jason L. Potter, Gregory Guy Goodin and Robert Martin Johnson, Christopher Chicky, Steven N. Schweitzer, Deborah R. Waite, Jared R. Marsh, Kimberly Ruth Goldsneider, Christopher-George Jacques, Brian G. Hall and Jarrod M. Sanborn. Although the circumstances of these deaths vary, what they hold in common is the profound sense of loss that was felt by our parents and families, our congregation and community. It was, however, precisely at these moments of tragedy when our faith triumphed most. I often quoted the words of Ernest Hemingway from his book, *A Farewell to Arms:*

> *The world breaks everyone, and afterward,*
> *many are strong at the broken places.*

I am in awe of the many who have become so strong at these broken places. Today, I am cognizant of my age, now seventy-five (75). The names are all associated with faces and personal stories made forever young by the unfair and always tragic touch of death. One death occurred when I was young but continued to speak poignantly about the power of the world to break us. A careless driver on a street in Malaga, Spain, killed Michelle Dawn McKinney on April 20, 1981. Michelle was only fourteen years old, a bright and beautiful girl, on vacation with her parents and brother, Michael. She stepped off a street curb at an intersection and was struck by a speeding car driven by a careless driver.

In April 1984, the church dedicated a sanctuary piano to her memory, along with that of Carol Bessette Carpenter. Our organist plays a special instrumental piece on Remembrance Sunday, so we will never forget Carol, Michelle, or the promises of God. At the Dedication, I made these remarks:

> *… This instrument will grace this sanctuary for a very long time, offering to those who worship new opportunities for the soul to be touched, the spirit to soar and our sense of being to express or experience itself as a part of the rhythms of the universe. Whenever it is played, we surely remember that Michelle died tragically at the age of fourteen (14) but let us not be trapped by death's encircling darkness. Rather, in remembering her, let us bask in the light of her natural beauty, goodness, and grace. Let us hear again the voices of the Junior Choir and the giggles of girls. Let us see bright eyes that invite others to join in on the song and dance of life with youthful exuberance. Let us remember and believe that out of the mouths of babes often comes the truth about life. This was especially true for Michelle. In 1980, she wrote this poem, as if for the occasion. It gives fresh meaning to the line from Isaiah that tells us that a little child shall lead us.*

"The Dove"
by Michelle Dawn McKinney, '80.
(Reprinted with permission)

The delicate little thing,
Beating its tiny wings
Hoping it would get there.
The sacred sign in its beak,
Only water could it see.
Until, it appeared, over the peak,
Could it really be?
When he got there,
Noah let out his hand,
The dove landed, gracefully.
They knew there was land,
Then over the horizon it rose,
A colorful promise, a rainbow.

We have a file folder in the church office, or perhaps the church archives now, that contains a copy of the above poem and Michelle's middle school picture. Each year on Remembrance Sunday, which is on the Memorial Day weekend, I brought out the folder and looked at her picture. Sadness always descended, but it brought with it her youth and beauty, and they reminded me of a Native American proverb.

The soul would have no rainbow, had the eyes no tears.

Where, O Death, Is Your Victory?
Where, O Death, Is Your Sting?
                    First Corinthians 15:55 (NRSV)

****

"Memorials and Metaphors"

To what do we owe this glory---
The glory that was bestowed,

In sharing life with one so loved
>> In heart and mind, in soul.

Our paths have crossed
>> Never to be the same,
For as our lives so touched
>> Our memories were born.
>> In quiet moments---
>> Or in those we share,
Our loved one still shares with us
This day and tomorrow evermore.

(Katherine Thon, as read at the memorial service for F. Pauline Little, March 15, 2003; source unknown)

There were so many other services over the years that gave us the opportunity to express or give voice to what we feel and believe. These are the services for our parents and grandparents, our sons and daughters, our spouses, and friends. They were for farmers and teachers and community leaders. They were always filled with heartwarming memories and sometimes, we happened upon metaphors that helped us make sense out of certain situations.

One of the largest funerals of my tenure as pastor of First Church took place on July 1, 1990, for Scott Wilton Rose. Throughout the records for First Church over the past seventy-five years, the family name of Rose appears often and figures prominently. Scott was surely one of our favored sons. Supported with a full measure of love from his wife, Sue, and his son, Christopher, and his parents, Fred and Louise, he battled cancer courageously and was only thirty-four years old when he died. When Dr. Bernie Seigel quoted the following much beloved saying from India, I'm sure he had someone like Scott in mind.

> *When you were born, you cried, and the world rejoiced. Live your life in such a manner that when you die, the world cries and you rejoice.*[54]

---

[54]   Bernie S. Siegel, M.D. *Love, Medicine, and Miracles* (New York: Harper and Row, 1986) p. 224.

Feeling broken, we cried that day, and yet, we never lost sight of our calling, not only to celebrate our faith but to rejoice in the riches of life. My eulogy for Scott, I hope, spoke to our needs, and I share it again as somewhat universally representative of what we have said and done at First Church for so many of our sons and daughters who have died too young.

"Safely Home"

Eulogy for Scott Wilton Rose
July 1, 1990
by the Reverend Dr. Bruce J. Johnson

"The outlook wasn't brilliant for the Mudville nine that day."[55]

So began "Casey at the Bat, A Ballad for the Republic, sung in the year 1888," perhaps the most famous American verse ever written. How well we all know that sometimes in life, the outlook isn't brilliant, and the outcome of the game is not what we wanted!

The concluding stanza of "Casey at the Bat" is almost as oft quoted as its first. It is a stanza that captures, at least in some respects, how we all feel, this because Scott has played for many a Mudville nine, always to the last out and he and his team haven't always won.

> *Oh, somewhere in this favored land the sun is shining bright;*
> *The band is playing somewhere and somewhere hearts are light,*
> *And somewhere men are laughing, and somewhere children shout;*
> *But there is no joy in Mudville--- Mighty Casey has struck out.*

We come here this afternoon with hearts that are burdened by grief, with eyes made red by tears, with voices stilled by the sorrow we feel because we will miss Scott.

---

[55]   Ernest Lawrence Thayer, "Casey at the Bat," 1888.

He was "The Natural" [56] in who he was, how he lived, the way he loved and in everything he did for us. To borrow a phrase from the movie, he was "the best there ever was, the best there ever will be." (The few exceptions are the few flaws that Sue revealed to Fred and Louise on Friday about something they never knew such as- how the snowmobile got its dent or why the transmission of the new Torino started to slip.)

His dearest loves were always obvious, starting with Sue, his beloved wife and childhood sweetheart and best friend, and son, Christopher, his parents, Fred and Louise, and his sisters, Karen and Barbara Jeanne. Then, there was the extended family of aunts and uncles, nieces and nephews, in-laws and out-laws and the extensive network of friends and friendships that always seemed to develop and mature naturally around him. (All we need to do is look around this sanctuary today with its condition of 'standing room only' to have this observation about Scott confirmed.)

There have also always been the dogs, especially the very talented, entertaining, and somewhat "news houndish" Shadrack! I list the dogs last simply not to embarrass those who have been mentioned first, for if the truth be known ... well, enough said!

Scott was an outdoorsman and sportsman in the truest sense of those words and representative of the best that the tradition offers. He was a competitor, or in the words of Larry Keeley, who wrote that poignant article for *The Chronicle*, a battler. He had a passion not only for the game of baseball but for life itself, whether in the woods while walking serenely on a crisp fall day or leading a noisy caravan of snowmobiles in a winter wonderland up north or on Long Island Sound pulling a lobster pot or baiting a hook for Chris in a boat he built or setting the decoys for a day of duck hunting. Scott had a healthy passion for it all.

At no time was his passion for life and his reassuring confidence in himself and the order of things great and small more evident than when *the outlook was not brilliant*. He had an exceptional last day with Sue and Mike, talking about things that mattered most and leaving them with this comment: "I'll ride out the storm."

He rode out the storm and died peacefully that night.

---

[56] The reference is to the title of a very popular movie of the early 1990's called "The Natural," starring Robert Redford. The story line involves a handsome, gifted baseball player.

And now, what remains for us is to grieve our loss in such a way that we might ride out our storm and come to know the peace and promise and joy of that SOMEWHERE that Scott would say is HERE, where the sun is shining, the band is playing, hearts are light, people are laughing, and children are shouting.

If I may close by once again relying upon the metaphor of baseball, I want first to share with you a bit of trivia and then through a piece of baseball poetry, the profound truth of our Christian faith which affirms our resurrection to eternal life.

First the trivia: As for the origins of baseball, there are two schools of thought. Some believe that it was a game created by a man named Alexander Joy Cartwright. Others contend it evolved from cricket, or a game called rounders. No one really knows. What we know, however, is that as early as 1796, Jane Austen mentioned the game of 'baseball' in <u>Nothanger Abbey</u>, and in 1744, an anonymous poem appeared in "A Little Pretty Pocket Book." That poem reads:

> "B" is for
> Base-ball
> The ball once struck off
> Away flies the boy
> To the next destined post
> And then... Home ... with joy.

This afternoon, what we affirm as true is this:
Away has flown our Scott
To his next destined post
He's Safely Home ... With Joy.
Amen.

"Safely Home" has always been the final and most essential proclamation of the church and its faith.

****

"For Everything Its Season"

For rural farming communities such as Coventry, many of our citizens live their lives close to the land. We have our share of farmers and dairies. They work from dawn to dusk, seven days a week and every day of the year and in my year, leap year, one extra day! I'll never forget my meeting with Edward Hill and Laura Woronecki in 1994 concerning their wedding plans. When asked about dates and times for the wedding, I first suggested a late afternoon wedding and an evening reception. Eddie said that my suggestion was much appreciated, but there was one problem with it: he would like to have his mother and dad and brother, Byron, at the wedding. I thought for a moment, not really understanding what he meant. Suddenly, I realized their herd of cows, who needed to be milked each morning and evening, didn't care much about the wedding. Indeed, as far as they were concerned, the wedding would have to take place between milkings! So, it did.

New England is also a place of spectacular beauty as one season yields to its successor. Whenever I quote from the *Book of Ecclesiastes*, heads nod and hearts note a basic truth in life:

> *For everything, there is a season and a time for every matter under heaven: a time to be born and a time to die.*
> (Ecclesiastes 3: 1-2, NRSV)

Farmers and farm families are the salt of the earth. It has been my honor to deliver a tribute to their lives multiple times. One of my most heartfelt tributes was for Lester Taylor Hill, Judy's husband, and Byron and Edward Hill's father.

Eulogy for Lester Taylor Hill
November 19, 1999
by Reverend Dr. Bruce J. Johnson

On October 29, 1988, I had the privilege of presiding at the funeral for Lester's father, Wilfred. I began his eulogy with a quote from Lester. (No, it wasn't off color and contained no profanity!) He simply said:

> *Even though you expect it, you're never really ready.*

On Tuesday morning, sitting at his bedside keeping vigil with Judy and watching her so lovingly hold Lester's tractor toughened hand, I thought to myself that contrary to what Lester thought, sometimes it goes like this:

> *Even though you don't expect it, you are, by grace, ready.*

Once Lester learned that his form of cancer was too aggressive for his treatment, he was ready. Maybe that's why his dying progressed so quickly. Besides, he always had <u>his</u> way of doing things. Why change the rules now?

As I watched Lester breathe his last breath so peacefully, Tennyson's lovely words came to mind.

> *God's finger touched him, and he slept.*

He's with God now, and I only hope that God is ready!

Lester was an original. Jesus once gathered a crowd in a field that had never seen a tractor and declared, "They were the salt of the earth." Lester was the salt of the earth, a salty old timer. He lived his entire life on Silver Street. He was born there, grew up there, got married and lived there, raised his family there, farmed there, hunted there, and loved it there.

The farm was his life, and Judy, the boys, Byron and Eddie, Laura and, of course, the one upon whom the morning's sun rose and will set tonight, his granddaughter, Heather, shared him with it. There was the corn, the hay, the tractor and the fields, the barn, and his beloved Ayrshires. (Byron, how do you spell Ayrshire?)

That

> *...friendly cow all red and white.*
> *I love with all my heart.*
> *She gives me cream to have with apple tart.*

Yet, by the looks of things last night at colling hours, the sheer numbers are an extraordinary tribute to a man and how his life has touched other lives. He must have gotten off the farm from time to time! I'm reminded of this verse:

> *He was a friend whose heart was good,*
> > *Who walked with me and understood.*
> *His was a smile men loved to see,*
> > *His was a hand that asked no fee,*
> *For friendliness or kindness done,*
> > *And now that he has journeyed on,*
> *His is a fame that never ends,*
> > *He leaves behind unnumbered friends.*

I understand that in his younger days Lester carried the nickname, "Lightning" and boasted often to the boys that in his younger days, for twelve years, he never went to bed on the same day that he got up. And judging by the number of signatures and messages in his yearbook, the "old timer" did all right for himself off the farm.

The quote beneath his yearbook picture reads:

> *Smiles from others are obtained from good wit.*

My favorite message:

Lester,

> *"Best of luck to one of the nicest guys I know. Remember the good times we had in 210 and walking back from homeroom. Also remember how you and your buddies made my face red." Donna*

Come to think of it, he has made my face red a few times!

He loved a good time and a good joke. Some of those jokes were not repeatable in some social settings! Lester was quite a square dancer and a card player.

His heart was good and as Byron said, he was always for the common man, down to earth, ready to help anyone. His involvements and commitments show this: The Grange, through civic positions he has held and what he has done for others in and through this church, where he served as deacon.

He could have done better at some things—like telling those he loved the most, that he loved them and that he was proud of them, which was how he actually felt!

He could have been a little less stubborn and less committed to his way as the best way. (Actually, I guess there might have been a time or two when his way may have been the only way!)

But when all is said and done, we end up with a good man who has lived a good life… a blessing to his family, his church, and his community.

There is a verse from Paul's Second Letter to the church at Corinth that seems to me to be appropriate. He writes:

> *The point is this: the one who sows sparingly will also reap sparingly, and the one who sows bountifully will also reap bountifully. Each of you must give as you have made up your mind, not reluctantly or under compulsion, for God loves a cheerful giver. (2 Corinthians 9: 6-7, NRSV)*

Lester's life, both on and off the farm, shows us he decided he would sow bountifully, so that the harvest, for him and others, would be abundant. Even though we didn't expect it, we are, by grace, ready.

So, today we honor him with the expression of our love,

With the memories we share,

With our thank you and our farewells.

Let me close with this last poem. I read it for Lester, as I have for others who lived their lives and made their living on the farms they loved.

"Farewell to the Farm"
by Robert Louis Stevenson (1850-1894)

The coach is at the door at last;
The eager children, mounting fast
And kissing hands, in chorus sing;
Goodbye, goodbye, to everything!

To house and garden, field and lawn,
The meadow-gates we swung upon,
To pump and stable, tree and swing,
Goodbye, goodbye to everything!

And fare you well for evermore,
O ladder at the hayloft door,
O hayloft where the cobwebs cling,
Goodbye, goodbye to everything!

Crack goes the whip, and off we go;
The trees and houses smaller grow;
Last, round the woody turn we swing;
Goodbye, goodbye, to everything!

****

"I'd Rather Play at Hug O' War"

Sometimes it was best for me to relinquish the pulpit for the time of remembrance, allowing and encouraging others to share what was in their hearts. The sudden death of Morgan B. Redfield, a beloved teacher in our school system, was one such occasion. One of his favorite poems was by Dr. Suess and was called "Hug O' War."

> *I will not play at tug o' war. I'd rather play at hug o' war*
> *Where everyone hugs, Instead of tugs,*
> *Where everyone giggles, And rolls on the rug,*
> *Where everyone kisses, And everyone grins,*
> *And everyone cuddles,*
> *And everyone wins.*

The Principal of Coventry Grammar School, Raymond Grasso, gave an eloquent tribute with a strong statement of faith. He did some "tugging" and some "hugging" through his words. (Such an excellent example of a "voice" from the pew!)

SOME WORDS FOR MORGAN[57]
by Raymond Grasso, Principal, Coventry Grammar School
May 21, 2003
(Reprinted with permission of the author)

Something wonderful is missing from our school right now, creating a great big hole right in the center of things that is going to take quite a lot of fixing. Oh, yes—we'll heal. We'll patch things up. And, oh, yes, we will eventually fill in the space. But will it be as bright and as warm and as welcoming a space as Morgan once helped make it? I hope so. For the children's sake, for our staff's sake, for my sake, I believe so. And with Morgan's spirit still guiding us, I know so.

Sometimes when I find myself struggling for the right words, I turn to my five-, six-, seven-, and eight-year-old consultants at Coventry Grammar School because they are wiser than I and not guarded in their words and thoughts as adults, sadly, are. Monday morning, at recess, a young friend of mine, one of Mr. Redfield's delightful students this year, summed it up for me and, I'm sure, for all of us. I found the little guy quietly folded within himself, a tiny pile of elbows and knees, sitting against the outer wall of our building. Usually, you can barely make him out at recess because he has that second-grade-boy superpower of being able to travel at the speed of light (except, probably, when cleaning his room).

But not Monday morning. I went over to him and sat down next to him. He looked up into my face, and I asked him how he was doing. It was the most unnecessary of questions. With a pause, then a sigh, he softly replied: "I feel like I just can't move right now." At that moment, I was sure that he was speaking for every one of his classmates and for many other children in our school. At that moment, I was also sure that no grown up could have spoken so honestly, so openly, so truly from the heart.

Here are the words that Mr. Redfield's students have been using this week to describe him in conversations and in cards and letters we have been writing: "caring," "loving," "lovable," "zany," "silly," "funny," "wicked funny," "fatherly." "He always makes us laugh. "He gets us to read even when we don't want to." (The past tense is so very hard for children when

---

[57]   Reprinted with permission.

someone dies, isn't it?) "He told me and my friend that we should always appreciate that we have each other."

It takes my breath away that these heartfelt expressions are so very similar to the ones that the children wrote to Mr. Redfield after his accident in January—I find it remarkable that his students' feelings are still as vital and as vibrant because, except for an occasional visit the past few weeks, Mr. Redfield had <u>not</u> been with them each day in their classroom in several months... Or had he?

You all know of Morgan's unique and special classroom antics because several have become legends, and rightfully so with such a proud legacy of twenty-eight years of classroom teaching. Here's a quick quiz for you—the legions of Mr. Redfield's students know this stuff, so the pressure is on.

Ok, first one. The eight best ways to become a better reader are (read, read, read, read, read, read, read, and <u>read</u>). And what's the very special thing that Mr. Redfield would do if all the students got 100 percent on a spelling test? (Dance on the desk)

Here are some descriptive words from earlier this week from Morgan's school colleagues and school friends (actually, there's no distinction because it was practically impossible to be one without also being the other): "witty," "kind, kind, kind," "kind-hearted," "light-hearted," "inspiring," "generous," "<u>genuine</u>." "He's been like a parent to me...and he made the best dill dip." Morgan always looks to the bright side." (The past tense is difficult for grown-ups, too, isn't it?) "Morgan could cool a hot moment with students or adults with a laugh or a joke or a gesture." "His was a life well-lived...and it was a privilege to know him." "Morgan gave the best hugs...and we will miss them terribly."

There were also many antics apart from the classroom involving Morgan and his school friends, but I <u>won't</u> quiz you on them now because we are in God's house. But I'll give you just a tease. Many of them are related to what one friend aptly described as "Morgan's subtle yet slightly roguish sense of humor." Hmmm.

One of the greatest regrets of my life is that I will never have as rich a knowledge of Morgan as his students or his teaching friends have. I had only worked with him for a relatively brief time but, even then, used to laugh out loud every time Morgan referred to me as "the boss," as if it were possible that anyone could actually be his boss. (Except Polly, perhaps...)

And yet, Morgan was respectful, supportive, kind, and considerate to me, cheering me on when he agreed with me and keeping his opinions to himself when he did not. I could <u>not</u> have asked for a more loyal colleague.

One morning early in this school year, during a particularly problematic week—one of those weeks when I knew I wasn't pleasing anyone, including myself–I got a note from Morgan delivered by a young messenger who needed to take a walk. "I have to see you at 10:37," the note said. Oh, no, I thought. Another problem. And from the president of the teachers' union. And 10:37, not 10:30 or 10:35. Morgan must mean business. Well, promptly at 10:37, Morgan appeared in my doorway (actually, <u>filled</u> my doorway). "Hi, boss. I needed to see you at 10:37." "Can I help you, Morgan?" I queried. "Nope. I just needed to see you at 10:37. Have a great day." I did!

Morgan would say to me, "You know, boss, we men have to stick together because, look around, there aren't a lot of us here." Which sidetracks me a bit because I have to tell you how much Morgan loved being one of the few men at Robertson and at Coventry Grammar, and how even so much more he loved being the ONLY man at his grade-level. Under such circumstances, Morgan raised the practice of teasing and cajoling to an art form. But because even a master teacher such as Morgan needed a lesson once in a while, his female colleagues delighted in driving him out of the room with detailed talk of "woman problems," and off he'd scurry, red-faced and shaking his head. But they also were charmed into doing Morgan's paperwork, putting together his bulletin boards, and periodically, dusting. (I think Morgan may have stretched the truth about the dusting…)

Several years ago, Morgan shared with his friends a letter he had received from a former third grade student. This was so uncharacteristic of Morgan because he was never comfortable with praise or self-promotion. Obviously, the young woman's words had touched him. Let me read to you from this letter.

> *Dear Mr. Redfield,*
>
> *I'm writing to thank you for all you have done for me. I don't know if you remember me. However, I remember you. I was in your classroom the school year of 1984-85. I walked into your room an awkward child with no self-esteem because*

I had stayed back in third grade. I had dyslexia and had a hard time reading and understanding math. I was told for a long time that I wasn't smart and wouldn't amount to anything. However, you helped me realize that I wasn't what people said about me and that I could be anything that I wanted to be. I decided that I wanted to be like you. I wanted to help children realize their self-worth. I wanted to help children learn, explore, and fly...When I left your class, I knew that I could achieve anything. You helped me love reading and school...After I learned to decode the words, I never stopped reading...You encouraged me to try to do my best. You helped me understand how important an education can be...

...I moved to Springfield, MA. (in fifth grade). I went to public school, and they helped me with my dyslexia. Some people kept telling me that I wouldn't graduate from high school. I told myself that I would show them...I went to high school and college (where) I worked full time and attended school full time...Through all my schooling, I had major setbacks, but I wouldn't let anyone tell me that I couldn't do it. I just remembered you telling me that I could...

I graduated (college) with high honors...(and) I'm now in my third year teaching in Springfield. I love teaching children, (and) I hope that I can change a child's life the way you changed mine...

I still have the monster book you gave me at the end of the year. You wrote a note telling me to keep my chin up, that I could do anything. Those words are forever in my head...

Among the many tributes that will no doubt follow Morgan's passing, may I humbly ask a favor of everyone gathered here this afternoon? No matter your age, if there is a teacher, tutor, coach, mentor, clergyman, counselor, or other caring person who taught you something that has stayed with you and has helped to form you, please write, call, or visit that person to thank him or her for the invaluable life lesson. Please. In Morgan's honor. Before it's too late.

And, if you do so, Morgan will be smiling down on you, no doubt taking a short break from his new teaching assignment. Can you see it? The angels are gathered around him (those few with self-esteem issues the closest by). Because the angels all want to be like Morgan, they're wearing sunglasses. And there's a new design to their angelic robes. Short sleeves, no matter how cold it gets. A pocket for whatever list an angel might keep (#1. Watch over someone. #2. Choir practice at 8 p.m. #3 Praise the Lord...)

Oh, yes, and I'm sure that Morgan is joined by the only team-teaching partner he was ever truly comfortable with—Taffy, the Wonder Dog.

And if the angels all get 100 percent on their spelling tests...

****

"Ideals Are Like Stars."

The ideals which have always shone before me and filled me with the joy of living are goodness, beauty, and truth.[58]
Albert Einstein

Eulogy for Ruth Elinor (Leach) Spink
By Reverend Dr. Bruce J. Johnson
January 7, 2000

There were only a couple of places marked in Ruth's family bible—the King James edition, of course. The first was the account of the birth of Christ according to Luke, a passage that was read every Advent and Christmas when the Spink family observed the lovely tradition of lighting Advent candles in preparation for Christmas.

The second marking was on a couple of lines from the third chapter of Proverbs:

---

[58] A. Einstein, "The World as I See It," an essay originally published in Forum and Century, Vol. 84, (New York: Simon and Shuster, 1931) pp. 193-194. Also included within *The Ultimate Quotable Einstein*, collected and edited by Alice Calaprice, Princeton University Press, 2011.

Trust in the Lord with all your heart; and do not rely on your own insight. In all your ways acknowledge him, and he will make straight your paths.

(Proverbs 3: 5-6, NRSV).

I think Ruth knew we would need those couple of lines someday, and that someday is today. So, I'm going to do as she says, namely invite you to join me in trusting in the Lord with all our heart, knowing that He will direct our steps to that place of understanding and acceptance where broken hearts are made whole, where tears are wiped away from our eyes and in the morning, our mourning is transformed into joy.

One of Ruth's favorite books is titled: *In the Vineyard of the Lord: Lights and Shadows from the Life of Helen Steiner Rice.* She turned down the page on chapter 23. Its chapter heading of "My Outlook on Life" tells us why. The chapter contains this poem: "Ideals Are Like Stars."

In this world of casual carelessness
   it's discouraging to try
      To keep our morals and standards
   and our IDEALS HIGH....
      We are ridiculed and laughed at
   by the smart sophisticate
      Who proclaims in brittle banter
   that such things are out of date...
      But no life is worth the living
   unless it is built on truth,
      And we lay our life's foundation
   in the golden years of youth...
      So allow no one to stop you
   or hinder you from laying
      A firm and strong foundation
   made of ***Faith and Love and Praying***
      And remember that Ideals
   are like ***Stars Up In The Sky,***
      You can never really reach them,
   hanging in heavens high...

> But like the mighty mariner
> who sailed the storm-tossed sea,
>> And used the **Stars To Chart His Course**
>> with skill and certainty,
>> You too can **Chart Your Course In Life**
> **with High Ideals and Love**
>> For **High Ideals are like the Stars**
> that light the sky above…
>> You cannot ever reach them,
> but **Lift your Heart Up High**
>> And your life will be as shining
> as the **Stars Up In The Sky**.

No person's course in life has been charted with higher ideals and more love, and no life has let its light so shine more before God, family, friends, and community, than Ruth Spink's life.

From that very first Christmas Eve back in 1973, our first year in Coventry, when Ruth invited the new young pastor and his wife to be part of their family on one of the holiest of nights, we have admired and loved her.

Especially in recent years, Lois and I would often tell Mark and Ruth that they were our idols—because of their closeness, their active and involved lifestyles, and because they always seemed to have so much fun! They were always doing or planning something neat!

Anecdotes abound, but none more illustrative than what happened to Mark and Ruth on their last trip to Florida. They would fly to Florida and meet Rich and Jane, Matthew and Mark. (I'm not sure whether Marissa was there on the last trip.) Mark and Ruth would supervise the activities of the kids, while Rich and Jane attended some business meetings. Ruth would begin the week with her favorite "knock, knock" joke. (Matthew—Mark—Help me out here!)

> KNOCK, KNOCK? WHO'S THERE?
> EMMA! EMMA WHO? —
> EMM- I GONNA HAVE TROUBLE WITH YOU?
>> Of course, they never had trouble with two such fine
>> young gentlemen!

At week's end, Mark and Ruth went to the airport for their 1 p.m. flight. When their departure time arrived, an airline staff person came out to announce that the flight was overbooked. He was looking for volunteers who would give up their seats for a couple of hundred dollars in vouchers and seats on the 5 p.m. flight. Mark and Ruth looked at each other and up went their hands. So, they waited for the 5 o'clock flight. The departure time arrived. A flight attendant appeared again, looking for volunteers for a few hundred dollars in vouchers and seats on the 9 p.m. flight. Mark and Ruth looked at each other as if to say, "Why not?" and up went their hands. When the departure time arrived for that flight, the same scenario unfolded yet again but with a new enticement. This time, the attendant promised $400 dollars in vouchers, an overnight stay at the airport hotel and an early morning flight to Hartford. This sounded like a grand adventure to Mark and Ruth! Before all the flights landed and took off without them, they had secured $1800 in flight vouchers!

I'm reminded of a wonderful poem by James Whitcomb Riley:

> What delightful hosts are they---
> Life and love.
> Lingeringly I turn away
> This late hour, yet glad enough
> They have not withheld from me
> Their high hospitality.
>
> So, with face lit with delight
> And all gratitude, I say,
> Thanks --- so fine a time! Good night!

I know Ruth would be the first to say that life and love have been wonderfully delightful hosts, having blessed her and hers with their highest hospitality. She loved life and the blessings of her life. Her face and way of relating to people were always lit with delight and gratitude and maybe that's why, when I remember Ruth, two very special words come to mind.

Hostess and hospitality are Ruth from start to finish.

Along with being the kindest, most generous, Christian woman I know, she is one of the best hostesses. Whether you are a guest at her home for a Monday afternoon Seeker's Bible study, or a Tuesday night bridge game or for Sunday dinner, or a reception here at the church, she did everything she could do to make it special. As a result, you felt it was just for you. The decorations, the dishes, the flowers, and, of course, the desserts were just right! She liked nice things, not only because they were nice, but because they could make guests feel special.

And she did the same for her Jane and Gail and their friends and, more recently, her grandchildren. The whole family was home in April for Easter, which always included a children's Easter egg hunt. I have here in front of me her 1999 list of Easter Eggs!

> There were eighty eggs-forty-six with money and thirty-four with candy, pencil sharpeners and plastic bugs.
> 10--orange with fifty cents in each--$5.00
> 10--pink with $1 in each--$10.00
> 5--blue with $1 in each--$5.00
> 10--green with twenty-five cents in each--$2.50
> 10--yellow with twenty-five cents in each--$2.50
> 1--Golden with $5.00 in it--$5.00
>
> 3 eggs in Marissa's basket and eleven extras.

I said last Sunday that for me, Ruth always spoke the language of affection. She was fond of calling people "love" or "darling." When she was a nurse at Windham Hospital, she was always the consummate professional, but how she cared for her patients was profoundly personal. I wouldn't have been surprised if she had entered a patient's room and said, "I'll be your hostess today, love!"

Ruth's light was the light of the spirit of hospitality. She naturally welcomed you into her life and wanted to be in yours. She could talk, but she was also good at listening. Her goodness was contagious, and her sense of humor was fun to be around. Her love was ever-present.

And it will remain so.

Ruth used to enjoy reading magazines like "Guideposts." Throughout her recent illness, she had a copy near the couch where she spent a good bit of her day. In a recent issue, Mitch Albom, the author of the enormously popular book *Tuesdays with Morrie*, shared what he called the story behind the best seller. His article ends with these words:

> *What he was trying to teach me from that first Tuesday was simple:*
> **'DEATH MAY END A LIFE, BUT IT DOES NOT END A RELATIONSHIP. LOVE, AS MORRIE TOLD ME, ALWAYS WINS.'**

Well, today we say that Mitch may have had his Morrie, but we have had our Ruth, and through both, love has truly won and always will.

CHAPTER IV

Voices from the Pulpit

(The longest tenured pastor of First Church was its first, the Reverend Joseph Meacham. After graduating from Harvard College in 1710, he came to Coventry in 1712, received a Master of Divinity in 1713, and was ordained in 1714. His pastorate extended from 1712 to 1752, a ministry of forty years. He is buried in Nathan Hale Cemetery. In his history of the church, the Rev. Henry Robinson laments that "None of Mr. Meacham's sermons were preserved." {p. 13.} Well, I am the second longest tenured pastor in First Church's history, and over the thirty-seven years of this pastorate, I have delivered a lot of sermons. In this final chapter, I have preserved a liturgical and thematic selection of those sermons for the historical record.)

Part I: Sermons on the Seasons of the Church Year

****

Advent

****

"A Green and Living Advent Hope"
by bjj
Scripture: Isaiah 11:1-10
Romans 15: 4-13

Meditation:

> *As lights twinkle in the ever-lengthening nights of the Northern Hemisphere, the earth's Southern Hemisphere is moving into the hot and dry days of summer. The old Advent custom of greening the home expresses both the yearning for fresh growth amid winter and the thirst for greenness in the drying summer heat. St. Hidegaard of Bingen understood this longing in the twelfth century when she wrote of the 'veriditas' or greening power of God. God in Christ brings 'lush greenness' to a 'shriveled and wilted humanity.'*
> (The Whole People of God, United Church of Christ Worship Resource)

This sermon originally started out with the line:

> *If the weather does not change, all hope for a white Christmas will be gone. The dreaming will be over and what we'll be hoping for is a continuation of what we have had the last few days—spring-like temperatures, green lawns, open golf courses and even, I am told by Cathy Hitt, a rosebud or two!*

The sports section of the Hartford Courant had a pleasant picture of a green ski slope. Below was the line "NO SNOW, SLOW GO."

Well, Mother Nature messed me up last night! We woke up this morning to a three-inch blanket of the white stuff, but I still want to talk about a 'green' Christmas.

Of course, the symbolic meaning of green as a Christmas color is central to some of our Christmas activities. (I am also fully aware that "green" is now closely associated with climate change challenges and energy alternatives.) For today, however, permit me to speak of the "greening" of our homes and how it has meaning, whether we are up here on top or down under! The evergreen up here in the mid of winter is as much a sign of life as it is in the Southern Hemisphere. Tom and Mary Wilsted could tell us some things about Christmas in New Zealand and Australia!

St. Hildegard of Bingen called it the greening power of God, the power of God to bring a lush greenness to arid places in life and in the heart where death at one time might have been considered the victor.

In this first season of Advent, after the tragic but transforming events of September 11th, how this time needs to be a time of hope!

I've always loved the old Scottish proverb:

> *Were it not for hope, the heart would break.*

The December copy of 'O' Magazine cited several quotes about hope. One was by the comic dramatist, Terrance.

> *Where there is life, there is hope.*

As true as that may be, I think that the following is equally true:

> *Where there is hope, there is life.*

The Swiss writer, Henry Amiel, said:

Hope is only the love of life.

Yesterday, I received a solicitation letter from some Christian mission organization called The Chariots of Hope. Their motto was:

Where there is hope, there is triumph.

That says it best of all. It sounds like St. Paul when he wrote to the Christians in Rome:

> *May the God of hope fill you with all joy and peace in believing, so that you may abound in hope by the power of the Holy Spirit.*
>
> (Romans 15:13, NRSV)

I like that phrase: abound in hope. I think that is what God wants for us, to abound in hope. So, without apology, we hope for a better world with less evil, greed, and hostility.

Both seasonal lessons from the prophet Isaiah, last week's and this week's, speak of such hope.

Last week's lesson spoke of swords being hammered into plowshares and spears into pruning hooks and no one learning war anymore. This week's lesson presents an image of the wolf dwelling with the lamb, the leopard with the kid, the calf with the lion, the cow with the bear and children playing confidently around snakes—with no one getting hurt!

Would that we could have such a world!

The other day, I came across a description of what it would be like to live in a perfect world. Here are a few of the thoughts.

> *In a Perfect World, a person would feel as good at fifty as he or she did at seventeen and would actually be as smart at fifty as he thought he was at seventeen.*

> *In a Perfect World, pro baseball players would complain about teachers getting paid contracts worth millions of dollars.*

In a Perfect World, the mail would always be early, the check would always be in the mail, and it would be written for more than you expected.

In a Perfect World, potato chips might have calories, but if you ate them with dip, the calories would be neutralized.

In a Perfect World, every once in a while, at least, a kid who always closed the door softly would be told, "Go back there and slam that door!"

Get the idea?

Of course, when we think of a perfect world, we have much deeper thoughts and hopes—of peace and prosperity for all, jobs, education and health services, an inclusive society, safety for our children and care for our elderly to name a few things. I always think that Advent and Christmas are just the best time to be green with hope for a better and more perfect world.

A French process theologian named Teilhard de Chardin penned one of those quotes that ranks among the best:

The world tomorrow will belong to those who brought it the greatest hope.

I believe in his observation, and I believe it is Christ and his gospel that bring us that hope. And that is the meaning of Advent. It is a time to call ourselves and the world to attention, so that we can see and respond to the birth of a certain child that wants to lead us and love us into the realization of our greatest hope for a better and more perfect world.

Last Wednesday, someone put on my desk a meditation written by Henri J. M. Nouwen about today's passage from Isaiah. Listen to these words:

Our salvation comes from something small, tender, and vulnerable, something hardly noticeable. God, who is the Creator of the Universe, comes to us in smallness, weakness, and hidden-ness. I find this a hopeful message. Somehow, I keep expecting loud and impressive events to convince me and others of God's saving power, but repeatedly, I am reminded that spectacles, power plays and big events are the ways of the world. Our temptation is to be distracted by them and made blind to the 'shoot that shall sprout from the stump.'

When I have no eyes for the small signs of God's presence--the smile of a baby, the carefree play of children, the words of encouragement and gestures of love offered by friends--I will always remain tempted to despair.

But the small child of Bethlehem, the unknown man of Nazareth, the rejected preacher and naked man on the cross never stops seeking after me and my attention—wanting me to take notice and have reason to rejoice and believe."[59]

Jesus Christ is the hope of the world because Christ shows us that God's love is inclusive and infinite. God loves us all as if we were but one, and each of us as if God had no one else to care for. And, if this Christmas we receive God's love incarnate into our hearts, we shall indeed find that there is something more. Christ's presence will displace our pettiness, our cynicism, our agendas, our self-indulgence, and our faultfinding. With Christ in our hearts, we shall hold the dying and dance with the living, put our arms around the assaulted, set a feast for the poor and preach peace to the nations. Candle by candle, we overcome darkness, and person-by-person, our goodness overcomes evil.

Let us then, today, as we stand in the snow, rejoice in the green and living hope of this Advent season.

Amen

****

Christmas

****

"What the World Needs Now Is Love"
by bjj
Scripture: Luke 2: 1-20

---

[59]   Featured in Henri J. M. Nouwen Quotes

Meditation:

> *We are all born for love. It is the principle of existence, and*
> *its only end.*
>
> Benjamin Disraeli

> *Be glad of life because it gives you the chance to love and to*
> *work and to play and to look up at the stars.*
>
> Henry Van Dyke

I once heard it said:

> *You can look at a window and see a window, or you can look*
> *through the window and see the world.*

Tonight, on this Christmas Eve, I want to suggest to us that the Christmas story has never been a story to be looked at but through. It is a window to the world.

Whenever we come here so late into the night, a time that is so dark, so cold and sometimes stormy, in the bleak midwinter, as we quietly sing, we are challenged to resist seeing and celebrating only the sentimentalized story and to embrace its import for a "worked up" and "worked over" and sometimes "worn-out world."

Several years ago, a Pastoral Counseling Center in Boston distributed a copy of their version of the Christmas narrative. It was written as a report by a social worker after the worker had made a house call in Bethlehem. The report reads:

> *On January 7^h, your caseworker went to visit the Ben Jacob*
> *family. These people were reported to be living in a barn*
> *owned by The Inn of Bethlehem. The report was made by the*
> *innkeeper's wife who claims that the woman had a baby there.*
> *Some neighbors suggested to the worker that these people were*
> *vagrants and would not live that way unless they wanted to.*
>
> *Mr. and Mrs. Ben Jacob seemed rather dazed, but they had*
> *fixed up the quarters very nicely, although the barn was quite*

cold. *He was a carpenter in Nazareth and apparently quite handy but unemployed. His wife is much younger, almost a child herself, but her baby seems healthy and cared for.*

I mentioned something about the unsanitary conditions that existed in the barn because of the animals, but they didn't see much of a problem. Although they were cautious in their communication, they mentioned something of visits by shepherds who were the first friendly people they had met and some 'foreign gentlemen.' When asked if they had enough money, they said that they did, because of the gifts brought to them by these foreign gentlemen, one of them being a Negro who said that they knew something about not being let into The Inn.

When asked about their plans for the future, they mentioned that they knew that they had to get out of Bethlehem. It was a bad place to bring up children. Indeed, officials and even some other families seemed to have it in for them. There were numerous reports of abuse, even killings. They were planning to go to Egypt, but there also, they were aware of the potential for bad times for Jews, but they had no other choice. Perhaps someday they could return home.

Mr. Ben Jacob seemed very knowledgeable about the world and, in fact, got quite worked up about the state of the world and how people treated one another. I attempted to calm him down by suggesting that perhaps someday his little son might have a big impact on the world, doing something about these things. The mother seemed to perk up at such a suggestion, but Mr. Ben Jacob said that, although he hoped that his son would, he suspected that it would take a very long time to change people.

Case closed.

A long time indeed! But He is still hard at work and the Christmas story is a story that is forever hoping to awaken in its tellers and hearers a renewed resolve to carry on His work. On Christmas Eve, we tell the story of His birth and expect it to be our own. We even sing our prayer, *"Be born in us this day."* We light a candle of hope and life, knowing full well that it will burn amid the realities of despair and death. When we say that the name of the child was Jesus, Our Emmanuel, we remember what his name means, "God with us" and wherever God is, there is also love, for God is love and that love is invincible, and we have the chance to rededicate ourselves as carriers of that love.

The great German philosopher, poet, and dramatist Goethe was reported to have cried out from his deathbed:

Light, the world needs more light.

Years later, someone responded, saying:

No, Goethe was wrong. What he should have said was, 'Warmth, the world needs more warmth.' We shall not die from the dark but from the cold.

Tonight, on this most sacred and silent of nights, we go even further and say,

Love, the world needs more love. We shall not die from the dark or the cold but from the heart-breaking feeling of being unloved, and the murderous feeling of being incapable of love.

Seeing the world through the window of the Christmas story, we know what our world needs, don't we? The world needs more love!

In his book *The Spellbinder's Gift*, Og Mandino recalls one of his favorite motivational stories, Oscar Wilde's fable (1888), titled 'The Happy Prince,' which was really about an unhappy prince. A partial summary of the fable goes:

There was this special and elegant statue of a happy prince that stood on a tall column high above a city. The prince's

body was covered with thin leaves of fine gold, for eyes he had huge sapphires and on his sword hilt there was a large red ruby.

One day, Bart, a little swallow who had delayed his winter journey to Egypt much too long, paused on his hurried trip south to put up for the night between the feet of the statue. However, the swallow couldn't sleep because of the sound of the prince weeping, so he flew up, landed on the prince's shoulder and asked him why he was crying.

The prince replied that although everyone called him the happy prince, he was not happy at all. How could he possibly be happy, he asked the little bird, when from his station high above the city he could see so many people who needed help, food, care, love and tenderness. 'Will you please help me, little bird? Will you help me give myself away?' The bird agreed.

First, the swallow removed the ruby from the prince's sward and carried it down to a frightened young mother tending her sick child in a cold attic. Then the little bird flew all the way back to the prince, removed one sapphire eye and carried it down to an old man in a small shack who had not eaten for two days. Then he flew all the way back to the prince once more, removed the other sapphire eye and left it in the city at the feet of a little match girl. One by one, the leaves of gold were removed from the prince's body and distributed to the poor and helpless children of the city.

And then the frigid blast of winter struck, and since the prince's body was no longer protected, his leaden heart cracked. And unable to protect himself from the cold, the tiny swallow perished.

One morning, God called his angels together and pointed down to the city, saying, 'Bring me the two most precious things from that place.' And when the angels returned, they *were carrying the cracked heart of the prince… and the body of the tiny bird.*

It's called 'love with no price tag,' my friend, and if we don't start learning how to live that way, <u>our</u> lives will be worthless. (p. 142)

In a baby born in Bethlehem, God is giving us a 'love with no price tag,' at least one that we won't have to pay. God gives us unconditional love, and it's for everyone. That's what makes the night so beautiful, the story so magical and the message so profoundly relevant and indeed redemptive for the world to which it comes.

Let me close with another story. I once read a vignette that came out of the canceled coronation of King Edward VIII. The city of London was filled with the rich and powerful and even royal from all over the world. When Alfred Deakin, the Prime Minister of New Zealand, arrived back home from the event, he was asked by news reporters what impressed him most. He was thoughtful for a while, and then he told how one night, while walking back from the state dinner to his hotel lodging, he saw something that moved him deeply. In a dark alley of a slum section, he saw a little boy about twelve years old, sitting on a stoop in a doorway with his arm around a girl of three.

It was late at night and quite cool. The boy had taken off his jacket and wrapped it around the shoulders of the little girl. And he had taken off his cap to cover her bare feet. Deakin said that he had traveled thousands of miles to witness a coronation of a King among the high and mighty, but the most kingly thing he saw issued from the heart of a little boy in a dark alley in a London slum. [60]

Well, tonight our focus is on a stable and the 'kingly' gift of God's love in a vulnerable little baby born in a feed trough. It is a birth that took place in the dark of night but beneath the white light of a star of promise and hope. And it finds its time to change us so that we too can love as deeply as we are loved.

Amen

---

[60] Source of story unknown.

****

Epiphany
****

"Arise, Shine- The Gift of a Bright Encounter"
by bjj
January 2002
Scripture: Isaiah 60: 1-6
Matthew 2: 1-13

Meditation:

> *The feast of Epiphany is a celebration of God's inclusive love for all the world, as revealed in Jesus Christ. The continuing revelation of God's rich and cosmic deliverance depends in part on the church manifesting in local settings the diversity of God's people and God's wisdom.*
>
> (The Whole People of God, United Church of Christ Worship Resource)

The University of Miami has won the NCAA football national championship. They beat Nebraska on Thursday evening, much the same as the University of Connecticut women's basketball team beat Tennessee yesterday. Last year, the *Wall Street Journal* told a story about Eli Herring, an offensive tackle from Brigham Young University. He was everybody's All-American and was expected to go high in the draft, possibly the first round, after all the highly valued quarterbacks and running backs. The Oakland Raiders had already announced that he would be their first pick. He was smart, hardworking, and deeply religious. Incredibly, he announced early that if drafted, he would **not** play because choosing professional football meant he would have to work on Sundays, and he simply would not do that. Instead, he intended to teach math and coach football at the high school level.

Ted Roberts, a *Wall Street Journal* columnist, learned about the story and the multi-million dollar contract the young man was turning down. He interviewed the six-foot, eight inch, 340 pound lad, and the following represents an excerpt of that interview:

> *But Eli, I asked him… What about your family and 18-month-old daughter who someday will cry for designer jeans and later, maybe a $40,000 dollar wedding?*
>
> *Well, Eli says, his family will be just fine and maybe a blessing from above is better than a bank account. Eternity is so long, and life is so short, you know. Hey, you can't be a beacon if your life don't shine.*
>
> *Hey, you can't be a beacon if your life don't shine!*

We come together on this Epiphany Sunday around this theme. The voice of the prophet Isaiah rings out with just this message:

> *Arise; shine, for your light has come! (Isaiah 60:1, NRSV)*

Just twelve days ago, we celebrated Christmas, affirming this fundamental truth of our faith, that God's light shines in our darkness and in us. Because Christ has come, we shine.

Last February I received a neat little book of faith and the art of living titled: *A Touch of Wonder* by Arthur Gordon. He introduces the fifth chapter by remembering one night:

> *…walking alone through the blackout in London during World War II. There had been an air-raid warning, with searchlights crisscrossing the sky, but now the sirens were sounding the all clear. Suddenly all the searchlights were extinguished except for four, one on each side of the city. These great shafts of light ceased moving and grew still, focused on a single point exactly overhead. I stopped walking. They remained there like silver sword blades quartering the tremendous blue-black vault of midnight. The sirens died away and there was no other sound. Nothing. Just a deep ringing silence. It was like being at the heart of a gigantic star! I have never forgotten that moment. I have always called it: 'the gift of a bright encounter.'*[61]

---

[61]   Arthur Gordon, *A Touch of Wonder* (Fleming H. Revell Company: Old Tappan, New Jersey, 1974) p. 125.

I wonder if that was what it was like for the wise men when they finally arrived at the place just below those brilliant and streaming bands of light? The experience might well have been a gift of a bright encounter, and, of course, epiphany's power is in the message. God guides and leads even people of other faiths and cultures, life experiences and hopes and dreams to that point where we can do nothing other than offer our precious gifts!

Arise and shine, the prophet Isaiah says, *for your light has come and the glory of the Lord has risen upon you.* (Isaiah 60:1, NRSV)

And Eli made it clear: *You can't be a beacon if your life don't shine!*

I have been over to St. Joseph's Living Center several times this week to see Jan McCauley. She died yesterday afternoon. When you leave her room, turn left and walk straight toward the nurses' desk, you can't miss the poster on the wall. I'm not sure whether it is meant for the staff or visitors or both! In bold, colorful print, it reads:

BE A BEACON OF LIGHT

Christmas and Epiphany are supposed to be gifts of bright encounters that awaken us to the wondrous happening of God showing us such incredible love. The experience fills us with that love and enables us to shine and challenges us to share it with others. And there is nothing mysterious about how that is done.

We are simply called and challenged:

> **To live with greater love and kindness,**
> To be more patient, tolerant, and forgiving,
> **To show more compassion in situations**
> **when we might prefer to judge.**
> To bless others as generously as we
> have been blessed.

Of course, it is not uncommon to feel somewhat of a letdown after the holidays. (Where would we be without UCONN basketball and now, what do we do with the Tennessee game in the "win" column?) The same can happen spiritually.

Tony Campolo, one of my favorite preachers, tells the story of an old guy in the backwoods of Kentucky who could always be counted on to show up at revival meetings whenever the evangelist came to town. At the end of each service, when the invitation was given, he would come down the aisle, get down on his hands and knees, raise his arms to heaven and cry out: *Fill me, Jesus! Fill me! Fill me, Jesus!*

Then, within a matter of a week or two, he would slip back into his old ways of living. But when the next round of revival meetings was held, he would once again go to the meeting, walk down the aisle, pray that same prayer repeatedly.

One time, he was down on his knees yelling to the ceiling, *Fill me, Jesus! Fill me. Fill me, Jesus!* when suddenly from the back of the church some lady yelled,

> *Don't do it, Lord! He leaks!*
> (Tony Campolo, *Let Me Tell You a Story*, p. 96).

The opportunity to be filled up and turned on through worship, prayer, song, sacrament, and service is given to us despite leaking and losing light and love from time to time. That's what being the church is all about---to gather where the star rests over the place where the Savior lay, offering the gift of a bright encounter that changes lives.

So, arise, shine, for our light has come, and we cannot be beacons if our lives don't shine.

Amen

****

Lent

****

"The Signs of God's Faithfulness"
by bjj
March 2003
Scripture: Genesis 9: 8-17
1 Peter 3: 18-22

Meditation:

> *Sin is not exhausted in describing individual acts which aren't very nice. 'Sin' is a description of our entire situation, one of separation from God, alienation from Him, arising out of our rebellion, our refusal to do His will, our insistence upon following our own wills.*
>
> Robert McAfee

> *Although we live in a culture that denies sin, the gospel gives us the resources whereby we can be honest about ourselves and our sinful state. Repentance is not a duty; it is a great gift, a byproduct of God's grace in Jesus Christ.*
>
> William Willimon

Lois and I saw a terrific movie a week ago, "Chicago," the movie version of the stage production of 1975. It's about life in Chicago during the 1930s and 40s when daily newspapers roared with headlines, killers were romanticized or vilified, and cops and lawyers and reporters lived in each other's pockets. The story line is about these women who were in prison for killing the men in their lives. Each claim in song that "They didn't do it but he deserved it!" Richard Gere is Billy Flynn, the slick, high priced attorney who boasts he can beat any rap for a $5000 fee. His motto:

> *If Jesus Christ had lived in Chicago and if he had $5000 and had come to me--- things would have turned out differently.*

Sounds somewhat sacrilegious to say during Lent, doesn't it?

Although there were some tense moments in his defense of Roxie Hart, who killed the man who was supposed to be promoting her entertainment career, he does the "razzle dazzle" to perfection! (Ebert, Chicago Sun- Times)

That is all I'll say. It is a terrific movie.

It gave me pause, though, to remember an oft quoted line from one of Carl Sandburg's poems from his collection called "Chicago Poems":

> *Can we be honest for five minutes, even though this is Chicago?*

As we begin this season of Lent and even though this is Coventry, it's appropriate for us to ask the same question: *Can we be honest for five minutes?*

This morning's lesson from the book of Genesis is about the story of Noah and the forty days and forty nights of rain that was meant to wash the earth clean of evil doers and doing. As we learn through today's lesson, however, at the end of that stretch of rainy weather, God is not all that certain that He has done the right thing. He vows never to do it again. As we all know, the rainbow is then established as a sign of God's everlasting promise to his creation and us, but it moves us far beyond that. God promises to place the rainbow in the sky as a reminder to Himself—a reminder of the promise never again to destroy the earth, never again to respond with that kind of blanket judgment on us for our sin and for our evil, no matter how bad we get!

And we can get bad, can't we?

Today, we remember Jesus's forty days and forty nights in the desert. Satan and wild beasts were there, and if it were not for the angels, we're not entirely sure how Jesus would have come out of it! At the beginning of this Lenten season, we are called to that same place with the same fears and same hope, called to examine and assess who we are and what we value and how we live.

A few years ago, *The Wall Street Journal* published one of its more provocative editorials. It began with a question:

When was the last time you had a good conversation about sin?

The editorial discussed the many moral issues seen on TV daily, such as corruption, teen sex, and addiction. Then it made the valid point that the word *sin* has been dropped from our vocabulary. Indeed, as I reflect on my priorities as a pastor, preacher, and person, I confess to some level of neglect.

As a society, we've been pretty good at getting rid of the word. Not good for self-esteem, we say.

Several months ago, I referred to a book by Dr. George Vaillant, a psychiatrist/educator at Harvard. The book was called *Aging Well*. He also wrote another book called *The Wisdom of the Ego*. It's a book about our complex system of defense mechanisms, those creative psychic means by which we protect ourselves, by which we cope with devastating onslaughts of reality. Far from being negative, says Dr. Vaillant, our defenses, these idiosyncratic means which the brain devises to shield us from the cold facts about ourselves, are positive coping mechanisms. If that is true, I can speak for myself at least. Don't expect too much raw honesty from me about my sin! In fact, Dr. Vaillant believes we become more adept at utilizing our defense mechanisms as we grow older, as we gain education and experience. Being well-educated myself and having just had another birthday, I guess I must be well *defended* and therefore, just maybe, somewhat psychologically dishonest!

(Indebted to William Willimon, Pulpit Resource, Vol. 245, #1)

But today can be different. In fact, I am asking for those five minutes of honesty!

For sure, we have enough moral dilemmas to consider, don't we?

Despite the opposition that exists in our country, our nation is heading toward war. It supports the United Nations Resolution #1441. Saddam Hussein and his regime are evil. They have produced, stockpiled, and have not accounted for some 8,500 liters of anthrax, 6,500 chemical bombs, 650 kilograms of growth media bioagents and stockpiles of VX gas. He has been ruthless with his own people and certainly is capable of terrorism toward the world. Their sin is great, perhaps as great as what is now being done in North Korea. Perhaps we should say of them, categorically, that it is a *sin* to build such weapons and agents of war. However, shouldn't we also look at ourselves from the same moral perspective?[62] Much has been written about the faith of President Bush and its role in this set of circumstances. No one questions the sincerity and genuineness of its role in his life. He was even asked the specific question on Thursday evening at his prime-time news conference. Shouldn't we be asking if it's all "righteousness" that designs the policy and positions the firepower for this war? Where is *our sin* in the preparation and making of war rather than showing restraint on behalf of peace?

---

[62] Multiple news outlets reported on July 7, 2023, that the United States had destroyed the last of its chemical warfare stockpile. President Joe Biden reported: "Today, I a proud to announce that the United States has safely destroyed the final munition in that stockpile..." (AP by Andrew DeMillo, Thomas Peipert and Dylan Lovan, July 7, 2023)

Where is our sin in the costs and consequences of war, especially in terms of human life and limb? How about its financial cost? Huge deficits and their effects on the economy, upon jobs (Yesterday's NY Times reported a rise in joblessness to 5.8 percent) or the resources that will not be available for education, health care, aid to our nation's poor?

Can we be honest for five minutes?

And other aspects of our lives deserve attention and some genuine honesty.

A few weeks ago, *The Wall Street Journal* printed an article under its "Houses of Worship" column. Gene Veith, professor of English at Concordia University, titled the article *Curse of the Foul Mouth*. He laments the prevalence of profanity from award shows to everyday conversations. Veith makes the case that "cursing" violates the obligation to love one's neighbor. When we curse, we call down harm, or we call someone a "name" so that we can insult or attack the legitimacy of someone's birth or a mother's virtue. The cavalier use of the Lord's name is the most egregious of violations.

How about this comment?

> *But I don't mean anything by it,* a modern-day unintentional blasphemer might say. *Exactly. Not meaning anything by it is what it means to take the Lord's name 'in vain.'*

Can we be honest for five minutes?

This Lenten season is a time for reflection and change, a time to be honest for as many minutes as it takes to get things on the right track. But so much has changed since Noah's day. Christ has made all the difference for us. In our New Testament lesson from 1 Peter, we have the writer identifying that difference. He says at the time of Noah, only eight people made it through the flood, but since the time of Jesus and his baptism and ours, we all make it through. And it's not about the removal of dirt from our body but the awareness of a clear conscience for having received God's forgiveness of Christ so preemptively (not sure I should use that word). We can boldly be honest about our sin. We can be in a different place and enjoy a renewed and redeemed sense of self!

There is an old and well-traveled story about a man who sent a floral arrangement to celebrate the expansion of a good friend's business at a new site. When the sender got to the grand opening celebration, he was shocked to find his flower basket with a card that read *Rest in Peace*.

Furious, he called the florist to complain about the mix-up. The florist said,

> *Hey, don't be upset. Think about it this way. Somewhere in town today, somebody was buried under a sign that said, 'Good luck in your new location.'*

Of course, there is no luck to it, either for here and now or later and there! It is simply the fulfillment of God's promises, something as sure as we're sitting here. And we have signs of God's faithfulness, the rainbow, the waters of baptism and, of course, and the cross.

We don't need Billy Flynn, and fortunately, Jesus didn't have $5000. Jesus accomplished the forgiveness of our sin through his death, and he secured eternal life for us by rising again. So, throughout this Lenten season, let us be honest about our sin, but with the clear conscience of sinners who have been forgiven, let us grow in our faith.

And let me close with this final quote. I've always loved a quote from Reverend Timothy Keller:

> *The gospel is this: We are more sinful and flawed in ourselves that we ever dared believe, yet at the same time we are more loved and accepted in Jesus Christ that we ever dared hope.*

Amen

****

Palm/Passion Sunday

****

"As the Parade Passes By"
by bjj
March 2002.
Scripture: Isaiah 50: 4-9
Matthew 21: 1-11

Meditation:

> *For most of us, our faithfulness to God is not spectacular,*
> *not dramatic. Yet, in our everyday, ordinary acts of fidelity*
> *and goodness, the great and cosmic purposes of God are being*
> *worked out.*
>
> William Willimon

> *We can't all be heroes because someone has to sit on the curb*
> *and clap as they go by.*
>
> Will Rogers

Some would say that it has been a great weekend for television. First, both UCONN basketball teams are still traveling on their respective *Roads to the Final Four!'* We had a Husky men's victory on Friday night; a women's victory yesterday, and the men play again tonight and then tomorrow, another women's game. In between those two games, though, we have the Oscars, the show that honors the movies and their actors and actresses for being the "best." In his book, *Living a Life That Matters,* Rabbi Harold Kushner makes some observations about Oscar that intrigued me. He writes:

> *Every year, on an evening in late March, tens of millions of*
> *Americans stay up late to watch the motion-picture industry*
> *present its Academy Awards. The coveted Oscars are given*
> *to the best director, the best actor and actress, the best movie,*
> *and the best in other categories. Among the prestigious awards*
> *given out are those for the best actor and best actress in a*
> *supporting role.*

> *I've always been intrigued by the supporting role category.*
> *I don't know what it is like to direct a movie. I have no*
> *idea what goes into composing a musical score or designing*
> *costumes. But I know the feeling--I suspect we all know the*
> *feeling--of being a supporting actor in other people's movies,*
> *not being in the spotlight but doing things that shape and*
> *drive the plot. (p. 126.)*

We come together this morning on Palm Sunday, a day that begins the most sacred of holy weeks in church life, a week filled with high drama for it leads to and through the Passion of Christ. Someone is in the spotlight, and we know who it is. All those other characters about whom we read, the disciples, the scribes and Pharisees, the Romans and the crowd, even the donkey, are cast in supporting roles. And in some ways, as we re-enact and reflect on our places in the drama, so are we, in like manner, cast in supporting roles, shaping, and driving the plot. However, the drama never ends with the final scene because it keeps inviting all viewers and listeners to its purpose and promise, into its mystery.

To prepare for this morning, I consulted my files. Three years ago, when I preached on this passage, I focused on the Lead Actor.

'Who is this?' was the question we asked.

This year, the question that seems most important, (maybe because of September 11th and the extraordinary responses made by so many ordinary people) is not *Who is this?* but *Who are we?* The emphasis is not on what He will do for us, but on how we will respond. For certain, as this parade passes by, knowing what we know about those in it, people such as:

The disciples, one who betrays Him with a kiss, another who denies Him and all who abandon Him,

The scribes and Pharisees, so fearful of losing their power, who plot to condemn Him,

The Romans who crucify Him,

And the crowd, who cheered him one day but called for his death only days later.

It is important to focus on them. Nobody comes off very well. But we are challenged to see ourselves in them and reflect on how we can be different.

So, the more pressing questions seem to be:

Who are we that we could do such things?
Who do we need to be not to do them?

Rabbi Harold Kushner tells a story about a Native American tribal leader describing his own inner struggles.

He said, *There are two dogs inside me. One of the dogs is mean and evil. The other dog is good. The mean dog fights the good dog all the time.*

Someone asked him which dog usually wins, and after a moment's reflection, he answered,

The one I feed the most. (pp. 58--59)

During this Holy Week, we are challenged to feed the "good inner self" so that in this time of darkness, our presence will be a source of hope and promise and goodness and faith.

There is an ancient Chinese proverb that goes:

If there is light in the soul,
There will be beauty in the person.
If there is beauty in the person,
There will be harmony in the house.
If there is harmony in the house,
There will be order in the nation.
If there is order in the nation,
There will be peace in the world.

My favorite line from any of the Palm Sunday narratives is taken from the Gospel according to Luke, where Jesus first weeps over the city before entering it and then laments:

If you, even you, had only recognized on this day the things
that make for peace!
(*Luke 19:42, NRSV*)

Of course, he knew that ultimately the thing that makes for peace is to have light in the soul, His light!

When I look at Holy Week, which begins with Palm Sunday, I see the commencement of a process during which the light in too many souls is extinguished and with it, albeit momentarily, the promise of beauty, order and peace.

This morning's lesson ends, as I have said before, with these words:

When he entered Jerusalem, the whole city was in turmoil, asking,
Who is this?
And the crowds were saying, This is the prophet Jesus from Nazareth in Galilee.

(Matthew 21:10, NRSV)

You know, I once read that a prophet is not a man who tells the future, but a man who tells the truth.

If that is true, and I think it is, then perhaps Pearl Bailey was also right when she said:

You never find yourself until you face the truth.

And it was the great Pascal who said:

We know truth not only by reason but by the heart.

As the parade passes by today, it is the heart that is on the line, specifically, our hearts, as they shape and drive the plot in a supporting role. "A Beautiful Mind" may well win the Oscar tonight, but it is the beautiful heart that changes the world.

Rachel Naomi Remen, in her book *Kitchen Table Wisdom*, tells an engaging Sufi story about a man who is so good and loving that the angels ask God to give him the gift of miracles. God wisely tells them to ask him if that is what he would wish.

So the angels visit this good man and offer him first the gift of healing by hands, then the gift of conversion of souls and last the gift of virtue. He refuses them all. They insist that he choose a gift, or they will choose one for him. *Very well*, he replies. *I ask that I may do a great deal of good without ever knowing it.*

The story ends this way:

The angels were perplexed. They took counsel and resolved upon the following plan: Every time the saint's shadow fell behind him, it would have the power to cure disease, soothe pain and comfort sorrow. As he walked, behind him his shadow made arid paths green, caused withered plants to bloom, gave clear water to dried up brooks, fresh color to pale children, and joy to unhappy men and women. The saint simply went about his daily life diffusing virtue as the stars diffuse light and flowers' scent, without ever being aware of it. The people, respecting his humility, followed him silently, never speaking to him about his miracles. Soon they even forgot his name and called him simply, 'the Holy Shadow.' (pp. 245-46.)

As the parade passes by this morning, we're not asking, Who *is this?* but *Who am I?* or *Who are we?* And the answer comes back that amid the shadows cast by persons whose light no longer shines, we choose to walk with light in our souls, love in our hearts and goodness in our deeds.

Amen

****

Easter

****

"Death Has No Victory"
by bjj
April 2003
Scripture: Isaiah 25: 6-9
Mark 16: 1-8

Meditation:

> *The Easter message says that all that tenderness and strength,*
> *which on Good Friday was scourged, buffeted, stretched out*
> *on a cross—all that beauty and goodness are again alive and*
> *with us now, not as a memory that inevitably fades, but as*
> *an undying presence in the life of every single one of us, if*
> *only we would recognize it. Christ's resurrection promises our*
> *own, for Christ is risen, pro nobis-for us to put love in our*
> *hearts, decent thoughts in our heads, and a little more iron*
> *in our spines. Christ is raised to convert us, not from life to*
> *something more than life, but from something less than life*
> *to the possibility of a full life itself. As it is written: 'The glory*
> *of God is a human being fully alive.'*
>
> William Sloane Coffin

Today is the church's big day, Easter Sunday. It is a day on which we celebrate the culmination of all that has preceded it and the commencement of everything that God intends to have us follow. Our journey has been from Bethlehem and its cradle to Jerusalem and its cross. And today we gather at an empty tomb, and it is decision time: does death or life and life eternal have the victory?

On this day, I'm supposed to work things into a crescendo, so I ask for all of us: "How far have we come?" Have we made it all the way from curiosity to commitment, through despair and death to the joy of resurrection, and the birth of a true and living faith?

I picked up the 'Life' section of the *Hartford Courant* on Friday and chuckled over the headline: *Caution: Moose Ahead.* It was an article warning the people of Connecticut, especially the state's drivers, *that the moose are loose!* Maine, though, has the largest population and the most accidents.

(Hartford Courant, 4/18/2003)

This reminded me of the well-circulated story of the two old codgers who went hunting for moose in the forests surrounding Moose Lake in the northwest part of Maine. As the pilot of the small airplane let them off on the shore of the lake, he reminded them,

Like I said, I'll be back in three days. But remember, this is a small plane. There is room for the two of you and one moose!

When, three days later, the pilot returned and taxied to the shore; he was irritated to see between the two boys, standing proudly with their rifles, not one but two moose, huge ones at that! (The article on Friday said that moose could be six feet tall and weigh 1400 pounds!)

Look, he said, I told you—the two of you and one moose.

The two old timers looked at each other in surprise and answered,

Funny, the guy who flew us in last year didn't complain.

The fear of his competition proving greater than all other fears, the pilot relented. Grumbling, he helped them pile both moose into the little plane, and the two old codgers crawled up and lay down on top of their trophies. The plane took forever to get off the lake, barely cleared the trees on the far shore, and about a quarter of a mile further clipped a high pine and crashed, sending pieces of its wings and moose antlers in all directions.

Finally, and fortunately, one of the old codgers came to, pulled his head out of the moss, spied his companion a short way off and asked, **"Where are we?"**

His companion replied,

Oh, about a hundred yards further than last year.

I guess it would be okay to ask this morning, *where are we?* Any further along than last year, in understanding what the resurrection of Jesus of Nazareth means to us?

What's so interesting about Easter when the Gospel according to Mark is read is that in some ways it brings us backward rather than forward. What I mean by that is that in this account, there are more questions than answers. It is not clear that these women believe that love has won, and fear and death have lost. It is not clear from the account that these women believe Jesus is raised. We hear early morning secrets, cries, and whispers. We read of terrified, terrorized women running away from an empty tomb! Worse yet, they are so afraid they are not telling anyone about the empty stone hewn cave they have just seen! Astonishment, fear, and trembling, rather than resurrection, recognition, and rescue, characterize this first Easter story. Mark tells it plainly with a little dressing up.

On that first Easter, at first light, with the first thin streaks of color in the sky, Mary Magdalene and Mary, the mother of James and Salome, came to the tomb expecting to anoint Jesus's body with their spices. It was not customary to bury the bodies of common criminals; usually they were left to the vultures and wild dogs. But a member of the Sanhedrin, Joseph of Arimathea, at odds with the conclusions of his colleagues on the Council, had saved Jesus's body from this indignity. With Pilate's permission, he had buried Jesus in a tomb; a great circular stone, which, like a cartwheel, ran along a groove across the opening, then closed the tomb.

Arriving at the tomb, the women are startled to see the stone rolled away and a youth sitting on the right side, dressed in a white robe. They are all shocked when he speaks to them.

> *Do not be amazed. You seek Jesus of Nazareth, who was crucified. Jesus has risen and is not here; see the place where they laid the body. But go, tell the disciples and Peter that Jesus goes before you to Galilee.*

In this first gospel narrative, no one sees Jesus; there are no tearful recognition or reunion scenes. There are no powerful earthquakes, no trembling guards, and no answers.

My heart goes out to this company of women, who on Good Friday had watched it all from a distance, in an agony of mind and spirit. Now is their first chance to anoint the body of their friend, and they are pushed out again into the darkness of fear and trembling. No wonder they fled the tomb and withheld the story from others!

Try to imagine this moment. There they are, standing in the dark and empty cave in which the body of Jesus had been placed only days before. Try to imagine the emptiness in the hearts of the women as they stood there in that empty tomb. It was when everything in their lives must have seemed like it came to a screeching halt.

Of the four gospel resurrection stories, Mark is the only one who dares to leave us in such a state of apprehension and suspense. As the women flee the tomb, they left us to wonder:

> *How did anyone find out about Jesus's resurrection if they were so dumbfounded and filled fear—so much so that their first response was to say, 'nothing to anyone!'*

Obviously, at some point, they moved beyond their grief and confusion, their fear and their immobility, but we are not told that. The gospel does end, however, with a footnote, showing that some accounts include post-resurrection appearances. I think the beauty of the Markan account of Easter is it leaves resolution up to us. We write the ending with what we do with the fact that the tomb was empty, and the reason given is that *He is risen.*

Do you all remember that wonderful movie that starred Richard Dryfuss, *Mr. Holland's Opus?* There is that deeply moving scene at the end when all his former students return for a reunion to honor him on his last day of employment and his first day of retirement. The Governor, a former student, gives a speech, claiming that all those who are now gathered to honor him are his symphony!

The truth of the resurrection stands on its own, but its transforming effect on people's lives and our lives, what we feel, what we think and how we live and why we choose to love is placed in our hands. We are the ending to Mark's Gospel and living testimonies to the power of the news of Christ's resurrection.

There was an article in yesterday's *New York Times* about the religious pilgrimage that Shiites are now free to take--- from every city or town in Iraq to the Holy City of Karbala.

Here is a quote:

> *Shiites can journey freely across Iraq now, with a song of joy.*
> (*New York Times*, B1, April 2023)

Our journey today is not to some Holy City but home, and we are encouraged to take it freely and with a song of joy because Christ is risen.

In today's Easter lesson, the women are told to tell the disciples and Peter what they had seen and heard and no matter what, to get back to Galilee where they have their homes and families, neighborhoods, and jobs and there, they would see him and talk to him. Today's fear will be transformed into confidence. Today's doubt will turn into faith and today's despair into joy and wherever they go, they will go freely with a song of joy!

Arthur Gordon, in his book, *A Touch of Wonder*, tells the following story:

> *One raw, cold day last winter, I found myself having lunch at the seaside cottage of some friends, an attractive young couple in their twenties. The only other guest was a retired college professor, a marvelous older gentleman, still straight as a lance after seven decades of living. We had planned a walk on the beach after lunch. But as gusts of wind shook the house and occasional pellets of sleet hissed against the windows, our host's enthusiasm dwindled visibly.*

> 'Sorry,' said the wife, '*but nobody's going to get me out of this house in this weather.*' '*That's right,*' her husband agreed comfortably.

> *So, we left them, finally, the professor and me, preparing to do just that. But when we went to our cars, parked some distance away, I was astonished to see the professor open the trunk of his ancient sedan and take out an axe. 'Lots of lovely driftwood out there,' he said, gesturing toward the windswept beach. 'Think that I'll get a load for my fireplace.'*

> I stared at him. *You're going out there to chop wood? On this sort of afternoon?*

> *He gave me a quizzical look. 'Why not?' he said. It's better than practicing the deadly art of nonliving, isn't it?' And with an axe slanted across one shoulder, he set off through the dunes.*

> *I watched him go with the sudden odd feeling that something*
> *was wrong here, something curiously inverted in this scene,*
> *and I was left with a choice and little time to make it.*

> 'Wait,' I heard myself calling to him, 'Wait, I'm coming!'[63]

I think that's the big choice Easter presents and especially the Gospel according to Mark. Shall we succumb to fear and confusion and remain passive, practicing the deadly art of nonliving, or go forth joyfully? For indeed, *Death has no victory,* and the risen Christ has gone on before us. And all that is required of us to shout out:

Wait, we're coming!

Amen.

****

Pentecost

****

"Pentecost People"
by bjj
June 2003
Scripture: Ezekiel 37: 1-14
Acts 2: 1-21

Meditation:

> *On Pentecost Sunday we celebrate the transforming nature*
> *of God's spirit at work in the early Christian community, in*
> *creation, through the prophets, always and everywhere... It*
> *is the 'whoosh!' of renewal and the crackle of excitement that*
> *followers of Jesus experience when blessed with the Spirit.*
> (Seasons of the Spirit: United Church
of Christ Worship Resource)

---

[63] Gordon, pp. 160-161.

On a Saturday afternoon in August 2000, I presided at the wedding ceremony for Robert Brown and Cheri Turkington at the home of Cheri's parents on Bolton Lake. It was a picture-perfect day. The sun was glistening off the lake. A light breeze cooled our faces, faces that were alive with joy. Yesterday, Rob and Cheri asked me to be with them again—this time on a Tuesday morning in June—to speak at the funeral mass for their son, Connor Francis Brown, who lived but ten days after being born on May 27th at the University of Connecticut Health Center. Connor died only hours after being baptized by the hospital chaplain. There will be no sun. Tears will fall from heaven, and they will not be tears of joy but of sorrow beyond words. Please keep them in your prayers.

How different it is for us today. We gather here in joy for the baptisms of Sierra, Dylan, and Aiden--- thank God, not because death may claim them but because lives of promise lay before them. We want them to live with a sense of God's guiding presence, the gift of God's love and the friendship of Jesus for life.

So, this morning, I am reminded of words written by Paul to the church in Rome:

> *We do not live to ourselves, and we do not die to ourselves.*
> *If we live, we live to the Lord, and if we die, we die to the*
> *Lord. So then, whether we live, or whether we die, we are*
> *the Lord's. For Christ died and lived again...*
>
> (Romans 14: 7-9, NRSV)

Baptism is all about affirming this truth: whether we live or whether die, we are the Lord's. And as grace would have it—we gather today as well on the day of Pentecost, fifty (50) days after Easter. The disciples are still hanging around Jerusalem, still trying to sort things out and set things up for what lay ahead of them. It is interesting to read what precedes this morning's dramatic account of the rush of a mighty wind and tongues of fire and being 'under the influence.' (Some said that it was the Holy Spirit, but others insisted that such behavior resulted from too much new vino.) What we read is that the disciples were going about filling a vacancy on the board of disciples. They needed twelve, and Judas' betrayal and untimely death had created a vacancy. There were two candidates—Joseph Justus and Matthias. The disciples elected Matthias.

So, they were at full strength again, of course, if strength is in numbers, which it isn't. And they were to find that out.

In today's lesson from Acts, everyone was together somewhere in Jerusalem when all heaven broke out. It must have been a wild scene with the wind howling, flashes of fire and people talking all at once! God changed everything; the disciples and those with them. He was pouring out the Spirit in abundance. See what will happen next!

Then, Peter preaches, and people worry and wonder and want to know what to do and how to respond to his message. In verse thirty-eight (38), something we didn't read, he tells them: *Be baptized! And receive the Holy Spirit!*

It is passages like these that sometimes get me wondering and questioning who we are and what we are supposed to do in the life of our church, where pews almost seem assigned, and everything is scripted and even the sermon is researched and written. Believe me, sometimes I'm up here and I want to say: *Someone—check for a pulse!* Last Sunday, Confirmation Sunday, was not one of them. When the decision was made by seven of our young people to confirm their own baptisms, something that Sierra, Dylan and Aiden will do in fourteen years, it was exciting. However, we did communion at the end of a long service, and I used the established words for the liturgy and sensed that it may have lacked energy and focus at that point. Then, when I turned to the worship aids for this morning, which provided a liturgy for communion, were we to be celebrating it today, listen to what was suggested:

Invitation to the Table:

> Parthian, Mede, Elamite, and Judean.
> Those from Cappadocia, Pontus, Phrygia and Pamphylia;
> Peoples of Africa, Asia, Europe, South America,
> North America, Australia, New Zealand,
> The Pacific, the Atlantic,
> The Indian and Artic Oceans
> First nations, last nations
> Hartland, Hartford, Coventry, and Columbia
> The Spirit calls you to gather, to come by this place and
> meet with heaven.

Come now and take your place at the front door of eternity.

This bread and wine lie silently on the table.
Harmless, still, gentle in the quiet of this place.
Yet voices of every language have cried aloud because of it.
Throats have been cleared in protests, inspired by its content.
Proclamations roared in response to its message.
Cries of anguish have been raised because of its consequences.
Pain and distress result from its politics.

We join these voices.

The quietest of places now becomes the loudest message to the world. As we remember you breaking bread, spilling with destiny and light, by spirit, surrounded by promise, as you ask us to eat and drink and join all heaven.

Pentecost appears to have been one of the 'loudest' of experiences---not just in terms of the wind and tongues of fire and all those people speaking, but the experience that awakens us to love's claim and love's power. And baptism is the act of the heart and mind and being, the open and public declaration---*Here I am!---fill me!* Or with our children, we parents present them. *Here they are---fill them!*

But that's not the safe route to take, of course.

I am very fond of reading reflections written by Barbara Brown Taylor. In her book, *Bread of Angels*, she writes of Peter and his preaching and those who heard and responded to him:

> *His world had just been turned upside down. He had just had his doors blown off their hinges and when the Israelites asked him, 'What should we do?' I do not believe he gave them a three-step prescription to fill. I believe he told them how to prepare for a holy hurricane.*
>
> *'Reorient your lives.' That is the truth of what he told them, knowing full well that that was what would happen the*

— 137 —

moment Jesus came to live in them. Forget everything you ever thought you knew about who is in charge in this world. Get ready to revise all your notions about what makes someone great, or right, or worthy of your attention. If you think you know which way is up, think again. If you think you know how things should turn out in the end, get ready to be wrong.

This Jesus I have been telling you about is one surprise after another. You cannot second-guess him. All you can do is love him and let him love you back, any way he sees fit. Sometimes it is so strong it can scare you to death. You want to know what you should do? Repent, return, revise, and reinvent yourself.

Then go get born again, by water and the Spirit. Walk into the river of death with him, and while you are down there, let the current carry away everything that stands between you and him. Then, when all your own breath is gone, let him give you some of his. Take his breath inside of you. Let it save your life, and when he rises, rise with him, understanding that your life is no longer your own. You died down there. You are borrowing life now. Let someone make the sign of the cross on your forehead to remind you of that and join the community of those who call themselves his body, because they believe his heart beats in every one of them.

Then, receive the Holy Spirit. Breathe. Deeply. Receive your life as a gift invisible as air and prepare to be astonished by all the forms that breath can take. Under the power of the Holy Spirit, shy people have been known to step up onto platforms and say audacious things. Cautious people have become daredevils; frugal people have become philanthropists and people who used to be as sour as dill pickles have become rich with friends.

I guess that's what it means to be a 'Pentecost People'—a people who in baptism, consciously and willfully, open themselves and their children to the gift of the Holy Spirit and its gifts and the changes it makes in our lives and us.

And no gift is greater than knowing His heart beats in us, that His capacity for love has become our capacity and that joy abounds in the lives of those who know and believe they belong to Him.

May God bless Sierra, Dylan, Aiden and Connor with this knowledge and joy.

Amen

****

"Thanksgiving"

****

"Now Thank We All Our God"
by bjj
Thanksgiving Day
Scripture: Joel 2: 21-27
Mark 4: 1-9

Meditation:

> *We stand in the midst of nourishment, and we starve...*
> *We dwell in the land of plenty, yet we persist in being so hungry.*
> *And not only do we live in a land of plenty, but we can be fulfilled....*
> Macrina Wiederkehl, *A Tree Full of Angels.*

I was thinking the other day that my favorite Thanksgiving hymn is # 715 in our Chalice Hymnal- *"Now Thank We All Our God."*

> Now thank we all our God, with heart and hands and voices
> Who wondrous things hath done, in whom the world rejoices
> Who from our mother's arms has blessed us on our way
> With countless gifts of love and still is ours today.

I think that the reason I so like that hymn is that the emphasis, the focus, is always so clear--- it is on God. While it gives thanks for the countless gifts of love, the focus is on the Giver. While it lifts the blessings of presence and providence, grace and guidance, the emphasis is, without apology, upon the One from whom all blessings flow.

Thanksgiving is a national holiday that struggles with its focus. Although not a religious holiday, it certainly has a religious dimension. As we all know, harvest festivals are present in most cultures, but Thanksgiving is uniquely American. In this time and place, in a nation such as ours, we profess to a deep and abiding religiosity. However, we are also on a path intent on removing the mention of God in public gatherings. I wonder today if, while we express our gratitude for the gifts of hearth and home, health, and happiness, for country, constitution and freedom, for family, friendship, community and church, for the blessings of earth and spirit, sea and sky, we will remember to acknowledge and thank the Giver. Thanksgiving is not just about counting created blessings but blessing the Creator.

Edward Bleier's book, *The Thanksgiving Ceremony: New Traditions for America's Family Feast,* was released in September and received impressive reviews. It really is a wonderful little book! William Safire, the columnist for the *New York Times*, wrote the *Forward*. In it, he acknowledges that Thanksgiving in America is no longer a religious holiday but a day that has redefined its focus. That focus is family. He writes:

> *...Thanksgiving is not only a family holiday but is a holiday of families. The Americans and their guests who come together on the fourth Thursday of November may be related by blood, or by marriage, by friendship, by common interest or perhaps just by neighborliness or ethnicity or some combination of all associations. Although some members of the feast may be bound by habit or driven by hunger, what brings almost all together at a time of harvest is the longing to be a part of a family, real, virtual, or amalgamated by remarriage... (p.15-16)*

As true and as good as that may be, it saddens me to hear that God may not be the guest of honor at so many of our tables.

I was astounded by our Governor's proclamation. It certainly focused on the need and necessity of giving thanks and addressing the needs of others, but it is also a proclamation with no mention of God! Did anyone notice that?

President Bush, often criticized for his public piety, released a proclamation with a religious focus and a patriotic tone. (2003) The opening paragraph makes it clear:

> *Each year on Thanksgiving, we gather with family and friends to thank God for the many blessings he has given us, and we ask God to continue to guide and watch over our country.*
>
> (President's Proclamation, Thanksgiving 2003)

Last Thursday, the *Hartford Courant* featured an article about 'The Original Thanksgiving' from 1621. There was some neat stuff in the article. First, the menu likely didn't include turkey, but probably featured boiled mussels and roasted goose/duck. Cranberries dotted the sauce for the fowl. A sweetish corn pudding, boiled cabbage, and stewed pompion (pumpkin) rounded out the meal. (I can't imagine Thanksgiving without creamed onions and brussel sprouts!)

Second, here is another note of interest. That first celebration in 1621 was not a single meal as we celebrate it today. They didn't have to get things done and over with to make way for the biggest Christmas shopping day of the year! Rather, it was a series of gatherings over the course of three days. The settlers may have viewed the event as a harvest festival instead of a Thanksgiving celebration, since for the Puritans, 'thanksgiving' was a religious act. They observed days of thanksgiving regularly, marked by morning and afternoon religious services rather than feasting. For them, the focus of thanksgiving was on God as the Giver and not the gifts, whereas the focus of the feast was on the harvest. As we all know, the Puritans were not famous for their 'parties.' We are. That's why we are all here this morning for religious services first --- before the feasting! For the Wampanoags, who were much more religious than the Puritan English, the idea of giving thanks to the Creator for the earth and its gifts was part of daily life and the underlying theme of every ceremony or feast.

Jesus tried to make people aware of God's goodness and generosity and to give thanks.

Paul was the one who said it well. While advising the Ephesians to get drunk on the spirit rather than wine, he tells them:

> *...but be filled with the Spirit... giving thanks to God the Father at all times and for everything in the name of our Lord Jesus Christ.*
>
> *(Ephesians 5:19-20, NRSV)*

Jesus's lesson from Mark today is unique as he uses parables to awaken and enlighten, but the disciples fail to understand it, so he makes them think about it. Here, however, he explains things after they complain. We all know the parable well and often our focus is on the seed and soil.

The most interesting thing about the parable is not so much what happens to the seed, although that is important enough. But the most intriguing thing about this parable is the generosity of the Sower, the sheer undisciplined and abundant distribution of seed by the Sower. Palestinians who listened to Jesus were just poor, and many were farmers, scratching out a living on only small parcels of arable land. Rainfall would be scarce, and they would have had to be very careful with their seed. No waste here because there was little money around to go buy more seed. Those farmers who sat there listening to Jesus on that day would never think of doing with their seed what this Sower did with his.

And so, it really puzzled these farmers as they listened to the story that Jesus was telling about the Sower. Why is he so undisciplined? Why so generous? Why is he so incautious? Why so silly?

Why? The answer is because that is just the way it is with God. God sows out of love anywhere, anytime, in all places, among all people, so that all may receive blessings in every way. The only thing that might limit the yield is how rich the soil of our hearts and homes, our lives, and our spirits!

The story is told of a monk who, in his travels, found a precious stone and kept it. One day, he met a traveler, and when the monk opened his bag to share his provisions with him, the traveler saw the jewel. He asked the monk to give it to him. The monk did so readily. The traveler departed, overjoyed by the unexpected gift of the precious stone, a stone worth enough to give him wealth and security for the rest of his life. However, a few days later, he came back in search of the monk. When he found him, he gave him back the precious stone, but then he had one more request.

Now give me, he asked, something more precious than this stone. Give me that which enabled you to give the stone to me.

And we all know what that is, don't we?

The gifts simply manifest the Giver, who with such a spirit of abundant generosity has sown the seeds of blessing all over the place, and today, on this family holiday and this holiday of families, we gather in gratitude and in a spirit of true thanksgiving to acknowledge the Giver.

SO, LET THIS BE OUR THEME AND OUR HYMN TODAY:

Now thank we all our God with heart and hands and voices
Who wondrous things hath done, in who the world rejoices
Who from our mother's arms has blessed us on our way
With countless gifts of love and still is ours today!

Amen

****

Part II: Thematic Sermons

Lay Sermons

I am very proud of the prominent role that the laity has played in the life and mission of the church. The foundational principle of this memoir is that voices from the pew contributed significantly to clarifying and communicating the essence and relevance of our faith and ministry. As a 'Lay Sermon,' that voice is personal and powerful, engaging, and inspiring. I include two superb examples here, and I am indebted to these 'lay preachers.'

****

"The Substance of Faith"
by Carla Kelly
February 1982

> ...*suffering produces endurance*
> *and endurance produces character*
> *and character produces hope*
> *and hope does not disappoint us...*
>
> (Romans 5: 3-5)

These words have enormous significance to me because they point the way to the acquisition of faith–faith, that illusive, yet simple complement which rounds out our lives, which gives our lives texture and taste and color. All my life I've searched for a way to God, but it always seemed that you had to have faith before you could get faith. That's where I always got stuck. Faith was like a closed circle, and I couldn't break in–I couldn't seem to get started. But I believe I've found a way, and I'd like to share it with you. It begins, of all places, with futility.

-2-

Sometimes our days seem to be full of nothing but junk mail and runny noses, insurance payments and leftover spaghetti. This produces a hand-to-mouth mentality. We lose sight of the quality and promise that everyone should have in his life to keep him vital. It leaves us sitting in a chair at 3 o'clock in the morning staring out at the black, deserted street wondering, "what's the point, why bother? I'm only repeating what everyone has done before me. Is this all there is to life? Why?"

-3-

I've been in that chair many times. And I've discovered something there in the hollow darkness. It's not what you do, but how and why you do it, and the secret ingredient is hope. Hope is what you have when love fails. Hope is the jelly that keeps the peanut butter of numbness from sticking to the roofs of our lives.

-4-

What is hope? The American Heritage Dictionary says that hope means "to entertain a wish for something with some expectation. To be confident; to trust."

-5-

There have been difficult, no, grueling times in my life; times when the fire of existence burned cold and, like some distant star, was too remote and barren to serve my human need. For example, in 1974, a fluke explosion blinded my husband. It was a gory accident; the kind of stuff that books are made of. We could not collect damages to pay for the extensive medical bills. Shortly before that, I had become totally unable to work because of a nervous disorder, which was rapidly threatening my ability to function on <u>any</u> level. I felt like I was dying, and the medical profession could not give me any cure or promise, or even relief.

-6-

Engraved in my mind is the day I found myself trapped at a wedding reception. I was shaking so badly, and in so much pain, that I began to panic. I had to get away by myself, but circumstances prevented it. Every room was packed with people I didn't know. Finally, in desperation, I snuck under a table which was draped to the floor, where I could finally compose myself: but too spent and frightened to appreciate what a bizarre scene I made, all primped and powdered, squatting approximately under the broccoli casserole.

-7-

Well, it was pretty dismal that year. The best doctors said Jim would never see again. Meantime, I was worthless. The savings of four years were spent, we were spent, barely thirty, both disabled.

-8-

Forget all the mountains to climb, bicycle rides and ball games and simple physical pleasures of vital youth. We were suddenly handicapped in an already tough world with nothing to live on and nowhere to go.

-9-

Well, today I stand here before you, shaking maybe, but not hiding under any tables. And today Jim has his vision restored. The doctors called it unprecedented, baffling—a miracle. "A miracle" they said—but still I hadn't caught on. But times they were a changing.'

-10-

Somebody clever once said, "the only constant is change" and deep in my heart, I knew and accept that as the formula for life. With that understanding, the trials of life are never a surprise and never a dead end, because things will change; and incidentally, become opportunities for growth and discovery. Maybe not right away, but eventually you will see through the desperation–there was a gift in there somewhere.

-11-

I believe that sometimes all you have left is hope; sometimes that's all you need. After you've come through the other end of a few disasters, you realize you've grown - you've gained endurance. So, the next time troubles hit, you can relax a little more because you say, "if I got through that (death, or divorce, or sickness or whatever) then I can get through this one too." You realize that things always work themselves out. If you have hope, then you recover more quickly; you respond to the promise of better things to come, and something else happens, something subtler; you find that you handle yourself more gracefully in the process. <u>Hope gives you the energy to act positively.</u> That's very important, because it means that when you have nothing else, at least you remain open. And I had hope, and so, I remained open–open to the inevitable change I knew would occur.

-12-

We got back on our feet and bought a house, and I was pregnant in 1978. Finally, we were getting somewhere. We worked hard on the house; Christmas came, and my parents were there; we had a wonderful New Year's party. Then I had a little girl in February. We named her Brie. She was so healthy and beautiful… As some of you know; we lost Brie two weeks later. Again, we were left with nothing. Nothing but more medical bills. Nothing but an empty crib.

-13-

So, I took a job to help pay the bills and keep from being dysfunctional. And time passed and my hope restored, and I was pregnant again. And today we have Adam. He's everything his sister promised to be. I don't think I'll ever take him for granted. We worked so hard to get him here.

-14-

A dear friend from my atheist years, were he to see me speaking to you here, today, would break himself laughing. I can barely believe it myself. But that's how unlikely are the changes in me. But you never know. Here I am.

-15-

I am here because one particularly rotten day last summer my mental health was on the critical list. Nothing more could go wrong, and I was powerless to unravel any part of the snarled mess in my life. Night after night I had stared into the yawning dark, into dawn…grown stiff in the chair…with no answers.

-16-

Then it happened. Without warning one day, while driving home, a feeling of calm and confidence washed over me like a warm tide. Without censuring, I looked up and said, "I give this one to you." It wasn't a challenge; more like a response–like a hug of gratitude and relief. I just knew that the knots were going to fall out,and one by one, they did. That was no accident; it was a gift of resolution. This time I caught on.

-17-

I have kept my hope, which is leading me to a burgeoning faith. Hope– even when that faith is sick, or tired, or as was my case, nonexistent, enables you to reach beyond the probable, and win.

-18-

Let me tell you what I mean. Not long ago I heard about a program in which I really wanted to participate. It would be a dream come true. Unfortunately, I didn't have anything like the credentials I needed to apply. But I really believed that I could benefit from it and that I was qualified even without the prerequisite credentials. Mostly, I just plain wanted a shot at something big. So, I spent a couple of weeks on the phone trying to get an appointment with the man who was in charge of the program. He didn't return my calls. The secretaries began to sound embarrassed. I wouldn't take no for an answer, though; I really wanted in. Well, he finally called, and I got the appointment, and we had a long talk; and you know what? He said yes. Just like that. I was so surprised (since I really expected to be thrown out of his office) that I asked why. Do you know what he said? "I figure that anyone with the guts to come in here with such a request deserves a chance." I applaud that man's receptiveness and compassion.

-19-

Now, I went there on nothing but raw hope; the same hope which, little by little, is leading me to the faith in God, which I've been seeking for so many years. And that man accepted me on faith. It's working everywhere.

-20-

The avenue to faith is clear to me now. The circle <u>can</u> be opened. And all along, the answers were in scriptures. For example, Hebrew 11, verse 1:

> Now Faith is the substance of things hoped for,
> the evidence of things not seen.

So, if your faith is faltering, or like mine, sometimes nonexistent, remember that. Remember also:

> suffering produces endurance
> and endurance produces character

and character produces hope
and hope does not disappoint us.

I'd like to carve that somewhere, where I can read it every morning of my life.

****

"Expanding the Circle of Compassion"
by Sandra Larson-Gilmore
April 2004

Meditation:

> *The greatness of a nation and its moral progress can be judged by the way its animals are treated. Vivisection is the blackest of all black crimes that man is at present committing against God and His fair creation. It ill becomes us to invoke in our daily prayers the blessings of God, the Compassionate, if we will not practice elementary compassion toward our fellow creatures.*
>
> Mohandas Karamchand Gandhi

Good morning!

A number of years ago, I was sitting with a Quaker friend of mine in her office in Boston. We were discussing the events in our lives that had led us to that moment in our careers. During that meeting, she read me this quote by Frederick Buechner:

> *The place God calls you to is the place where your deep gladness and passion and the world's deep hunger meet.*

That quote had a profound effect on me, and I thought, "How true." I believe God calls each of us to satisfy that deep hunger by expanding our own circles of compassion to include not only human beings but also all of creation. My deep passion has always been helping animals. I believe that is what God has called me to do. Compassion for animals is something I have felt ever since I can remember. I recall as a child in third grade taking out my wrath on a sixth-grade boy in our neighborhood who was shooting at doves with a BB gun. I remember my mother and I rescuing an emaciated stray dog from a parking lot.

I told my mother when I was four that I wanted to be an animal doctor —because I thought that was the only way that one could truly help animals. However, that belief changed as I gradually came to new levels of understanding by having my awareness raised by people I encountered or things I experienced. I was fortunate to have many animal companions as a child and spent many hours with them. Later, my college science education was centered on my getting into vet school. However, God had other things in mind for me. My experiences during the next ten years, working for vets, working in labs, including research at the Harvard Medical School, and going to graduate school, brought me to where I believe I started my life's work. This work finally allowed me to truly express my deep passion.

For the next twenty years, I became a national advocate for animals- a voice for the voiceless. I worked as the director of education and scientific adviser for the oldest and largest animal protection organization in the country. I also founded Kitty Angels, my cat rescue organization. Through all this work, my own perceptions of the other creatures that share this world with us expanded greatly. I saw pain and suffering that I could never have imagined and saw the whole of creation through the "veil of tears" that James Herriot describes in *All Creatures Great and Small* during his work at Skeldale House.

My relationship with God dramatically changed. For many years, I had what I can only describe as mind wars with Him. How could He allow such widespread, horrendous cruelty toward innocent beings to exist? Where was this compassionate God? Where was this merciful Christ? For many years, I carried around tremendous anger. And this anger buried my relationship with God.

When I thought that my relationship with God had ended, my passion for my work quickly faded. He who had put that spark within me had also sustained it. No matter how I tried to rekindle that force within me, I could not. Without God directing my life, I was lost.

Even though I didn't realize it, Jesus was still with me. I eventually came to know that his compassion and love never failed me, nor had it failed the rest of creation. Christ on earth was compassion incarnate. Then, as now, he calls us to live a life of compassion — to expand our circle to include not only all of humanity, but all of creation. Because his new covenant is with all of creation, we must ask ourselves what grounds we have for excluding animals from the proper exercise of Christian responsibility. No longer can we justify our behavior with empty rationalizations like, "Well, they aren't as smart as we are." or "They don't have the same language as we do." Because the question is not "Can they reason?" nor "Can they talk?" but "Can they suffer?"

Yes. They do. They suffer like us and bleed when wounded. Under the skin, be it smooth, furred, or feathered, we are all related. Animals, like us, are living souls. They are not things. They are not objects. Neither are they human. Yet, they love. They dance. They suffer. And they mourn.

Pioneering heart transplant surgeon Dr. Christiaan Barnard said in his book, *Good Life, Good Death*, "I had bought two male chimps from a primate colony in Holland. They lived next to each other in separate cages for several months before I used one as a donor. When we put him to sleep in his cage in preparation for the operation, he chattered and cried incessantly. We attached no significance to this, but it must have made a great impression on his companion, for when we removed the body to the operating room, the other chimp wept bitterly and was inconsolable for days. The incident made a deep impression on me. I vowed never again to experiment with such sensitive creatures."

In that one experience, Christiaan Barnard had his awareness and understanding raised, and his circle expanded.

I'd like to relate to you one other very moving story I discovered when writing this sermon. It is from the book *When Elephants Weep: The Emotional Lives of Animals* by Jeffrey Moussaieff Masson and Susan McCarthy.

Unlike most other animals, elephants recognize the dead bodies or skeletons of their own kind. When an elephant encounters another's corpse, he or she explores the body carefully and inquisitively with feet and trunk, smelling it and feeling the shape of the skull and tusks, perhaps in an effort to recognize the individual that has died. Even a bare and sun-bleached skeleton will elicit the interest of other elephants, who inevitably stop to inspect the bones, turning them with their trunks, picking them up and carrying them from one place to another, as though trying to find a proper "resting place" for the remains.

Even more striking is the elephant's response when a family member dies. Because elephants live almost as long as people, the bonds they form are lasting. In 1977, hunters attacked one of the family groups studied by Cynthia Moss, Director of the Amboseli Elephant Research Project in Kenya. An animal Moss had named Tina, a young female about fifteen years old, was shot in the chest, the bullet penetrating her right lung. With the larger herd in a panicky flight, Tina's immediate family slowed to help her, crowding about her as the blood poured from her mouth. As the groaning elephant began to slump to the ground, her mother, Teresia, and Trista, another older female, positioned themselves on each side, leaning inward to support her weight and hold her upright. But their efforts were to no avail. With a great shudder, Tina collapsed and died.

Teresia and Trista tried frantically to resuscitate the dead animal, kicking and tusking her and attempting to raise her body from the earth. Tallulah, another member of the family, even tried stuffing a trunkful of grass into Tina's mouth. Tina's mother, with great difficulty, lifted the limp body with her mighty tusks. Then, with a sharp crack, Teresia's tusk broke under the strain, leaving a jagged stub of ivory and bloody tissue.

The elephants refused to leave the body, however. They began to dig in the rocky dirt and, with their trunks, sprinkled soil over Tina's lifeless form. Some went into the brush and broke branches, which they brought back and placed on the carcass. By nightfall, the body was nearly covered with branches and earth. Throughout the night, members of the family stood in vigil over their fallen friend. Only as dawn broke did they leave, heading back to the safety of the Amboseli reserve. Teresia, Tina's mother, was the last to go.

I'm sure Bruce has witnessed many times family members staying at a graveside after everyone else has gone. They too, like the elephants, linger to say their final goodbyes.

Can we open our hearts to the animals? Can we greet them as our soul mates, beings like us who possess dignity and depth? To do so, we must learn to revere and respect the creatures that, like us, are part of God's beloved creation, and to cherish the amazing planet that sustains our mutual existence. We must join in a bio-spirituality that will acknowledge and celebrate the sacred in all life. The Jains have accomplished this. In Jainism, non-injury to living beings is the highest religion. All beings hate pain; therefore, one should not kill them. This is the quintessence of Jain wisdom — not to kill anything. According to Buddhism, all beings seek happiness. One must let one's compassion extend itself to all. Because he has pity on every living creature, therefore is a man called "holy."

On the other hand, I believe many Christian clergy have shown almost total indifference toward the infliction of suffering on other species, present company excepted. They have gone to great lengths to justify, using biblical references, our diabolical treatment of nonhuman life.

But what matters most in a society less bemused by doctrinal abstractions, is the conviction that cruelty is negative, evil, and self-defeating, whereas pity and compassion are positive, humanizing, and life enhancing.

Christ was the embodiment of compassion. He gave his life for us. He taught us "no greater love has he than to give his life for a friend." It's interesting to see this concept reflected in the behavior of monkeys. In an experiment, two monkeys were put in cages side by side. One had food, but the other could only obtain food by pressing a lever that gave a painful shock to his companion in the next cage. The unfed monkey would starve rather than press that lever. The same cannot be said, however, of students in similar experiments in psych labs.

What is significant are not the differences between creatures, but their common origin. In the long course of our moral and spiritual evolution, says Darwin, we have gradually learned to broaden the circle of concern for others. Perhaps it is now time to bring not only other races and nations, but also other species within that arc. Expanding our circle will be the next stop in our moral and spiritual evolution.

Animals, like us, are microcosms. They, too, care and have feelings; they, too, dream and create; they, too, are adventurous and curious about their world. They, too, reflect the glory of God.

Jesus was power expressed in powerlessness; strength expressed in compassion. If selflessness and walking in love are the hallmarks of true discipleship, then we use Jesus as our example for living. Our actions should be as Christlike as we can make them. Christ challenges us as

Christians to be a light in a dark world. Paul expresses this by saying, "You will know them by their fruit." We are called upon to shine brightly by doing all that we can do to develop kindness and mercy in our lives.

Sometimes when I'm in our cat shelter doing chores in the evening, I turn the radio to WJMJ. They broadcast a series of prayers and chants, which often include, "Lord have mercy, Christ have mercy, Lord have mercy." We call upon Him to be merciful toward us. Should we not model this attitude in our dealings with the animals if we are to be Christlike? The cats even react to this portion of the programming. They become very quiet and peaceful, lie down on their beds, and actually bow their heads and close their eyes. It looks for the entire world as if they are praying.

Writer Henry Beston concluded in *The Outermost House*:

> *We need another and a wiser and perhaps a more mystical concept of animals. Remote from universal nature, and living by complicated artifice, man in civilization surveys the creature through the glass of his knowledge and sees thereby a feather magnified, and the whole image in distortion. We patronize them for their incompleteness, for their tragic fate of having taken form so far below ourselves. And therein we err and err greatly. For the animal shall not be measured by man. In a world older and more complete than ours, they move finished and complete, gifted with extensions of the senses we have lost or never attained, living by voices we shall never hear. They are not brethren; they are not underlings; they are other nations, caught with ourselves in the net of life and time, fellow prisoners of the splendor and travail of the earth.*

I will close, therefore, with this prayer by Virginia Fuller:

> *Almighty God, we entreat Thee on behalf of Thy animal creation. We ask Thy protection for all creatures that dwell upon the Earth. Help us to know before it is too late that in destroying them, we diminish the beauty of Thy handiwork, the fullness of Thy world, the sanctity of all life, and most of all, ourselves. Bless all who work for the common cause of protecting those of*

Thy creatures, who have no voice, but cries of pain, no words but those spoken on their behalf. O Lord, teach us gentleness and peace, and spread the mantle of Thy compassion over all Thy creatures, that they may be refreshed and comforted. Amen.

****

Stewardship Sermon

****

"What Matters Most-A Stewardship Sermon"
by bjj
April 1, 2001
Scripture: Isaiah 43: 16-21
John 12: 1-8

Meditation:

The chill of charity is the silence of the heart; the flame of charity is the clamor of the heart.

St. Augustine

Three weeks ago, before Leonard Gillon had his surgery, and during a visit at his bedside, he handed me this slip of paper from the 'Jesta minute' page of his January issue of a VFW magazine. The little 'Jesta' that he wanted me to read falls under the 'proud of daddy' category and goes:

Three boys were in the schoolyard bragging about their fathers. The first boy says: 'My dad scribbles a few words on a piece of paper. He calls it a poem and they give him $50.'

The second boy says: 'That's nothing. My dad scribbles a few words on a piece of paper. He calls it a song and they give him $100.'

The third boy then says: 'I got you both beat. My dad scribbles a few words on a piece of paper. He calls it a sermon, and it takes eight people to collect all the money.'

Every year, the Board of Stewardship asks me to deliver this sermon before the annual pledge drive to support our budget, and I'm glad to do it. However, this year I said that they had better have eight ushers on hand rather than just two. Such will be the power of my few scribbled words!

I was reading through my most recent Church Call and was so impressed by how this church is such a happening place! Indeed, as soon as word gets out, as announced in our most recent Church Call, that our own Bruce John will have a *SIN-ALONG* with the Friendly Circle on April 17th, two days after Easter no less. Everyone likes a good *Sin- Along!* People will come to our church in droves, throwing money at us.

--- FRIENDLY CIRCLE, INDEED!

(PS Marcia Campbell has already e-mailed our little church bulletin blooper to Reader's Digest!)

The board has mailed out their material, a cover letter, the 2001-02 budget and pledge cards. Mindful of the uncertain economy, the extraordinary generosity of this congregation to the Habitat for Humanity project and the other ways in which so many give so much, there is a minor change in next year's budget. The actual increase is only $695, from $239,700 to $240,395. I encourage all of you to review it critically and share your thoughts, but most important of all, I hope that together, we will support it with our pledges.

Whenever the subject of money comes up, especially these days, corruption comes with it. We read daily about the effects of money on politics, government and sports.

In the last week or so, there has even been quite a flap over the sale of the face and voice of the Rev. Dr. Martin Luther King Jr.'s very famous "I Have a Dream Speech." Have you seen the television advertisement? Dr. King is out there all alone, speaking about his dream to an empty mall in Washington… and then comes the tag line:

Before you can inspire,
before you can touch,
you must first
---and here comes the key word for the communications network--
connect.

Then you see the name of the company Alcatel America, followed by the actual footage of the original speech. Some, of course, have said that the advertisement debased the memory of Reverend King, and that the family has sold out. When I first saw the ad, I agreed and wondered how Alcatel got to use that footage, thinking that the family would never sell it. But they did. Money can be persuasive.

Yet, this morning, I would like to 'connect' our numbers to faces and dreams. I'm sure most of you read the front page article in the *Hartford Courant* this week, *Is This the Face of Jesus.* Of course, there is no physical description of Jesus in the New Testament. He never had his picture taken or posed for a portrait!

We have, however, stories that tell us of the man and his message.

Today's lesson from the Gospel according to Luke is poignant and, in some ways, stands distinctively on its own. For John, the story is part of the passion narrative. It expects Jesus's death and burial and shows us an example of true discipleship. In a few days, at his last meal with his disciples, Jesus will wash his disciples' feet and dry them with a towel as an example of how they are to love and serve one another in humility and with charity. But this day, it is all about Him and what Mary, the sister of Martha and Lazarus, does to show love for Him in an act of self-giving. So, Mary, over the objections and complaints of Judas, who saw only denarii or dollars in the jar of anointing oil, expressed her love and devotion in what might have been a costly way. At that point in her life, this mattered most, showing her love, and giving herself in devotion to Jesus.

The Board of Stewardship is asking that we all see the face of Jesus in our budget and in the ministries that make such a difference in people's lives. As I look at this budget, everything is distributed across the individual budgets of the boards and their expenses but behind the numbers is a wonderful appreciation of our humanity and our common search for or experience of God.

A budget is all about our house of worship and the worship that takes place here and what happens for us these few hours before the beginning of another week and amid the problems we face and the joys we celebrate.

It is about a pastoral presence that provides support and a message of hope in the most difficult of circumstances and the sometimes deepest of sorrow. Seeing all these daffodils reminds me of all those people for whom

I have done services this year, twenty-six (26) funerals, but only two of them were members of the church. For me, that's significant because it says that we try to be a visible and serving presence, a sign of Christ's inclusive love in our community.

It's about music, Mary and Christine, and about songs and the voices of adults and youth and cherubs.

It's about Melissa and her teaching staff, it's about Mary Ellen and Jim and about the youth of our church, what we teach in the classroom or at Pilgrim Fellowship or what they learn in a third world country.

Our focus is on missions and housing, and we strive to provide a safe place for all individuals, regardless of age, to learn that they are appreciated and cared for.

So, over the next couple of weeks, I invite you to set aside 'jesta minute,' put a few numbers on that bright canary yellow piece of paper you received in your mailing, a pledge card and rejoice in it as a gesture of love to Jesus himself.

AMEN

****

September 11, 2001

****

"Days of Images and Words"
by bjj
September 14, 2001
Scripture: Psalm 46
Matthew 5: 38-48

Meditation:

> *Nonviolence is a power which can be yielded equally by all- children, young men and women and grown up people- provided they have a living faith in the God of Love and have therefore love for all mankind.*
>
> Gandhi, 1936

Upheaval after upheaval has reminded us that humankind is traveling along a road called hate, in a journey that will bring us to destruction and damnation. Far from being the pious injunction of a Utopian dreamer, the command to love one's enemy is an absolute necessity for our survival.

The Reverend Dr. Martin Luther King Jr.

The opening paragraph for an article in Wednesday's *Hartford Courant* dealing with the role of religion in times of adversity and tragedy reads:

Religion, the philosopher William James said 100 years ago, is what man does in his solitude. It's the thoughts you think when nobody else is around, when you find yourself resting in the crook of a tree or surveying a glorious vista from a mountaintop. It is the deep thoughts you write in your journal at bedtime.

(*Hartford Courant*, Mark Oppenheimer, AA2)

The unthinkable tragedy of this week and the human stories that break your heart render that definition of religion trivial. Along with a resurgence of patriotism, we have become a nation that has turned to religion for comfort, for wisdom, and for hope. Religion is not just a solitary practice, but also something we do in the face of hardship and major life events. And certainly, one of the most obvious insights from this past week is that it is also something we don't do alone but in community. That community is even ecumenical. Yesterday's *New York Times* highlighted the unity of our nation's religions in response to this tragedy.

Evil has slashed into our lives and seared horrific images into our psyche. No words can express what we feel. We have needed to come together in prayer and conversation, in relief efforts ranging from heroic rescue teams to those contributing whatever they can.

This is another set of "defining moments" for President Bush and his administration, and for us as citizens and church members. In some ways, there has never been a more significant moment in my twenty-nine (29) year pastorate here at the church. I've never seen so much positive reference to the role of religion in people's lives, or the power of prayer.

There are as many clergy persons being interviewed as representatives of other organizations. I have had a sense of that importance resting upon my heart for days and this sermon must rise to the level of its calling. And yet I have found my thoughts and feelings to be in a state of constant movement. What I thought I would want to say when I did the bulletin on Wednesday isn't in some ways what I think I should say today. The images keep coming at us and the words, printed and spoken, keep us thinking and reflecting and processing.

Of all the challenges that face us now, none is greater than the decision we must make about what to do in response to this tragedy, this evil act of terror. Friday's front page of the Hartford Courant presented two faces--- The Face of Terror in Bin Laden and the Face of Resolve in President Bush. I can only trust that we as a nation are resolute in our efforts to bring to justice those who committed this heinous act, to bring them before the international court of justice and hold them accountable for these crimes against humanity, and I think that from the outpouring of support and solidarity from around the world, it is understood as just that!

Yet, revenge and retaliation are not justice. They represent judgment. The *Hartford Courant* headline for Friday's National Day of Mourning was upsetting.

A PRAYERFUL PAUSE ----AMID TALK OF WAR

I have been concerned about the direction of our planned response as a nation. Initial polling suggests Americans overwhelmingly support of retaliation, and they would retaliate against whoever is responsible, even if it meant killing innocent people. Two-thirds, according to a CBS poll, favor a military response. Just 20 percent oppose it.

Such a response is not compatible with our Christian faith. The archbishop of Canterbury said it well when he issued a call for justice, but reminded everyone who was gathered in St. Paul's Cathedral in London that as Christians, we are called by our Lord to a higher standard of human behavior. Tom McMillan said on Thursday evening that although it may always be true that we may wish that Jesus had never said:

> *You have heard it said — 'Love your neighbors and hate your enemies, but I say unto you, love your enemies and do good to those who persecute you.'*

HE DID SAY IT!

This means that even though we may be awash with images and words that anger us and break our hearts----we are called to a higher standard of human behavior, a deeper process of understanding and responding.

Mary said to me yesterday that she has had a "g-zillion" emails, all kinds of stuff. We all have. Kris Jacobi shared an email from President David Carter of Eastern Connecticut State University.

> *As I too search for answers and meaning to these unparalleled events, I am reminded of the words of the late Rev. Martin Luther King Jr.:*
> *"Darkness cannot drive out darkness; only light can do that. Hate cannot drive out hate; only love can do that. Hate multiplies hate, violence multiplies violence. The chain reaction of evil- hate begetting hate, wars producing more wars, must be broken ...*

But how do we break the cycle rather than perpetuate it?

I think we can take our initial steps even today by grappling with a few insights we need to understand.

First, Thomas Friedman wrote a column for the *New York Times* that reported from Jerusalem some comments made by the Israeli foreign minister, Shimon Pères. Listen:

> *Several decades ago, he notes, they discovered that smoking causes cancer. Soon after that, people started to demand smoking and non-smoking sections. 'Well, terrorism is the cancer of our age,' says Mr. Peres. 'For the past decade, a lot of countries wanted to deny that, or make excuses for why they could go on dealing with terrorists. But after what has happened in New York and Washington, now everyone knows. This is a cancer. It's a danger to us all. So, every country must now decide whether it wants to be a smoking or non-smoking country, a country that supports terrorism or one that doesn't.'*

Mr. Pères is correct; this sort of separation is inevitable—we must pay attention to who's in the smoking and non-smoking worlds.

As Mr. Pères himself notes, this is not a clash of civilizations—the Muslim world versus the Christian, Hindu, Buddhist, and Jewish worlds. The actual clash today is not between civilizations, but within them— between those Muslims, Christians, Hindus, Buddhists, and Jews with a modern and progressive outlook and those with a medieval one. We make a great mistake if we simply write off the Muslim world and cannot understand how many Muslims feel themselves trapped in failing states and look to America as a model and inspiration.

Second, there was a quote from a column written by Susan Campbell that has remained with me. It comes from an African proverb and was important to the struggle for justice and peace in South Africa:

You can't hate someone whose story you know.

I have heard it often said that as a nation, we would never be the same. I hope that this is true. In some ways, we need to place this experience within the broader context of human experience.

One of the most popular spiritual gurus of our time is Deepak Chopra. He has contributed something significant to the process. In a personal reflection on the events of September 11th, which he titled "The Deeper Wound," he writes:

> *As fate would have it, I was leaving New York on a jet flight that took off forty-five minutes before the unthinkable happened. By the time we landed in Detroit, chaos had broken out. When I grasped the fact that American security had broken down tragically, I couldn't respond at first. My wife and son were also in the air on separate flights, one to Los Angeles, one to San Diego. My body went absolutely rigid with fear. All I could think about was their safety, and it took several hours before I found out their flights had been diverted and both were safe.*

> *Strangely, when the good news came, my body still felt like it had been hit by a truck. Of its own accord, it seemed to*

feel a far greater trauma that reached out to the thousands who would not survive and the tens of thousands who would survive only to live through months and years of unbearable suffering. And I asked myself, why didn't I feel this way last week? Why didn't my body go stiff during the bombing of Iraq or Bosnia? Around the world, my horror and worry are experienced every day. Mothers weep over horrendous loss, civilians are bombed mercilessly, refugees are ripped from any sense of home or homeland. Why did I not feel their anguish enough to call a halt to it?

As we hear calls for tightened American security and a fierce military response to terrorism, none of us have any answers. However, we feel compelled to ask some questions.

1. Everything has a cause, so we must ask, what was the root cause of this evil? We must find out not superficially, but at the deepest level. Such evil is alive all around the world and is even celebrated. Does evil grow from suffering and anguish felt by people we don't know and therefore ignore? Have they lived in this condition for a long time? What is the root cause of such evil?

2. Can any military response make the slightest difference in the underlying cause? Is there not a deep wound at the heart of humanity? If there is a deep wound, doesn't it affect everyone? … If all of us are wounded, will revenge work? Will punishment in any form toward anyone salve the wound or aggravate? Will an eye for an eye, a tooth for a tooth, and limb for a limb leave us blind, toothless, and crippled?

3. Everyone is calling this an attack on America, but is it not a rift in our collective soul? Isn't this an attack on civilization from without that is also from within?

When we have secured our safety once more and cared for our wounded, after the period of shock and mourning is over, it will be a time for soul searching. I only hope that these questions are confronted with the deepest spiritual intent. None of us will feel safe again behind a shield of military might and stockpiled arsenals. There can be no safety until the root cause is faced. In this moment of shock, I don't think anyone of us has the answers. It is imperative that we pray and offer solace and help to each other. But if you and I are having a single thought of violence or hatred against anyone in the world at this moment, we are contributing to the wounding of the world.

Over the years, I have been fond of quoting in certain circumstances a line from Frederick Buechner:

The story of any one of us is the story of us all.

I'm not sure I ever really understood that until this week. There are no simple answers to this complex problem, but what we know for sure is that any solution begins with what is in our hearts. We will continue to be flooded with images of profound hurt and inspiring heroism. The flow of words will continue--- some will comfort and strengthen; others will alarm and worry. On my way to the funeral yesterday, the Walgreen's advertisement board out front had no promotions but carried this message:

In God We Trust--- United We Stand.

When I read that line, I hoped that someday we would all get the message. We stand united in trusting God to show us the way to stop hate, stop violence and make peace and to start that process with ourselves.

Amen

****

Gulf War- 2003

****

"As One with Authority"
by bjj
February 2003
Scripture: Deuteronomy 18: 15-20
Mark 1: 21-28

Meditation:

> *Today's scripture passages help us recognize the authority*
> *of those who speak and act on behalf of God's realm. The*
> *passages also help us claim our own authority to make God's*
> *realm visible in word and deed. We are challenged to express*
> *the gracious kingdom that is, indeed, at hand.*
>
> *Woven through the texts is the affirmation that God gives*
> *authority to teach and heal. What are the unclean spirits in*
> *our world, and how do we call them out? Whatever it is that*
> *trembles, that's what we need to call out, preaching, healing,*
> *and restoring to community.*
>
> (Seasons of the Spirit: United Church
> of Christ Worship Resource)

First, a pair of brothers heard His call coming unexpectedly, breaking into the ordinary routines of their fishing, daring them to follow Him, which they do! Then this man enters a Capernaum synagogue on the Sabbath and teaches, as no one has taught in recent memory---with such a presence and power, as someone who obviously spent hour upon hour with his media consultants. That day, in that place, He spoke as one with authority.

We don't know what he taught, but he shows us his true purpose when he helps a poor man with an unclean spirit. We all know what is unclean about that spirit, don't we? It is the bad stuff inside that distorts our self-image, corrupts our identity, and perverts our thoughts. But when someone challenges the unclean spirit, does it recognize the truth?

This reminds me of a story about a certain Army man who had been a heavy drinker for thirty-five years. He had the temperament of a vicious sergeant long after he had become a colonel. Finally, he encountered Christ and his whole life changed around.

He was speaking once before a group of medical people. He told them of his personality change, how he was now... as temperate as he had been intemperate; as considerate as he had once been severe, as concerned for others as once he had been selfish and self-serving.

A psychiatrist, who believed that personalities are so firmly set in early life that no one can change, protested to the Colonel that at his age a person could not have such a radical transformation.

> *Well, replied the Colonel, that may be true. But I am under new management now—I answer to another authority—the highest and truest there is. I am under new management now—I answer to another authority.*

In these trying times, with war seemingly imminent, Christians are struggling to understand what role their faith should play and how to act as disciples. As a pastor, I wrestle with finding a voice that follows the gospel, follows Jesus, and speaks to the current issues.

I've read that 50,000,000 people listened to President Bush the other night deliver masterfully an extraordinarily well crafted "State of the Union" address. As of this morning, the polls show that two-thirds of Americans support the administration's position, the case being made by not only the President but others as well, from those in government and out of it. Many voices are part of the debate, including religious figures. President Bush is a religious man, a Christian, and from what I heard in this address, he understands his policy and plan as a kind of divine mission. He invoked God four times during the speech.

> *The liberty we prize is not America's gift to the world; it is God's gift to humanity.*

> *We Americans have faith in ourselves but not in ourselves alone. We do not know--- we do not claim to know all the ways of Providence, yet we can trust in them, placing our confidence in the loving God behind all life and all history.*

Then, in addition to his use of phrases from some gospel hymns, he closed the speech with a changed benediction. Instead of saying,

> *May God bless America,* he said, *May God continue to bless America.*

Finally, as he has done so well before in times of crisis, he spoke to the nation yesterday- emotionally and eloquently and with the conviction of his faith:

> *In the skies today, we saw destruction and tragedy. Yet farther than we can see there is comfort and hope. In the words of the prophet Isaiah, 'Lift your eyes and look to the heavens. Who created all these? He who brings out the starry hosts one by one and calls them each by name. Because of his great power and mighty strength, not one of them is missing.'*
>
> *The same Creator who names the stars also knows the names of the seven souls we mourn today. The crew of the Shuttle Columbia did not return safely to Earth; yet we pray that they are all safely home.* (Isaiah 40: 26) (President George W. Bush, 2/1/2003)

I commend this sincere expression of faith, but in the matters of war and peace, we must, as Christians, ask of what kind of voice do the teachings of Jesus have in our lives, especially as compared to other voices. How authoritative are they?

On Tuesday, Kris Jacobi sent me an article from the *New York Times*, which was written by Joseph Loconte, a fellow at the Heritage Foundation. It was titled: *The Prince of Peace Was a Warrior Too.* I have since followed the responses on the op-ed page. I was so taken by the article that I shared it with the Diaconate and the Church Council at this month's administrative meetings. He writes:

> *Everyone, it seems, wants Jesus on his side. Nutritionists publish books with titles like "What Would Jesus Eat." Environmentalists issue policy statements asking, "What Would Jesus Drive?" With talk of war, we're now hearing "How would Jesus Vote on Iraq?"—assuming that He were a member of the United Nations Security Council.*

A growing number of religious leaders have decided that Jesus would veto a war with Saddam Hussein. Back from a fact-finding trip to Iraq earlier this month, a delegation from the National Council of Churches said it harbored no doubts:

> *As disciples of Jesus Christ, the Prince of Peace, we know this*
> *war is completely antithetical to his teachings...*

Loconte then presents the other side, rightly noting that Jesus preached that we have a moral obligation to confront evil and resist the darkness. He rightly observes that Jesus rebuked hateful mobs, cast out demons, and chased religious charlatans out of the temple with a whip. (Mind you, as far we know, no one was injured, and no one died!) And then most interesting of all, he cites the oft misinterpreted or misapplied line from Matthew 10:34.

> *Do not think that I bring peace on earth; I have not come to*
> *bring peace, but a sword.* (Matthew 10:34, NRSV)
> > (*New York Times.com*, 1/28/03)

What he fails to mention, astonishingly, is that the tenth chapter of Matthew is all about Jesus's commissioning of the disciples and sending them out as *"sheep in the midst of wolves"* (v. 16) and to a life of *"floggings and draggings"* (vvs.17-18) and yes, *even death.* (v. 28).

The tenth chapter is where, against this background of sacrifice and hardship, Jesus reassures them of their essential worth, even much more than that of the sparrow! The point, of course, is that discipleship sometimes puts individuals at odds with the authorities, your family, and the world.

The paragraph ends with a call to carry the cross and the promise:

> *Those who find their life will lose it, and those who lose their*
> *life for my sake will find it.* (Matthew 10:39, NRSV)

On Friday, the Reverend Bob Edgar, the General Secretary of the National Council of Churches, responded with these words:

> *Jesus could certainly be tough. He chastised those in his own*
> *community who did not live up to the moral standard of their*
> *professed faith. Conversely, he sought to forgive and redeem*
> *his enemies, even in a time of brutal oppression, steadfastly*

refusing to lead an insurrection despite pressure from some of his followers.

How we handle this crisis with Iraq is ultimately not about what kind of person Saddam Hussein is but what kind of people we want to be. I cannot believe that the Prince of Peace would condone a war in which the most powerful country in the world causes the needless death of thousands of innocents, even to remove the likes of Saddam Hussein.

Jesus by his example would call us to find a better way than war.
(New York Times, 1/31/2003)

I agree.

And they went into Capernaum; and immediately, on the Sabbath, he entered the synagogue and taught. And they were astonished at his teaching, for he taught them as one who had authority.

Eventually, he found himself on a hillside overlooking Galilee. A huge crowd gathered about him and among his teachings were these:

Blessed are the meek for they will inherit the earth.
(Matthew 5:5, NRSV)

Blessed are the pure in heart, for they will see God.
(Matthew 5:8, NRSV)

Blessed are the peacemakers. For they will be called children of God
(Matthew 5:9, NRSV)

You are the salt of the earth--- you are the light of the world!
(Matthew 5:13, NRSV)

> *You have heard that it was said, "An eye for eye and a tooth for tooth but I say unto you...* (Matthew 5:38, NRSV) (Well, you know what he said about that!)

> *You have heard that it was said, 'You shall love your neighbor and hate your enemy. But I say to you, love your enemies and pray for those who persecute you.'* (Matthew 5, selected verses, NRSV)

I accept that there are many voices, and that allowing these voices to speak their truth is what our beloved country and freedom are all about. However, as we listen, evaluate, and decide, let us remember Jesus longs to speak to us and teach us as one with authority.

There must be a better way than war.

Amen

****

"Our House of Prayer"
by bjj
March 23, 2003
Scripture: Exodus 20: 1-17
John 2: 13-20

Meditation:

> *...our Christian existence will be confined today to only two things: prayer and acting justly among people. All thinking, speaking, and organizing of the things of Christianity must be born out of praying and this acting.*
>
> Dietrich Bonhoeffer

> *Prayer always creates a new situation.*
>
> George W. Stewart

*The basic purpose of prayer is not to bend God's will to mine
but to mold my will into His.*

Rev. Timothy Keller

Our nation, one nation among a coalition of forces, is now at war. Coverage of the war is an unbelievable spectacle. We log on to our internet server, and we get invitations to read stories and see coverage with come-ons such as.

Rolling Thunder in the Desert
Stunning Blasts Shake Baghdad
Visit our Complete Interactive Guide: Live, See 'Shock and Awe'

In the days leading up to the final decision to go to war, questions about 'relevance and effectiveness' were raised not only about the United Nations but also about the church. Interestingly, just yesterday there was an op-ed piece in the *New York Times* about the United Nations. The *New York Times* titled its op-ed piece *Making the World Safe for Hypocrisy* and raised concerns about the effectiveness of not only the United Nations but also the church. (*NYTimes*, Luck, 3/22/03)

And just as interesting, if not compelling, are the discussions about the role of the church and the influences of the 'religious voice.' I listened to several interviews on CNN and MSNBC, and maybe even on Fox that raised the same question:

*… from the Pope on down to local congregations, whose voices
had been raised in opposition to war, why so little effect?*

Indeed, I imagine that just about every major newspaper in the country carried the recent findings of last week's poll by the Pew Forum on Religion and American Life and the Pew Research Center for People and the Press.

What I read did not surprise me. For a few weeks now, I have had at my desk an article from a February issue of the *Wall Street Journal*'s "Weekend Journal." It was about the church in these troubled times, and it was titled: *A House Divided,* and its sound bite about the tension that exists in the pew went:

> *Peace or war? Worried about losing members and money, more clergy are preaching both sides--- even in the same church.*

That sounded worse than the point being made, which was that some churches were simply trying to minister to everyone and each perspective in the parish.

(Weekend Journal, *Wall Street Journal*, 2/21/03)

But this Pew Poll is significant. Among the interpretations of the data were the following two:

First, I may as well use the headline from the *Hartford Courant: Clergy, Flocks Differ on the War. (Hartford Courant,* 3/22/03, p. A6.) There is a gap between pulpit and pew.

Second, few people are persuaded when religious leaders speak out, and only a small percentage of respondents said that their religious leaders and beliefs were influential. Ten percent of respondents said religious leaders and beliefs were influential. When grouped by influential groups such as family and friends, media and politicians, religious leaders ranked only above celebrities. OUCH!

The polls that I have seen indicate that the church is as divided as the nation in our post 9/11 world, where nothing seems simple anymore. Other polls show President Bush's ratings increasing, and support for military intervention remains high. The most recent wave of anti-war marches notwithstanding, the most recent number that I saw was 76 percent of the nation is supporting this military action in Iraq.

None other than Elie Wiesel wrote a highly controversial op-ed piece for the *Los Angeles Times,* which was then carried by the *Hartford Courant* favoring military intervention. He said:

> *Peace is not possible in the face of evil.*
> (*Hartford Courant,* 3/13/2003)

Lois, Peter, and I went to the movies on Friday evening to see *Tears of the Sun*---a thematic movie about the rescue of a doctor and her people from a Christian mission in Nigeria during a rebel pogrom of brutal ethnic cleansing. It was a powerful movie that challenges, no, forces, the viewer to think about evil and what to do when you face it. All that I will say here is that it ends with the oft-cited quote by Edmund Burke:

> *The only thing necessary for the triumph of evil is for good men to do nothing.*

So, we come here to worship this morning, struggling with our relevance and influence, wrestling with the question of what to 'do' in the face of evil—how to be the church!

I, for one, am both intimidated and inspired by today's New Testament lesson from the Gospel according to John. In it, we have Jesus at the temple. The story is commonly called "Cleansing of the Temple, and he is aggravated over what's going on there. It is a story that appears in all four gospels. There is only one difference between the stories in the account of Jesus's life, which is where they are placed. In Mark, Matthew, and Luke, the 'Cleansing of the Temple' takes place as part of Holy Week, just before the end of his life and ministry. After arriving in Jerusalem on Palm Sunday and witnessing all the activity that was taking place in the temple, he retires to Bethany. On Monday, he enters the city and heads straight for the temple. He grabs some rope that was on the floor and makes a whip, and in a rage, drives man and beast from the courtyard and then sends the money flying from overturned tables. We are told that he was angry at what they had done to the temple, making it a den of liars and cheats rather than what it is supposed to be 'a house of prayer.' As placed by Mark, Matthew, and Luke, we can understand his rage. He had had enough. Maybe he was feeling irrelevant and ineffective himself---that all has been for naught! So, he loses it, as we say these days! He goes in "to clean house" and reassert what the temple should be, not a house of politics or commerce, not a place where righteousness is for sale and certainly not a place where you lie and cheat. It is a house of prayer, a place where you go to talk to God and where God talks to you! Where you feel God's presence and draw upon God's power!

John's account is the same, except that John places the story right at the beginning of his ministry. Oddly, it is a story that follows the joyous occasion in Cana—the wedding feast—the event, you will recall, at which he changes water into wine! You talk about 'up one day and down the next!'

I guess he wanted to set the tone for what follows, to define the mission. You know what follows in chapter 3, the story of Nicodemus and the need to be born anew in the Spirit and John 3:16!

> *For God so loved the world that he gave his only begotten so that everyone who believes in him may not perish but may have eternal life.* (John 3:16, NRSV)

I wonder sometimes what He would say and do to us if He were to show up this morning.

The following is a French proverb and speaks all too truthfully:

> *He who is near the church is far from God.*

His mission today would be the same, to cleanse this place and drive out from within us all that impedes our relationship with God and living with such a profound sense of power and purpose and possibility! He would assert the same thing today as he did then. He wants this place to be "our house of prayer" and he wants us to be "a people of prayer!"

> *To pray,* observed the late Rabbi Abraham Joshua Heschel, perhaps the greatest modern theologian of the spiritual life, is *to bring God back into the world... to expand God's presence.* (Newsweek, 1/6/92)

Throughout this week, the media splashed the images of "Shock and Awe"in print and on the screen. Some are skeptical of its accuracy.

Well, the New Testament warns us about its own shock and awe and it's not misinformation. It tells us we offer *to God an acceptable worship with reverence and awe, for indeed our God is like a consuming fire.* (Hebrews 12: 28-29, NRSV)

But the yawn of familiarity has often replaced reverence and awe. We have tamed the consuming fire into a candle flame, adding a hint of sacredness, but no heat, no bright light, no power to purify.

I have always liked the writings of Annie Dillard. She once asked:

> *Why do people in churches seem like cheerful, brainless tourists on a packaged tour of the Absolute? On the whole, I do not find Christians, outside of the Catacombs, sufficiently sensible of the conditions. Does anyone have the foggiest idea what sort of power we so blithely invoke? Or, as I suspect, does no one believe a word of it? The churches are children playing on the floor with their chemistry sets. It is madness to wear ladies' straw hats and velvet hats to church; we should all be wearing crash helmets. Ushers should issue life preservers and signal flares; they should lash us to the pews for the sleeping God may wake someday and take offense or the waking God...*

If this is true, then it is no wonder that Jesus was so animated and insistent. The temple needs to be a house of prayer. This place must always be foremost, the place where we pray. There we get to talk to God and God talks to us, filling us with 'shock and awe' over the measure of his love for us and what we can do with His power.

Indeed, Fred Anderson, once the pastor of the Madison Avenue Presbyterian Church in New York City, defines prayer as:

> *That conversation we have with God in those moments of powerlessness and says, Prayer changes things.*
> (*The Living Pulpit*, p. 25-26.)

Prayer changes things, especially changing the powerless into the powerful. Jesus laments over our modern-day world, saying, *"Would that you knew the things that make for peace?"* We gather here to consider our relevance and effectiveness. Let us bring God into our lives and our world and here into this HOUSE OF PRAYER. Amen.

****

(The following reflection was offered roughly two years into my retirement and as the Pastor Emeritus of the First Congregational Church of Coventry. I wish we could say that the horrific tragedy at Sandy Hook Elementary School in Newtown, Connecticut, was an inflection point in our nation's fervent obsession with guns, but alas, it was not. In 2022, the *New York Times* labeled our present time as "the era of the gun" in a provocative piece. Our nation is awash in guns, and sadly, gun violence has become the leading cause of death among young people in our country. Mass shootings happen daily and the unthinkable, unimaginable is an ever-present reality. Voices from pulpit and pew need to speak out more forcefully with an equally fervent prophetic witness.)

"A Reflection on the Massacre of 'Our' Children"
at Sandy Hook Elementary School, December 14, 2012
delivered by Bruce J. Johnson on December 16, 2012

The unthinkable is now reality; the unimaginable is now the gruesome story told in picture and print. To comfort the nation, President Obama spoke both with emotion and eloquence on Friday:

> *Most of those who died today were children -- beautiful, little kids between the ages of 5 and 10 years old. They had their entire lives ahead of them -- birthdays, graduations, weddings, kids of their own. Among the fallen were also teachers, men and women who devoted their lives to helping our children fulfill their dreams.*
> *So our hearts are broken today for the parents and grandparents, sisters and brothers of these little children, and for the families of the adults who were lost.*
> *Our hearts are broken for the parents of the survivors for as blessed as they are to have their children home tonight, they know that their children's innocence has been torn away from them too early and there are no words that will ease their pain.*
>
> (President Barack Obama, 12/14/2012)

We are here this morning with broken hearts and with tears needing only the slightest provocation to flow. Never have we been in something together as much as we are since Friday. I met yesterday with a couple that wants to get married this June. Jenna is a second-grade teacher in Portland, CT. Like most of us this morning, she couldn't talk about it without tearing up! We feel heartbroken, and no words can ease the pain.

When I think of those children and that classroom, I am reminded of a verse from one song from Les Misérables, sung by Marius and poignantly titled:

"Empty Chairs at Empty Tables"

There's a grief that can't be spoken
There's a pain goes on and on.
Empty chairs at empty tables
(Now, our children dead and gone. These are my words
in parentheses)
Les Misérables

The first of the funerals was held yesterday, 12/17/2012 and the headline for this morning's USA Today read:
Tiny Coffin Rendered Me Speechless.
Indeed, there is a grief that can't be spoken and this is it!

I'm reminded as well of both the voice and verse of the one who gave us the classic, *A Christmas Carol*. These few lines are from another of Dicken's great works- *Dombey and Son:*

And can it be that in a world so full and busy,
the loss of one weak creature makes a void in any
heart, so wide and deep that nothing but the width
and depth of vast eternity can fill it up!

Charles Dickens
Dombey and Son

On Friday, we got a message from Chuck Wildman, our Conference Minister, that said:

As news unfolds and more tears flow, we will support one another as a Conference family of churches. For now, please hold Newtown in your Sunday prayers and honor God's life and salvation among us in this season of Advent Good News by continuing with pageants, concerts, children's programs. These life-affirming activities make a statement that God is with us and evil will NOT have the last word.

Peace and love, Chuck Wildman

I want to thank our Christian education staff and of course, the children who told us anew in the narrative about Jesus's birth that God is, in fact, with us…. the only fact whose width and depth can even come close to filling the void created by evil's ruthless assault on the precious children and their teachers at the Sandy Hook Elementary School. And today you have helped us make room and say 'Yes' where we kneel in our spiritual Bethlehem. (*My reference to 'Say Yes' is because of a beautiful and meaningful song that was sung during the pageant. "Say Yes"- lyrics by Bob Franke*)

I was asked the other day what preacher I most admired and maybe from whom I learned the most… The answer was easy- Rev. Dr. William Sloane Coffin.

And the sermon I most remember was delivered ten days after his son, Alex, died in a car accident. He delivered it to his congregation at The Riverside Church in New York City. It's about grief and condolence giving. An excerpt is reprinted in a book called: *A BROKEN HEART STILL BEATS- after your child dies* by Anne McCracken and Mary Semel. Coffin shares two theological insights that were transformative for me.

First, he said:

The one thing that should never be said when someone dies is 'It is the will of God.' Never do we know enough to say that. My consolation lies in knowing that it was not the will of God that Alex die; that when the waves closed over the sinking car, **God's heart was the first of our hearts to break.**

I believe with every broken piece of my heart that at Sandy Hook Elementary on Friday, '*God's heart was the first of our hearts to break.*' Second, he said:

> *I mentioned the healing flood of letters. Some of the very best, and easily the worst, came from fellow reverends, a few of whom proved they knew their bibles better than the human condition. I know all the 'right' biblical passages, including 'Blessed are those who mourn,' and my faith is no house of cards; these passages are true, I know. But the point is this. While the words of the Bible are true, grief renders them unreal. The reality of grief is the absence of God — 'My God, my God, why hast thou forsaken me?' The reality of grief is the solitude of pain, the feeling that your heart is in pieces, your mind's a blank, that 'there is no joy the world can give like that it takes away.' (Lord Byron).*

> *That's why immediately after such a tragedy people must come to your rescue, people who only want to hold your hand, not to quote anybody or even say anything, people who simply bring food and flowers - the basics of beauty and life - people who sign letters simply, 'Your brokenhearted sister.' In my intense grief I felt some of my fellow reverends - not many, and none of you, thank God - were using comforting words of Scripture for self-protection, to pretty up a situation whose bleakness they simply couldn't face. But like God herself, Scripture is not around for anyone's protection, just for everyone's unending support.*

> *And that's what hundreds of you understood so beautifully. You gave me what God gives all of us - **minimum protection, maximum support**. I swear to you, I wouldn't be standing here were I not upheld. Excerpt: pg. 217.*

I was thinking, no hoping, at this point that the congregation was remembering the last verse of *Say Yes*, which goes:

When the legion of angels call you blessed, Say yes.
And 'Were you faithful in every test?' Say yes.
And when they ask you, in story and in song,
'were you upheld and supported all along?'
'And did the power of the Spirit keep you strong?'

SAY "YES.")

Lois and I received a beautiful Christmas card the other day. It portrayed the front door of a home with a beautiful wreath and the message—*Welcome Christmas.*

What does that mean if not: life is lived with minimum protection, but Christmas assures us that God is with us all, our Emmanuel, and with Him comes the promise and reality of maximum support at all times, but especially when hearts are broken, when the grief goes unspoken and the pain goes on and on.

AMEN

Following this brief reflection, I read the names of all who died that day and with the reading, members of the congregation came forward and lit a candle in honor and remembrance of each child and adult. We formed a circle around the congregation and then listened to the Bell Choir play… *O Come, O Come, Emmanuel.*

Beautiful and meaningful and, of course, tearful.

****

Remembrance Sunday

(First Church has a lovely tradition of remembering those who died during the church year. We read their names. We place a flower in a chancel vase for each person, and do it on Memorial Day. The following sermon represents what we preach that day.)

****

"A Resurrection Faith"
by bjj
Memorial Day Sunday
(May 30, 1999)
Scripture: 1 Corinthians 15

It was Robert Lewis Stevenson who wrote these lovely words:

> *When the day returns, call us up with morning faces and with morning hearts, eager to labor, happy if happiness be our portion, and if the day be marked for sorrow, strong to endure."*

The night has now passed. The day has returned, but at least on one level, it does not call us up with morning faces and morning hearts. Death changes the return of this day, for we have marked it with sorrow, and it challenges the heart to endure.

In her truly blessed book, *After the Darkest Hour, the Sun Will Shine Again,* Elizabeth Mehren tells "The Parable of the Mustard Seed."[64]

> Gotami was a young woman whose every wish was fulfilled when she gave birth to a son. Her son was barely old enough to run about and play on his own when, suddenly, he died. Gotami was stunned into disbelief. She bundled the boy in blankets and strapped him onto her hip. From house to house she went, calling, 'Give me medicine for my son!'

> The neighbors were puzzled. How could they offer cures for a child who was so obviously dead? Finally, one friend urged her to knock on the door of the nearby monastery. The monk praised Gotami for seeking treatment, and by way of remedy, he gave her an assignment. Go to each house in the city, the monk told Gotami. And from every

---

[64] Elizabeth Mehren, *After the Darkest Hour, the Sun Will Rise Again* (New York: Fireside, Simon and Shuster, 1997) p. 47-48.

house where no one has ever died, fetch tiny grains of mustard seed.

In every house, the answer was the same. Here, Gotami was told again and again, someone has died. In one house, Gotami was told that no one can count the dead. At the next door, she was also left empty-handed. There would be no mustard seed. Here, once again, someone has died.

At last, in sadness and in resignation, Gotami went to the edge of the city and buried her son. Dear child, she said as she completed this tearful mission; I thought that you alone had been overtaken by death. I was wrong.

With her soul heavy, Gotami trudged back to the monastery. She expected that the monk would fault her for returning without a single mustard seed. But he embraced her and bestowed high praise. 'You have faced your grief and now you will find release from your numbing bitterness.'

GOTAMI KNEW THAT HE WAS RIGHT.

In some ways, I trust that we all know that the monk was right. Probably there is not a household here represented that could offer a single grain of mustard seed. Yet again, we have gathered on this Memorial Day weekend on our Remembrance Sunday to remember and honor those who have died this year. We come together to show to those who grieve that they are not alone and are surrounded by those whose grief is fresh and those whose pain and loss have been ongoing.

Shelley once penned these words:

> *Winter has come and gone,*
> *But grief returns with the revolving years.*

Grief is always unfinished.

But we gather also to remember the fundamental truth of our faith—"A Resurrection Faith."

Oscar Wilde wrote:

Hearts live by being wounded.

Helen Keller said:

Although the world is full of suffering, it is also full of overcoming it.

This is also the central purpose of the Christian faith! Overcoming our sadness and sorrow, overcoming our sense of vulnerability when tragedy strikes with a harsh swiftness. It's about living with certainties in the middle of uncertainties, with hope during illnesses that claim our loved ones. It is about life, about death, and about life eternal.

We read twenty-nine names this morning. They are our sons and daughters, our mothers and fathers, our husbands and wives, our friends, and neighbors. Felicia Marie had but a few breaths before dying in her mother's arms. Walter Wolf enjoyed seasons in two centuries.

As I read the names and remembered the circumstances and the services, I remembered the prayer of the poet Rainer Maria Rilke:

Oh Lord, give each of us his own death.
The dying, that issues forth out of the life
In which he had love, meaning and despair.

I wish that could have been the case for each name and life that was read this morning, and I am sure that the cruel incongruence of some deaths wound even more. Coming to terms with the most personal aspects of a loved one's death is the most pressing duty of the journey we take through grief. The complicated process requires time and attention and sometimes, some hard work through some major pain.

And one of the major emphases of scripture, especially in the words of Paul, is how we grieve. Writing to the church at Thessalonica, he wrote these words:

> *But we do not want you to be uniformed, brothers and sisters, about those who have died, so that you may not grieve as others do who have no hope. For since we believe that Jesus died and rose from the dead and through Jesus, God will bring with him those who have died.*
>
> (1 Thessalonians 4: 13-15, NRSV)

I have read Paul's words to the Corinthians many times, with a focus on his two primary concerns.

1. To address the doubts that arose in the Corinthian community concerning the reliability of news accounts concerning Christ's resurrection.
2. Its implications for them and their lives.

His argument is enthusiastic and convincing based on:

1. Tradition
2. Resurrection logic. How can any of you say there is no resurrection of the dead. He came not just for this life!

The gospel truth is this: *Death has been swallowed up in victory.*

(1 Corinthians 15: 54, NRSV)

On this Remembrance Sunday, our resurrection faith marks the occasion. This is what we believe: *In Christ, all will be made alive!* (1 Corinthians 15: 22, NRSV)

Amen

****

Week of Prayer for Christian Unity
Annual Pulpit Exchange

Throughout my tenure at First Church, we nurtured a firm commitment to ecumenism, locally and globally. One of the eagerly anticipated Sundays was the Sunday on which pastors and priests occupied the pulpits and preached the sermon at our sister churches. I preached this sermon at St. Mary's Catholic Church, Coventry, Connecticut.

****

"Together, We Know Jesus"
by bjj
January 19/20, 2002
Scripture: Isaiah 49: 1-7
John 1: 29-42

Meditation:

> "Follow me"
> No greater introduction than that.
> A hint of something better down the road.
> An Invitation to adventure.
> An offer of a new purpose in life, hazy.
> No money-back guarantees, no assurances,
> No display of credentials as to why we should trust him.
> Just that call breaking into our fishing.
>
> That's often how it comes. Out of the blue, yet curiously close to us,
> Touching our deepest yearnings.
> No time for careful consideration and weighing the alternatives.
> Just that dare to follow."
> Richard W. Chilson, *Yeshua of Nazareth.*

It is yet again a privilege for me to be here among you tonight on this the second day of our "Week of Prayer for Christian Unity." By the look of the weather outside, however, God is not smiling at our effort. Nevertheless, I always look forward to my time with you. Because Father Ray's schedule couldn't accommodate us for tomorrow, but had to be put off until next week, I get you tonight and my congregation tomorrow.

What an opportunity!

This reminds me of my favorite story from the great Danish philosopher Soren Kierkegaard, a story he calls: *'The Parable of the Ducks.'*

> He describes a town where only ducks live. Every Sunday the ducks waddle out of their houses and waddle down Main Street to 1171 Main to their church. They waddle into their sanctuary and squat in their proper pews. The duck choir waddles in and takes their places. Then, the duck minister comes forward, opens and reads from their duck Bible. (Ducks, like all other creatures on earth, seem to have their own version of the scriptures.)

He reads to them:

> *DUCKS! God has given you wings!*
> *With wings you can fly!*
> *With wings you can mount up and soar like eagles!*
> *No walls can confine you! NO fences can hold you!*
> *You have wings! God has given you wings! And you can fly*
> *like birds!*

In response to the inspirational duck gospel, all the ducks shouted in unison and with great fervor, *AMEN!*

> *And then they all waddled home!*

I do not want to see anyone waddle home tonight or tomorrow, but upon our wings of faith, we will not only fly, but fly as one!

The month of January always brings a flow of magazines that highlight the previous year's top stories. At the top of every conceivable list this year, of course, was the story of those murderous flights of September 11th and their effects on the nation and the world. Our congregations got together then as we do today---**as one**—praying for peace and for the victims of the bombings and those grieving so many deaths. We came together to give thanks for the heroic efforts of police, firefighters and first responders, all heroes and the countless ordinary citizens—who, out of their common humanity, rose to extraordinary levels of compassion and sacrifice.

Mother Teresa once said:

Not necessary to do great things but little things with love.

(The writings of Mother Teresa of Calcutta © by the Mother Teresa Center, exclusive licensee throughout the world of the Missionaries of Charity for the works of Mother Teresa. Used with permission.)

On 9/11, it was clearly necessary for some to do great things in the face of such horrific, terrorist violence, but in the long run, the measure of our recovery and the restoration of our shaken American identity will depend on all the little things we do with love.

Many have said that we will never be the same. Perhaps that is not only true but also good.

There is a song at the top of the country charts by Alan Jackson, titled "Where Were You When the World Stopped Turning?" We observed the "Week of Prayer for Christian Unity" each year on or near my son Peter's birthday. In the early years, I always had a story about him. More recently, because of his singing talent, he had a song for us. He is here tonight on the eve of his last year as a teenager. He's going to help his dad with this sermon by singing that song for you.

PETER SINGS: "WHERE WERE YOU?" by Alan Jackson

I love the chorus of that song:

I know Jesus and I talk to God, and I remember this from when I was young: Faith, hope and love are three things that he gave us and the greatest of these is love.

Like all of you, I often wonder what it would have been like to be in the physical presence of Jesus. In today's lesson from the Gospel according to John, Jesus appears, and maybe the world seemed to stop turning for those who looked into his eyes or heard his voice. Two disciples of John the Baptist heard him call Jesus the **Lamb of God** and they follow him. Jesus spins and asks them: "What do you seek?" Surprised, they only manage a lame response: "Where are you staying?" The Lord sees through it and tells them to "Come and See. I wonder what they saw and experienced!

Where was he staying? With whom? Who else was there? What did they talk about?

We're not given any of that information, but we know this, and maybe this is all we need to know: that they got to know Jesus and felt like they had talked to God and as a result, were called to a life in community, a community of neighbors who care for one another.

And Andrew, being so taken by the entire experience, rushed to tell his brother, Simon, that he had found the Messiah!

You know, every occasion of our being together in Christ's name is an opportunity for Him to turn to us and ask: "What do you seek?"

Every time we are together is an opportunity for us to be with God and find joy in faith, hope, and love.

And tonight, in our being together, He is here.

  — in worship, prayer, and preaching,
  — in song and sacrament and service!

What we seek and celebrate tonight is that together, we know Jesus, and we talk to God, and we remember what we know by heart—that faith, hope and love are three things that He gave us and the greatest is love!

AMEN

****

Annual Meeting Sunday
"Beyond the Ordinary for 292 Years"
by bjj
June 20, 2004
Scripture 1 Kings 19: 1-15a
Luke 8: 26-39

Meditation:

> *Faith is closest to worship because, like worship, it is a response to God.*
>
> Frederick Buechner

*What members find most compelling, what causes them to
make time for the church in their busy life, is a sense that they
get something there that they get nowhere else.*

Penny Edgell

The Rev. Fred Craddock, Bandy Professor of Preaching and New
Testament at the Candler School of Theology in Atlanta, delivered one
of my favorite sermons of all time. It was an entertaining and highly
provocative sermon about things that kill a church and things that keep it
alive and vibrant. Although I don't remember it all, I remember his musing
about how church buildings make excellent restaurants that could carry
catchy names like: The Fisherman's Catch for seafood, or the Carpenter's
Bench for a steak house, or The Master Chef for gourmet cuisine. I am
embarrassed to say that this idea hits close to home. In fact, Tim's senior
project in his major, Building Construction, at the University of Florida,
was to convert a church building to a sports bar! This was to be done by
a minister's kid!

Last week's *Hartford Courant* had an article about the Catholic
Church's sale of sixty properties in the Boston Archdiocese. As church
attendance declines and the real estate market heats up, developers are
expressing a keen interest in purchasing churches that will be converted
into condominiums. Here is an excerpt from the article:

> *At St. Peter and Paul, the one-to-three-bedroom condos are
> priced at between $300,000 for the smallest one-bedroom
> unit to 1.2 million for the 2400 sq. foot penthouse--- and get
> this—with cathedral ceilings and the bell tower of the 1840s
> church. Hartford Courant, (B-5)*

Do you know what else? I got a chuckle out of the divine irony struck
by the *Hartford Courant* when they put that article on its obituary page!

These are tough times for many churches, locally and denominationally.
Certainly, the Roman Catholic Church in the United States is struggling.
Many, if not most of the mainline Protestant churches, are being forced
to deal with declining numbers in both money and members. Our own
Connecticut Conference of the United Church of Christ made the news

and the op-ed page recently when Wethersfield's First Church of Christ, the largest United Church of Christ church in New England, voted to disassociate from the United Church of Christ and to drop out of our Connecticut Conference. That vote and the withdrawal of Wethersfield's First Church from the Connecticut Conference is going to hurt the ministries of the church and has set off alarms throughout the United Church of Christ.

Our relationship with the Connecticut Conference is also strained, and the issue isn't sex or faith but the very nature of what it means to be in covenant, the conference and local church. We'll need to work together to resolve our differences.

Then, just this week, the Southern Baptist Convention, the world's largest Baptist denomination and America's largest protestant denomination voted to leave the Baptist World Alliance and many other groups to which it belongs. The debate and disagreements, as best as I can tell, stem from tensions between the liberal and conservative factions.

These are difficult times for the church and the 292nd year of our church has not been easy either, but we've made in through, and I think we are strong in faith and works. First Church in Coventry is not dead.

One question being asked of candidates for the proposed part-time assistant minister's position is:

> *Please identify and discuss what you consider to be characteristics of a 'healthy' church?*

That's not a bad question for us all to think about and answer. How strong and healthy are we?

I would like to do a David Letterman with you this morning. There is a useful little book hot off the press this year that can be of help to us. Its title: *Beyond the Ordinary: 10 Strengths of US Congregations* by Cynthia Woolever and Deborah Bruce. I've included the following list in each of your bulletins so that you each can follow along.

Here goes:

☐ STRENGTH 1: GROWING SPIRITUALLY- a church is healthy when a majority of it members recognize the need for change and growth and believe that their needs are being met by worship and work at, in and through the church. "Someone asked the poet Longfellow how he had achieved a long and happy life. Pointing to an apple tree, Longfellow replied, "The secret of the apple tree is that it grows a little new wood each year. That's what I try to do." Frederick Buechner said it this way:

When faith stops changing and growing, it dies on its feet.

☐ STRENGTH 2: MEANINGFUL WORSHIP- What a challenge this is, and the study admits to this particular strength being one of the toughest to assess simply because--- those who haven't found worship to be meaningful aren't there. One thing is for certain, though, providing meaningful worship requires a dialogue between those who are happy with what you have and those who long for something tweaked or changed.

☐ STRENGTH 3: PARTICIPATING IN CONGREGATION- a strong church is one that involves its members, and I would claim too that it involves anyone who wants to be involved!

☐ STRENGTH 4: HAVING A SENSE OF BELONGING— "Congregations with a healthy heart touch the feelings of their participants. Someone said that home, in one of its many forms, is the great object of life. "Home is the place where we rest; home is the place where we find ourselves; home is the place where we feel safe." The church needs to be like home—a place of safety, a place with supportive friends and a place of acceptance--- and this means of course, all God's children--- the emphasis on ALL!

☐ STRENGTH 5: CARING FOR CHILDREN AND YOUTH.

☐ STRENGTH 6: FOCUSING ON THE COMMUNITY- George Bernhard Shaw once said: "My life belongs to the community and as long as I live, it is my privilege to do for it whatever I can." That goes for the church as well. It is our privilege to serve the community.

☐ STRENGTH 7: SHARING FAITH- This is one of the biggest challenges. Growing spiritually is most often quite a private and internal matter. Sharing faith, telling others about what has transformed our lives is not an easy thing to do, but strong congregations are made up of members who do just that. In today's lesson, we have a great example--- the man who is healed wants to follow Jesus, but Jesus tells him to stay home—tell his friends, tell his neighbors and tell his community.

☐ STRENGTH 8: WELCOMING NEW PEOPLE.

☐ STRENGTH 9: EMPOWERING LEADERSHIP—Ralph Nader once observed: ...*the function of leadership is to produce more leaders, not more followers.*

I suspect that is why Jesus did not hang around long but sent out those whom he taught and trained to go and do likewise. Strong congregations equip ordinary people to find their gifts and accomplish extraordinary things.

☐ STRENGTH 10: LOOKING TO THE FUTURE—"The heroine in the romantic comedy MY BIG FAT GREEK WEDDING complained to her future groom that her huge Greek family was somewhat over-controlling and irritating. His response to his future bride was classic advice:

Don't let your past dictate who you are, but let it become part of who you become.

Well, these are the ten strengths of US Congregations. Those who have them have moved beyond the ordinary in their faithfulness and service in the name of Jesus Christ. In this our 292nd year, we would do well to reflect on them.

So, what do you think? Should we put the building up for sale?

Amen

ADVENT

There is a time
for everything, and
a season for every
activity under heaven:
Ecclesiastes 3:1

HAPPY THANKSGIVING

† IN REMEMBRANCE OF ME †

EASTER

FLOWER CO.

DAFFODILS

Pilgrim Fellowship

Working Together

Music

Our Room

Working Together

EPILOGUE

Voices from Pulpit and Pew

In his brilliant best seller titled *Habits of the Heart: Individualism and Commitment in American Life*, Robert Bellah defines the essence of the church as 'a community of memory,' memories that tie us to the past and turn us toward the future. [65] This is an insightful definition of the church in general and First Church, in particular. I like that image; the church being tied to the past but turned toward the future.

The essence of this memoir, the memories and lessons implanted by voices from pulpit and pew, is a rich compilation of people and their operational theologies, the ones that informed and sustained our life of faith. On its pages, I have tried to share some memories and identify the messages in them. Our memories are young by comparison to the messages. The messages are as old and true as the bible story itself. Our memories are as young and as fresh as those who have had the courage, commitment, and conviction to be the church in this time and place. They remembered the story and used their voices and their very lives to make it come alive and relevant in and around First Church.

[65] Robert Bellah, Richard Madsen, William Sullivan, Ann Swidler and Stephen M. Tipton, *Habits of the Heart: Individualism and Commitment in American life* (Berkeley: University of California Press, 1985) pp. 152-55.

Many years ago, Linda Hodgkins gave me a verse by Mary Loberg that I have since quoted often:

> *Memories are like pictures, taken through the years,*
> *A smiling face, a happy time, a favorite place.*
> *These treasures time cannot erase.*[66]

First Church values its memories and their power, considering them to be sustaining and inspiring treasures.

In 1967, Gabriel Garcia Marquez published one of my favorite novels, translated from Spanish to English in 1970. The author is the Colombian novelist who won the Nobel Prize for Literature in 1982. The book's title is, *One Hundred Years of Solitude*.[67] It is a novel that tells a story of a strange disease that invaded the village of Macondo from somewhere in the surrounding swamp. The sickness was insomnia so powerful that it infected the whole town. One symptom was an inability to sleep because the body felt no fatigue. At first it seemed a marvelous lark; people had so much to do that they did not mind working instead of sleeping. Then, they encountered a more problematic symptom, an increasing loss of memory. The infected persons became unable to remember the names of simple things around them. As the disease progressed, they forgot memories of childhood. They forgot things they had learned long ago, information that had sustained them daily and indeed, from one generation to another, and eventually, even the names of those people closest to them. Finally, they sank pathetically into a loss of awareness of their own being, leading eventually to idiocy.

In the novel, one man in the town conceives of an imaginative way to stave off forgetting. He not only carries it out in his house, but also convinces the whole town to follow his example. One of the passages reads:

> *With an inked brush, he marked everything with its name:*
> *table, chair, clock, door, wall, bed, pan. He went in the*
> *corral and marked the animals and the plants: cow, goat,*
> *pig, hen. Little by little studying the infinite possibilities of*

---

[66]   Mary Loberg, Inscription in a popular Hallmark Card.

[67]   Gabriel Garcia Marquez, *One Hundred Years of Solitude* (New York: Harper and Row, 1970) pp. 48-49.

a loss of memory, he realized that the day might come when things would be recognized by their inscriptions, but that no one would remember their use. Then he was more explicit. The sign that he hung on the neck of the cow was exemplary proof of how the inhabitants of Macondo were prepared to fight against a loss of memory: 'This is a cow. She must be milked every morning so that she will produce milk, and the milk must be boiled in order to be mixed with coffee.' Thus, they went on living in a reality that was slipping away, momentarily captured by words, but which would escape irremediably when they forgot the values of the written letters.

Two of the most touching signs, however, were for the name of their village, Macondo, and for the faith reminder, a sign at the center of town that said simply:

'GOD EXISTS.'

Without that sign, they would have surely forgotten even that.

I am in awe of First Church's generational years of faithful witness. It has functioned as a sign at the center of town, reminding the citizenry not only that God exists but that the power of the Christian faith and the insights and inspirations of its stories can change hearts and save souls and transform lives. That is our message, true and tested, yesterday, today, and tomorrow.

I have worried, though, that perhaps someday some unnamed disease would creep up from the swamp of secularism or the corruption of our most cherished institutions, those that are foundational to our democracy, to create a similar, albeit a more contemporary, type of crisis of memory. I am not alone in that worry. A few years ago, as was mentioned in Chapter IV, the theme for the Pastor's Conference in Florida, Consultation XV on Parish Ministry was *Pastor as Preacher*. Dr. Fred Craddock was the featured preacher and for his concluding sermon he chose the first eight verses of the third chapter of Revelations.

> *And to the angel of the church in Sardis write: The words*
> *of him who has the seven spirits of God and the seven stars.*
>
> *'I know your works; you have a name of being alive, but you*
> *are dead. Wake up and strengthen what remains and is on*
> *the point of death, for I have not found your works perfect in*
> *the sight of my God. Remember what you have received and*
> *heard; obey it and repent.'*
>
> (Revelations 3: 1-8, NRSV)

Craddock calls this passage the obituary for the urban church at Sardis and suggests that should we want to know the cause of death; we would only need to consult the medical examiner in charge of ecclesiastical deaths. We would find amnesia listed. They forgot what they had received and heard. So, the church died.

Amnesia can kill the church, but First Church has not forgotten. Indeed, its proud and animated history has been written and told by ordinary folk who remembered what they had received and heard, not just for the preservation and enhancement of their lives in the present but for that of future generations. In this book, I have tried to highlight their efforts and honor them for what they have learned, preserved, and transferred to another generation.

Perhaps no writer/philosopher of our time has understood and written more profoundly about the role of memory in our lives and the responsibility we have to future generations than Elie Wiesel. In a three-volume collection of his work, a collection titled *Against Silence: The Voice and Vision of Elie Wiesel*, edited by Irving Abrahamson, page upon page, address upon address, speak of what it means to be a Jew, with an 'historic identity' defined by the 'collective memory' of a people transmitted from generation to generation through letters that make up words, and words that tell stories told by storytellers. Wiesel, of course, is one of the best and most effective. We have some good ones at First Church as well. These stories are remembered and told for a purpose, that we might know who we are and what we are about and who we must be in a world where good is threatened by evil, light by darkness, and life by death. For Wiesel, not only is the quality of life but our actual survival dependent upon memory and how we handle or mishandle it.

He concludes one brief reflection with a credo, advice for life:

> *Study more, live more intensely and keep the questions open. As long as it is open, you will look for more commitment, for more love, for more faith, for more knowledge and, above all, for more memory, without which we (Jews) could not survive.*
>
> (Statement, Temple Sholom, Chicago, Illinois, October 25, 1981)

The church is 'a community of memory' that is not only tied to the past but in significant ways, dependent upon it for its sense of identity, calling and survival for the future.

The church is always challenged to remember that we are 'a community of memory' that is turned toward the future. We live in very troubled times. There is a wide agreement that the events of September 11, 2001, changed America forever. And, more recently, the pandemic of 2020 has had a profound impact on both America and the church and on how it functions in the world, 'now more virtually than in person.' And there is a plethora of issues on America's agenda. They continue to demand serious attention and resolution such as race relations and issues of war and peace, the war on terror, foreign and domestic, renewed concerns about nuclear proliferation, national security, poverty, health care, cultural diversity and several social and moral issues, ranging widely from reproductive rights to the rights of our LGBTQ+ brothers and sisters and the alarming and dangerous rise of white Christian nationalism. (And, as I edit this manuscript, our nation is being terrified by an epidemic of gun violence.) So many questions are open, and they require more study and more knowledge, more commitment, discussion and debate and more faith. The church struggles to clarify its own vision and find its own voice. Our United Church of Christ designed and implemented a national initiative to address these issues. It is called:

> *Never place a period where God has placed a comma. (Gracie Allen) God is Still Speaking*'

Reflecting on these five decades of ministry, I believe with all my heart that God has spoken to us and through us, and that is why we have heard so many authoritative voices from the pulpit and pew. God will continue to speak, and we will listen as we move forward as the church.

Eleanor Roosevelt once opined:

> *The future belongs to those who believe in the beauty of their dreams.*[68]

Almost forty years ago, members and friends at First Church adopted a motto. It appears on all our bulletins and most other informational and promotional material:

> *The First Congregational Church of Coventry*
> *Where Dreams and Visions Become Reality.*

Warren Bennis, somewhat of a guru for training in leadership skills, defined leadership in the following way:

> *Leadership is the capacity to translate vision into reality.* [69]

First Church is dedicated to meeting the challenges and opportunities of the future. We welcome the chance to assume a leadership role because we believe in our dreams and are committed to translating our visions of a better and more just and peaceful world into reality. I mentioned in a previous chapter that the church has a 'Mission Statement.' Including it again seems appropriate:

> *THE mission of the First Congregational Church of Coventry is to worship and serve God through word and deed. In the name of Jesus Christ, we welcome and include all people as sisters and brothers.*

---

[68] Eleanor Roosevelt, quoted in Providence Journal Bulletin, 8 June 1994.
[69] "Executive Portfolio of Model Speeches for all Occasions." Book by Dianna Daniels Booher, 1991.

WE pledge and dedicate our lives and resources to God, working to transform both church and society into more just and compassionate communities.

WE fulfill this mission by faithfully preaching the Gospel, by educating our adults and children and by living out the teachings and example of Jesus Christ. (Adopted January 23, 2000)[70]

The more I read this mission statement, the more I appreciate the genius and hard work that created it and the integrity by which it asserts its relevance. In the end, 'church' is 'a community of memory,' that is, a community that remembers and acknowledges the Creator who calls it into being and defines its message and mission. We are tied to and dependent upon our past, but we are always turned toward the future, committed always, from pulpit and pew, to preach and teach Jesus Christ and to live as His disciples in a sacred covenant and calling to transform both church and society into more just and compassionate communities.

These troubled times and our uncertain future require that we be effective and faithful. In a book by Stephen R. Covey, *The 8th Habit: From Effectiveness to Greatness,* which was published in 2004 as a sequel to his enormously successful *The 7 Habits of Highly Successful People,* Covey defines the 8th habit as the finding of your own voice and the inspiring of others to find theirs to support a single guiding ethic- service above self.[71] That habit captures the essence of what I think happened repeatedly at First Church over these five decades of ministry. This collection of memories and messages has been precisely about your voice and mine, coming forth from pulpit and pew. I hope that my voice has motivated each of you to discover and employ your own in the pursuit of our common objective. I have referred to the voices of our fathers and mothers, sons and daughters, friends and neighbors throughout this book and have done so with admiration and appreciation for their truths and their insights. I was, therefore, not surprised to learn that when Covey was pressed to identify

---

70 Much to the great credit of the church, it has since adopted a more explicitly inclusive mission statement- an Open and Affirming Statement

71 Covey, The 8th Habit, p. 299.

the source of his greatest life truth-teller, it was his grandfather. As a grandfather, now settled in retirement, I respectfully choose to conclude with his sagely wisdom, fully appreciative that it simply captures and presents the wisdom of the ages and sages.

> *Life is a mission and not a career, and the purpose of all our education and knowledge is so that we can better represent Him and serve that mission of life in His name and toward His purposes.*[72]

---

[72]   Covey, The 8th Habit, p. 316.

APPENDIXES

APPENDIX #1

The Vestry Project
1965-1975

The Man from New London
(Stanley John Carpenter Harris)
and
The Woman from Coventry
(Ethel Crickmore Cargo Harris)

by
Glenden Dunlap

August 31, 1994
(Reprinted with permission)
****

Preface
by Bruce J. Johnson, Pastor

In 1965, while a 'Man from New London,' Stanley J. C. Harris, and a 'Woman from Coventry,' Ethel C. Harris, were organizing the members and assessing the resources of the First Congregational Church of Coventry before tackling what is now proudly referred to as 'The Vestry Project,' I was a senior at Branford High School. My heart thought that it had a reasonable sense of where I would go and what I would do, college and then a career in some professional field. (By my senior year in high school, I knew that I would not be playing for the New York Giants, Boston Celtics, or New York Yankees!) The ordained Christian ministry was not among the serious choices. Some eight years later, on April 29, 1973, the members of First Church called me to be their thirty-fourth pastor. Indeed, while I was preparing for ministry, they were getting ready for me! On June 15, 1973, at the First Congregational Church of Branford, I was ordained with Leonard Gillon, representing the congregation in Coventry, participating in the symbolic 'laying on of hands' ceremony. To this day, Len lists that moment as one of his most significant. It was special for me too!

Today, some twenty-two years later, I often wonder what would have become of my life, my ministry and me had Len not participated in my ordination service? From the very beginning we have been right for each other, and I don't doubt for a minute that when Len placed his hand upon me that night, the spirit of faith, good-heartedness and generosity that have been so characteristic of this congregation were among the bestowed gifts. When Lois and I showed up in September, I simply took my spot and joined in on both the serious and comical aspects of our adventure of faith. The strength of our church, at least from my perspective as pastor, has always resided in and emanated from the living faith and hard work of the membership. The few pages that follow are about the accomplishments of the congregation during the decade of 1965-1975. This record connects names and faces to all the wonderful things that have been done. These accomplishments, as extraordinary as they were, however, have proved to be but the first phase of two more decades of physical expansion and spiritual development. Who could have known back in 1965 that both the "project" and "spirit" Stan and Ethel awakened would grow and come to fruition many times over during the next thirty years? Perhaps only them. This paper is a tribute to their faith, their dedication, their love of First Church and their record of accomplishment, and it is included here as it was originally written by Glenden Dunlap, without edit, but throughout, the reader can enjoy the comments and reminiscences of one Stanley John Carpenter Harris. Be sure to read the footnotes. A colorful and sometimes comical narrative indeed!

Finally, with the completion of this account, we are assured that what was done and remembered will be preserved. Glenden is to be congratulated and thanked for his effort.

****

In 1965, as you went down Main Street, the only part of the church you saw was the steeple. Right next to the church, and closer to the street, was a large two-story red house, known as the Smith property, and just this side of that was Burnham's store.

Burnham's store had a couple of gasoline pumps in front. Inside you could buy ice cream, penny candy, and you could play cards, have a haircut, there were two barber chairs, and there were three pool tables in back. You could also buy fireworks for the Fourth of July.

The 1849 Meeting House was set back from the street, so its beautiful proportions were not revealed until you passed the Smith property.

Church Lane ran from Main Street along the south side of the Meeting House to serve two houses in line behind it, the Kenyon property and the Lang property. The Meeting House had been built in 1849 on the front part of the Kenyon property. [*][73][74]

In the twenty-two years after 1965, the scene was transformed. The church bought the Kenyon property (1969), which provided some parking space, and, until it was torn down in 1985, the Church Lane House was used for church school and community services. The church bought the Burnham property (1972) and later tore it down. The church bought the Lang property (1982) and converted it to three rental apartments. The church bought the Smith property (1984) and moved it next to the Lang house. It now provides more rental apartments and the headquarters for Human Growth Services. This cleared the way for the (1985-1987) construction of the new education wing leading off the rear of the Meeting House. Church Lane was blocked, and the enlarged parking area provides access to all parts of the church property.

The land slopes down from Main Street. The granite block walls that support the wood frame Meeting House create a large basement at ground level. The north side wall has five large eight over eight windows to match

---

[73]   'Jr. Miles, what a big help he was to me and the Church project. We bought sods of grass from East Windsor for the front lawn, we had the sign made up that says First Congregational Church. We sold raffle tickets for a new car. And together many other things. To improve the looks of the church, Bob Olmstead was my right arm, thanks Bob. We did it. God Bless

[74]   'Wes Hill and I met with the Kenyon's about buying their house and all their land. Which was a big area.

the lower row of windows in the Meeting House. The granite block wall in the rear had no openings in 1965. The south side wall on Church Lane is the same as the north wall except that the only outside door directly into the basement takes the place of the second window from Main Street. The only other way to get into the basement was the curved stairways from inside the Meeting House above. [75]

The curved stairways in each corner at the front of the 1849 Meeting House extend from the balcony to the basement. In the basement, the space between the staircases has served various purposes over the years. Herb Crickmore remembers how, as a child, he played in the coal bin there. In 1965, it was the space for a kitchen and toilets. By that time, the Meeting House was heated by oil from a furnace room in one corner at the back of the basement. The minister's study was in the other corner, with a stage in between. The large open area in the basement was the vestry, enjoying the light from the three middle windows of the five in the north wall, and the two windows and the door in the south wall.

But the wooden floor of the basement, and the perennial drainage problems under it, ultimately led to the Vestry Project that engaged the congregation for a period of about five years, beginning in 1970. [76]

In 1965, the church had three ministers. After being our pastor for eight and a half years, The Reverend James A. MacArthur announced in January 1965 that he had accepted a call to Valley City and Sanborn, North Dakota Congregational Churches and would be leaving March 31. Dr. Allison Heaps, appointed by the Diaconate, served as interim minister from April 1 to September 12. The Conference Minister, Dr. Nathaniel Guptill, helped to set up the procedures for the Pastoral Committee to follow in obtaining a new minister. On July 25, 1965, the congregation, by unanimous vote, called the Reverend William E. Beldan, Jr., who became our minister in September.

---

[75] 'We the congregation use to park in the street in front of the church and across the street and sometimes block the driveway of our neighbor. Wow, would he get mad. We had a paint stripper working for us, Herb Custer. The columns we bought were all black paint. Herb stripped them and painted them pastel colors they came out looking great.

[76] 'When I saw the condition of the floor. I scarred the Board of Trustees, there was no money for repairs.

Two problems were brought to the attention of the congregation: the parsonage, and the facilities for Christian education and community service. Neither was solved immediately. [*77]

The church had built its first parsonage in the 1870s on Wall Street after the Ladies' Society had provided funds for the purchase of the land. [*78] In 1956, the church bought a new parsonage on Nathan Hale Drive. It was used by the MacArthurs, The Beldans, the McBrides, and the Johnsons until October 1977, when the church approved the request by Rev. Bruce Johnson to receive a housing allowance instead of the use of a parsonage. In March 1978, the parsonage was sold.

The big yellow house on Main Street at the corner of Mason Street, opposite the Booth and Dimock Library, housed Phillips's Drug Store, and later, Dr. Bowen's office. The church bought it in 1954, during the pastorate of The Reverend Truman Ireland, to be used for Church School and community services. It was named the Kingsbury House in honor of Louis A. Kingsbury, who had been clerk of the church for a long time and a benefactor. The carriage house on Mason Street was remodeled and used as a worship center and meeting place for the youth of the church. It was named Quandt Memorial Hall in memory of Ruth B. Quandt, who had been active in church and community affairs.

In her January 1966 report on the activities of 1965, Mary Carlson, church school Superintendent, wrote, "The fall session opened with two sessions - 16 classes involving approximately 170 children," she also described the many program changes that had to be made after a fire damaged Quandt Hall, October 24, 1965. "Two classes (the Confirmation class and the Junior High class) were moved to the vestry. Group worship services had to be discontinued and class worship services substituted. The Church School Christmas worship service was held in the vestry for both sessions."

---

[77] *Frank Kristoff was a good friend of Burnham. He came up with a price of $7500.00. Bob Olmstead and I went out and raised $3300.00 to buy the property for the church.

[78] *We brought in tons of sand for the cellar of the church that had to be moved around evenly on the floor. Wes Hill said he had a large snowplow he could move the sand around with. He worked one evening and finished half the job. He had to come back the next night. The next night we had a flash flood, the snowplow ran for high ground in the basement. The flood moved the sand around perfectly for us.

After the fire in Quandt Hall, the Senior Pilgrim Fellowship met in the vestry.

Mark Spink, as secretary of the Board of Trustees, reported arrangements had been made with the insurance company and a contractor to repair the fire damage.

Mark Spink also reported a new septic tank and drain field were installed at the church.

Susan Cochrane's report for the Senior Pilgrim Fellowship read, in part, "we had charge of the Sunrise Service as usual this year (1965), but we could not hold our annual breakfast due to the plumbing situation at the church."

In 1965, the trustees "granted use of the rooms on the east side of the Kingsbury House to the Coventry Cooperative Kindergarten and Nursery for the 1965-1966 school year on the same basis as last year."

Walter Elwell, secretary of the Men's Club, reported "member Stan Harris repainted the vestry single handed."[79]

Walter Thorp was the program chair. The Men's Club met in the vestry, early in the morning, on the first Sunday of each month for the program, and "specially to enjoy the fine breakfasts prepared by chief chef Arnie Carlson." The membership provided labor and materials for redoing the minister's study.

The Friendly Circle, as reported by Arline Donovan, purchased two drapes and three new chairs for the minister's study.

After Mr. Beldan came, in September 1965, the congregation bought land at the top of Manning Hill, with frontage on Main Street (Route 31) and some frontage on Springdale Avenue. The long-range plan for the 21.3-acre site was to build a parsonage, a church school building, and either move the 1849 Meeting House or build a new church building.[80] With only the immediate goal of paying for the land and building a parsonage, a Land and Building fund-drive for $50,000 was conducted in 1966.

---

[79] 'My gratitude to my wife Ethel, for allowing me time off from her and her chores that should of have been done by me, while I worked on the church. Also, we missed going on trips, which we missed very much. But we made up for it later on when we went across country.

[80] 'Bryce Honeywell and I fought this move. Going up on the hill.

The Board of Trustees, as reported by its secretary, Mark Spink, "provided for the installation of permanent boundary markers on the new property." The Men's Club planted 500 evergreens.

At a meeting on May 9, 1967, the church adopted a new set of By-Laws, including one that set the fiscal year as beginning June 1 and ending May 31. The next annual meeting was held in June 1968.

Holding Sunday school classes in the Kingsbury House ceased in April 1968, when the property was leased to the Watt family as a store for used and rare books. The property was sold in 1971. Stanley Harris had succeeded Mary Carlson as Church School Superintendent in June 1967. Here is part of his June 1968 report. "All furniture, fixtures, books, and papers had to be moved - either to Quandt Hall loft or to the church vestry. Only a few people appeared to do the job that many should have been deeply concerned with. Those who did help seemed to me about ten feet tall that day and have my sincere thanks."

"Conditions will become worse in the fall, as we must then also vacate Quandt Hall. How can we possibly run and organize a Church School with such inadequate housing? Can all these classes be held in the church itself, or the vestry?"

William A. Smith was the Treasurer and Richard E. Young was chair of the Board of Finance and Auditor. Here is part of his Auditor's Report for the seventeen months ended on May 31, 1968.

"The Treasurer was forced to use money in other accounts that was ear-marked for other purposes. I cannot condone this borrowing, but it has been sanctioned by the vote of the congregation, which has given this privilege to the Treasurer. I looked with extreme apprehension on the finances of the church. I am definitely opposed to the procedure of borrowing money with no provision being made for reducing these loans by periodic payments."

As Stan Harris remembers those years - "we were broke, the church mice had left us. Our two treasurers, Dick Young and Bill Smith, both told me to nail up the front door and file for bankruptcy."

In November 1968, the congregation accepted with regret the resignation of the Rev. William Beldan, to be effective February 1969 when he became the assistant minister at the Storrs Congregational Church.

The Rev. Albert B. Kittell, Pastor Emeritus of the Somers Congregational Church was our temporary minister from February 1, 1969, until June 22, 1969, when the church called the Rev. James W. McBride of Greenfield, Mass. to be our minister.

In May 1969, the congregation voted to obtain releases from the subscribers to the Land and Building fund and to sell the property at the top of Manning Hill and buy the Kenyon property, including the land on which the Meeting House stood, and the house on Church Lane.

Wednesday evening, September 17, 1969, the steeple was struck by lightning and badly damaged. The greater feeling was that it is an essential part of the beautiful design of the 1849 Meeting House. The Board of Trustees "made the necessary arrangements through the five insurance companies" to have it repaired. The required scaffolding was around it for a few months. It was unsafe to ring the church bell until the repairs were completed.

For the Diaconate, Clifford Safranek, Chair, and Leonard Gillon, Secretary, reported, "This year the church acquired the Church Lane House, which now houses a portion of our Sunday school, and we also have a much-needed parking lot."

Mark Spink, secretary of the Board of Trustees, reported - "obtained furnishings and made necessary plumbing and electrical changes to rent the upstairs apartment, furnished, in the Church Lane House. The larger apartment in the downstairs east end of the building is rented from February 1970 to another family." "The parking lot was completed in April. In addition to contracting to have the excavation completed, a good amount of time was spent in obtaining releases for permission to go upon land" from the owners of adjoining property; this required the services of an attorney."

Harriet Eaton, Church School Superintendent, reported, "In September (1969) we held classes for kindergarten through third grade in the near side of the newly acquired Church Lane property, behind the church.... In February 1970, we moved to the far side of the house to allow the apartment to be used by someone else. This move gave us a larger room to meet in for worship together, but class facilities were poorer. Class facilities in the vestry and sanctuary are very poor."

This use of part of the Church Lane House for rental housing ceased in 1971, when the entire building was made available for Sunday school classes and community service.

June 22, 1969, the Rev. James W. McBride had been called to be our pastor.

February 6, 1972, the congregation granted, "with deep regret the request of the pastor," that he be retired from the ministry and this church effective September 1, 1972. His retirement was because of ill health. Mr. and Mrs. McBride moved to their home area in Michigan.

The church's annual reports in June 1970, 1971, and 1972 give eloquent testimony to the many ways their presence and spirit had blessed the congregation.

Mr. McBride's June 1972 report includes:

"When it was decided to remain in the present location, a committee began to explore the possibilities of renovating the vestry. It was discovered that the flooring and underpinnings had rotted away, and a drastic program was innovated to place the church's foundation on solid and secure pinions. This necessitated the tearing out of the entire vestry from wall to wall and rebuilding from the ground up. A drainage problem also required extensive piping of water. The vestry has been rebuilt with the volunteer labor of the membership and friends and contributions and financial support of the membership for materials and supplies."

His report continues:

"An interesting byproduct of the vestry renovation has been that it has united the membership in working together for a common goal.... Any divisiveness that there had been among the members was replaced by a sense of oneness in working toward a common goal and purpose."[81]

Here is part of the June 1971 report of the Decorating Committee by Barbara Hill.

"First, a basic floor plan was necessary for the complete renovation of the vestry, kitchen, minister's study and furnace room areas. The new layout changed the sizes on these rooms a little and put a door through the wall near the Church Lane House, with a hallway between the minister's study and the secretary's office, to facilitate entry from the parking lot.

"The kitchen required a lot of thought and planning, and ideas were completed in a very detailed layout, drawn by Harriet Eaton, with a mock-up.

---

[81] *NOTE: Forgive me fellows and gals if your name isn't mentioned. I'm 85 years old. Names come hard to remember after so long.

"Many men worked long, hard hours during the summer and early fall of 1970, excavating the basement area to prepare for the new concrete floor. Stan Harris led the workforce that did such a tremendous job. Then Frank Kristoff took over as "head carpenter" and he and Ernie LeDoyt have done a beautiful job in the vestry and the minister's study."

At a church meeting on October 21, 1970, the Decorating Committee's proposed floor plan was approved. [*82]

The Board of Trustees is responsible for the care and maintenance of church property, so it was appropriate for Jay Gorden, Chair, and Mary Carlson, Secretary, to report in June 1971, "Direction and supervision of the rebuilding and redecorating of the vestry by the Property Development and Vestry Decorating Committee has been maintained throughout the year."

In June 1971, Mildred Truax, Church Treasurer, reported:

"And spent $4,944.82 to buy sand and gravel to fill the basement of the vestry, lay pipes, cement the floor, buy new support columns, new windows, the lumber, the wiring and lights, cut the new rear door and buy and install the new fire door."

> The June 1971 Auditor's Report shows:
> Vestry Renovation receipts: $9,347.13
> Disbursements: $9,245.21

In the 1971 report of the pastor, Rev. McBride wrote:

"There has been considerable progress in the remodeling of the vestry and the securing of drains outside the church. The church kept the cost of labor to a minimum. Funds for the renovation have come in steadily so we have been able to pay for materials as we went along."

Mr. McBride also wrote: "The Vestry Fund has renewed efforts by our membership if we are to carry through to completion of our renovation of the kitchen, lavatories and other projects inside and outside the building."

Who could have been so bold as to lead the men of the church in totally tearing out the basement of the 1849 Meeting House? None other than the man from New London, Stanley John Carpenter Harris. He was born on February 4, 1910. He moved to Coventry in 1950 from New London. He was a building, bridge, and water tank painter for UCONN,

---

[82] 'NOTE: Frank and Ernie,, "What would I have done without you two?" Stan.

both at the New London campus and at Storrs. July 27, 1963, Stan married the woman from Coventry, Ethel Crickmore Cargo, who had grown up in the church. The Rev. James MacArthur conducted the ceremony.

In the summer of 1970, Jay Gorden was chairman of the Board of Trustees. Herb Crickmore remembers how shocked Jay was when they first ripped a hole in the 1849 wooden floor and saw muskrat tracks in the mud below. As Stan recalls: "A small river ran underneath the church from the north side to the south side, onto private property. The owner gave me a rough time about the water. Later, Jr. Miles bought the property next door and put in his deed that we had the right to run water on his property."

They moved the minister's study upstairs to a corner of the sanctuary behind the choir. They took out the basement windows. They took down the stage, the partitions for the minister's study, and everything else to free the whole basement. They took up the 1849 wooden floor and all of its rotten underpinnings. Where did they put this stuff? *[83]

The floor of the meetinghouse above was supported not only by the granite block walls, but also by 5-inch support columns in the basement. They came from the State Theater, on Village Street in Hartford, demolished in urban renewal. They were so heavy it took several men and great effort to set them in place, even with the help of some green tree trunks Stan got from Fred White.

The muddy ground was dug out and leveled, Orangeburg drainage pipes were laid. Many truckloads of sand and gravel were delivered to Church Lane from Desiato's Sand and Gravel in Eagleville and spread by the men working with Stan. It was not just men of the church. One day, three young strangers going by asked Stan what was going on, and they worked a few hours for fun. As Stan remembers, "Hired a mason I did not know for laying the cement floor for $300. He was alone, and I was running scared." Cement trucks delivered cement and when Ethel went there at noon, the floor had been laid.

The finished cement floor was nine inches lower than the original floor. It is interesting in 1994 to go in the basement and notice the way

---

[83] *NOTE: It was Bob Olmstead and I who took it upon us to look at the rotted out wooden floor. The Board of Trustees said we have no money; we can't do anything with the project. I told them I would raise the money. I hired one mason to lay that big floor.

broad concrete steps were provided at the bottom of the curved stairways. The step down at the Church Lane door was later made safer when Bob Olmstead and Garland Reedy made two broader, shallower steps. There was also a step down at the new back door. Later Bob Olmstead put in a long gentle ramp almost to the door of the minister's study. [84]

When the new wing was built (1985-1987) the outside of the rear wall became an attractive inner wall. The rear doorway was cut down and the basement floor of the new wing is even with the 1970 vestry floor.

Once the new cement floor was ready to be used, new windows were installed, and the restoration of the interior proceeded.

Here are excerpts from the Decorating Committee's June 1972 report.

"The first project was the minister's study: the carpet on the floor, the material for draperies, the paint for the walls and bookcases - and the same for the hallway and the secretary's office. Before we had finished the study, we were working in the vestry: floor tile, wall and trim paint, and, last but not least, draperies and rods for the windows. (In April 1972, the church sponsored a film-lecture by William Stockdale for the benefit of the Vestry Fund. $100.00 of the proceeds plus $50.00 from the Friendly Circle was used to purchase draperies and rods for the vestry.)"

This Stockdale Travelogue proved to be the first of thirteen annual events, held in the High School Auditorium, with Stan Harris as master of ceremonies, and the Senior Pilgrim Fellowship selling refreshments at intermission.

"While the vestry was underway, so was the kitchen and it kept us hopping trying to keep ahead of the men who gave so much time to the whole project. We found some Formica cabinets that were just what we needed in the kitchen and at a church meeting, it was decided to have them installed. The Ladies Association donated a new side by side refrigerator-freezer, to make the kitchen more complete."

"There have been donations from many people of time, labor, and material things. A few of the many who have given their time and labor are Frank Kristoff, Ernie LeDoyt, Stan Harris, Herb Custer, Herb Crickmore, Bob Olmstead, Ralph Hoffman, and Warren Little."

---

[84]   'NOTE: In front of the church, the porch was rotted out. Chic and Betty Bearce, at their own expense put in iron grating where the porch was and an iron ramp leading into the church. A 40ft. timber was in front of the porch holding it up. I went to a sawmill and bought two twenty footers (ash).

The report lists many material donations. "Without the many generous gifts placed in the 'little church' on Sunday mornings we wouldn't have been able to carry the project through successfully."

The "little church" is a very well made, white painted, wooden mode of a church building not unlike our own. It has a slot in the peak of the roof to receive donations. Frank Kristoff made it, and in 1994 it sits up in the balcony.

Sunday morning, July 23, 1972, the Rev. James McBride, as one of his last acts as our minister, dedicated the new vestry.

The Rev. Robert Heavilin served as our interim minister while the Pastoral Committee conducted a thorough search for a new pastor. The Rev. Bruce J. Johnson became our pastor, September 1, 1973.

The Vestry Project continued until the kitchen was completed and the Men and Ladies' rest room had been rebuilt. In her June 1974 report, as chair of the Decorating Committee, Joan Kristoff wrote, "we visited local church rest room for ideas to use in our church. Recently, we went to the Willimantic Redevelopment Agency and toured buildings that are to be torn down, looking for reusable fixtures. This wasn't an experience we would soon forget!" Bruce still remembers going with Frank Kristoff and Ernie LeDoyt to bring back a lavatory and lighting fixtures from the Methodist church. The closets and restroom were finished in April 1975.

In her June 1975 report, Joan wrote: "This year has seen the completion of our vestry renovations. We wish to give special thanks to Ernie LeDoyt, Frank Kristoff, Stan Harris, Herb Custer, and Joe Eaton for their fine work and cooperation in finishing the work. The financial support of the entire congregation has been most gratifying." For some time, the third Sunday of the month had been called Vestry Sunday and contributions for the work received.

Anticipating having adequate facilities, the Church Council, on January 28, 1975, voted "That a committee be formed to put on dinners once a month, headed by Herb Crickmore."

The church hosted the May 18, 1975 Tolland Association Spring Meeting.

The first Supper of the Month was served on June 14, 1975. Herb has led them to this day, with great benefit to the community and to the church.

In June 1975, the congregation, the Board of Trustees, and the Decorating Committee were already engaged in many other necessary activities to preserve and improve our property.

All of our property is only a tool to enable the congregation to do what it believes to be God's will. The Vestry Project is an example of a dramatic effort to give us a better tool.

List of names of some of those who helped on this project.

Nelson and Elizabeth Bearce
Arnold and Mary Carlson
Herbert and Theresa Crickmore
Herbert and Evelyn Custer
Joseph and Harriet Eaton
Leonard and Priscilla Gillon
John Grayson
Marcus and Marissa Krest
Stanley and Ethel Harris
Wesley and Barbara Hill
Ralph and Etty Hoffman
Bryce and Ethel Honeywell
Margaret Jacobson
Frank and Joan Kristoff
Ernest and Doris LeDoyt
F. Pauline Little
Janice McCauley
Orin and Sheila Miles
Robert and Catherine Olmstead
Garland and Beverly Reedy
David and Lillian Robbins
Clifford and Joyce Safranek
Mark and Ruth Spink
Grace White
Fred White

We extend thanks to Glen Dunlap for the work he did, researching, interviewing people and gathering this information. Stan Harris has been instrumental in the accomplishment of this report, and we thank him for his time and effort.

APPENDIX # 2

"Ten Years with Bruce at First Church"
(October 2, 1983)
(Unsigned)

In his paper "FOUNDING OF THE CHURCH" given during Old Home Week, the celebration of the 200th anniversary of the organization of the Town of Coventry and the First Congregational Church of Coventry, the Reverend Mr. Nestor Light, serving his twelfth year as pastor of the church, in his closing remarks said, I quote, "Restrictions on conduct as respects amusements have passed away, but the restrictions of the Christ spirit and the law of love abide. The gospel is the same yesterday, today and forever.

"As the church has lived to see Congregationalism come to believe and become a national force whose educational institutions have become typical of the nation, their doors open to all comers. The churches have become organized for great missionary operation. Our church is associated with thousands of like-minded churches for evangelization of the nation and the world. The church faces the third century, 113 strong, some three times as it was in meeting the second century when it was alone in the field. She meets it too with the advantages of a first century. The church edifice is beautiful without and within, well and comfortably heated as compared with a hundred years ago. How a father and mother of a hundred years ago would rub their eyes to see it lit in an instant with electric lamps! It has two fine musical instruments. It has a parsonage hard to match with its Hale Library and its steam-heater. What it needs is faith! Faith strong enough to work and to forget itself. Love is the life of the church–love to God and man. It can be nourished alone by Communion with God. It faces the future with a modern interpretation of Christianity in which it has been trained for twelve years or more. It should be a modern church with a modern creed, a modern organization doing its work in an up-to-date way. But its faith must be the faith of Christ. If so, it will be three hundred years old, one hundred years from today." End of quote.

Now, seventy-one years later, were he to return here, what would Mr. Light find? Would he be pleased or disappointed? By all means I am sure he would be most pleased to find a modern church with a modern creed, a modern organization doing its work in an up-to-date way, carrying out the works of God through its deep faith in Christ.

Who, for the last ten years, has been the leader of the members of the church or the shepherd tending his flock? None other than our beloved pastor, minister, counselor, confidant, friend or what other name you may wish to call him, lovingly known as Bruce to all, but more formally, the Reverend Bruce J. Johnson.

I shall attempt to give you the highlights of the past ten years of the activities at First Church and the influence Bruce has had on them. On April 29, 1973, at a special meeting of the church, the members voted unanimously to accept the recommendation of the Pastoral Committee that a call be extended to Bruce J. Johnson to become the thirty-fourth pastor of the First Congregational Church, starting September 1st. The call was accepted.

The Pastoral Committee reported at the annual meeting that it took its time in the search for the right person to become pastor of the church and the committee made the right choice. The committee read over 125 profiles, contacted over forty prospective candidates, interviewed twenty-two and of that number heard fifteen preach, which involved traveling to towns in Connecticut, central Massachusetts, and outskirts of Boston. I quote from the Pastoral Committee report, "The facts are presented in an attempt to shed some light on the amount of effort that went into finding a minister whom we feel will carry on the good work of this church and who will minister to our spiritual need in the best possible manner." (Please stand.) The committee members were Leonard Gillon, Marion Spencer, Doris LeDoyt, Herbert Crickmore, Jane Eastman, Harriet Eaton, Kenneth Gillon, Jay Gorden and Margaret Jacobson. Not one of us has been disappointed in our choice.

In his short statement of his view of the ministry, made at the time he was presented as the candidate, Bruce stated: "The heart of all Christian ministry rests in the words of Jesus when he said 'There is no greater love than this, that man should lay down his life for his friends,' The laying down of one's life in the form of an invitation to share in the ups and downs of human experience will surely be part of our calling. Open space for the stranger and the friend must be created in one's life in order for them to share the love of Christ which has sustained us in the past, supports us in the present and protects Christ's promise for us in the future. This is the heart of everyday Christian ministry to which I feel called."

A service of ordination was held for Bruce at the First Congregational Church, his home church, Branford, Connecticut, on June 15, 1973, and attended by several from this church. The Service of Installation as thirty-fourth minister of our church was held on February 10, 1974, here in our sanctuary.

Since Bruce and his wife, Lois, many things have taken place at First Church and in the community. I will first mention some of those things that pertain to the physical properties of the church. The renovation of the vestry, restrooms and closets completed, church chancel remodeled, monitor speakers for the organ installed, a new piano purchased for the sanctuary, hearing aids for the hard of hearing, cushions for the pews, new drapes at the windows, fans in the ceiling, display cabinet for artifacts of the church and a hand-printed roll of the ministers who have served this church since 1712, all within the building. Now to go outside, repairs to the pillars and porch, the front lawn graded from the front porch to the street, making the sanctuary more accessible to all, a new sign on the front lawn, purchase of the Burnham property and repairs to the Church Lane House. All these improvements have been made possible by the generous personal donations of money, also money from the Memorial Fund and by the many dedicated church and non-church members, who have shared their skills, talents and time to work together harmoniously. Last but not least, has been the purchase of the house and land at the end of Church Lane, known as the Lang property. For the first time in the church's history, the church owns the land upon which the church building stands. The parking lot has been enlarged, thus providing a much needed space for parking as the result of the ever-growing attendance at regular church services and other functions. Thanks to the leadership of our minister, these improvements to our properties have been accomplished.

Since Bruce has been with us, he has brought new life and new ways of doing things to the church, working for a family-oriented church. New families are joining with us as they are finding that there are programs for all, from the youngest to the oldest. We have the Nursery, the Church School, Pilgrim Fellowships, the Adult Bible Study groups, Prayer Explorers, Friendly Circle, Couples Club, the Supper of the Month, Adult Choir and Junior Choir for those who sing to mention a few. All the above are possible because of the cooperation of all who work with these groups. Not to be left out are those persons who carry on much of the work of the church by being officers or serving on the various boards and committees. The women of the church have contributed financially to the church and to the various missionary projects. More members are taking part in the administrative and pastoral duties connected with the ministry of the church, such as home and hospital visitation. The church facilities have been opened to organizations of the community, providing a meeting place for each. Some of these are the Coventry Co-op Nursery, Alcoholics Anonymous, Senior Citizens, Mother's Club, Jr. Women's Club, Eastern Connecticut Dairy and Goat Association.

First Church and Second Church worshipped together during the summer, one month at one and one at the other during the vacations of the pastors. Other joint services have been held at Thanksgiving, Christmas, Easter, and other times and have been joined at times by St. Mary's Church. The combined choirs have added much to the services.

For the first time in years, and possibly the first in the history of the church, one of our members has entered the ministry and soon leaves to become minister of a church in Plymouth, CT Elizabeth Caine, better known as Leslie, was ordained at our church on March 13, 1983. She has said that Bruce has shared with her as well as the congregation what he has learned in his ten years here. He gave her support, creative suggestions and showed his enthusiasm for his church family. Leslie has shared her talents with us, serving as parish associate, interim minister, pastoral assistant, choir director and church secretary. We wish her well in her new venture. And now two more of our members are planning to enter the ministry. Like Leslie, one has been involved in the church serving as secretary, singing in the choir, and leader of the Prayer Explorers, Marie Ford. Joining her and receiving the same enthusiasm and help from Bruce that Leslie received is Susan Vannais. Both Marie and Susan are serving as parish associates. We hope that in a few short years, we may hold a service of ordination, with Bruce still our minister, for Marie and one for Sue.

Like Leslie, I am sure, many worship services are much out of curiosity as out of reverence and have continued to come. The present membership is over 430. We now also have a coordinator of youth activities, Mike Mansfield, who has just recently joined us. We welcome him.

Bruce has been active in community affairs, having served as a member of the Housing Authority, the Committee for the Needs of the Aging and currently serves as the administrator for the Coventry Clergy Fuel and Food Banks and Chair of the Human Services Advisory Committee.

When Bruce and Lois decided that they wanted a home of their own, the church sold the parsonage. In December 1977, they entertained with an open house at their new home on Barnsbee Lane. Since living there, they have been blessed with two sons, Timothy now five years of age and Peter eight months. Lois keeps as busy as does Bruce. She is a member of the adult choir and at one time, directed the junior choir. As a teacher at Coventry High School, she has endeared herself to the students and is most respected by them. As Bruce has touched the lives of so many in the community, so has Lois touched the lives of her pupils and associates.

Bruce has been furthering his education by attending Boston University School of Theology, working toward a Doctor of Ministry degree in clinical pastoral psychology. He spent several months at the United States Penitentiary, at Lewisburg, Pa. He makes return visits there in connection with the project he is carrying out with some inmates. He has shared some experiences he had there with us. We sincerely hope that he will not be, one day, kept as a permanent resident.

The Sunday morning worship services are never dull or lacking in surprises. To make a point, Bruce often says, "Isn't that so?" while looking at a person in the audience and calling them by name. The sermons for the children, or rather the children's stories, are not only interesting to them but to the adults too. When it comes time for the children's story, everyone is looking to see what Bruce is going to pull out of the hamper he has. Will it be a toy, a costume he will don, food, pennies, pictures or possibly a woolly lamb or a cute little puppy? And, oh, for the answers and remarks made by the youngsters. Morning worship has its serious moments interspersed with the more humorous ones.

After ten years as our minister, pastor, counselor, leader, Bruce may be as stated in his own words, "a few pounds heavier and a few hairs thinner on top but neither the result of being overburdened with pastoral, administrative or financial responsibilities." I believe this is all because as a leader of the flock, no task is too menial for him to do, be it shoveling the snow from the walk, moving stones onto the wall, splashing paint where it is needed, wearing an apron and slicing turkey for a church supper or out in the field where I spotted him one morning, hammer in hand, helping a member nail the rafters in place in the framework of his new home. One never knows where you may find him. Bruce has the knack for getting things done by delegating responsibilities. He has gained the cooperation of the members, staff, boards and committees, all involved in church worship, Christian education, world missions and community projects. An alive and active membership.

What would be your answer if you were Mr. Light and could witness what has taken place during the past ten years? Pleased or disappointed? I'll let you answer that.

With all of us working together, we hope, Bruce, that you will have more time to be out chasing that little ball about the golf course and, of course, more time to be with your family, Lois, Timothy and Peter.

To Bruce, a friend of all the members of the church family and all those in the community whose lives he has touched in some manner.

He listens when we need an airing.

He smiles to show real care.

He cries when we are hurting.

He laughs at joys we share.

He gives when we are needy.

He speaks what we need to hear.

He prays for God to sustain us.

He loves with trust, not fear.

May God bless you, Bruce, your family and the church as you enter the next decade of your ministry here.

October 2, 1983

APPENDIX #3

"A Celebration of Twenty Years (1973-1993) with Bruce J. Johnson, Pastor"
by
Glenden Dunlap

Regular attendance at the Sunday morning worship service with this congregation has been an important part of my life ever since I married Grace White fourteen years ago. She was Financial Secretary and Harriet Eaton was Treasurer. Since then, Paul Watson has been Treasurer, and a succession of people have served as Financial Secretaries, Doris LeDoyt, Joyce Knowlton, Joan Kristoff, Janice Hall, and currently Kris Jacobi and Marcia Campbell.

We are here to celebrate and be grateful for the Christian spiritual leadership Bruce has given us during these twenty years he has been our pastor.

> Bruce is a son and a son-in-law.
> He is a brother and a brother-in-law and an uncle.
> He is a husband and a father.
> Since the congregation sold the parsonage sixteen years ago, Bruce and Lois are householders, with a home of their own with their two sons.
> Bruce is a golfer and a jogger, at least, he was.
> He is an expert turkey carver as a part of Herb Crickmore's Supper of the Month crew.

Bruce is an unusually well-educated man. A graduate of Bucknell University, he came to this congregation twenty years ago, fresh from

Yale Divinity School with a Master of Divinity degree. While being our pastor, he has continued to study, and two years after coming here, earned a Master of Sacred Theology degree at Yale Divinity School.

Bruce's academic program took a detour when he spent his 1982 sabbatical leave in the chaplain's department in the Federal Penitentiary in Lewisburg, Pennsylvania, the town where Bucknell University is located and where Lois's family lives.

Early in his ministry here, Bruce helped found HUGS, Human Growth Services, Inc., a counseling agency. So it was natural for him to study pastoral counseling, and in 1989, the School of Theology at Boston University awarded him the Doctor of Ministry degree.

Bruce wears these academic achievements with great modesty. He does not expect us to call him Doctor or Doc. or to note the three doctoral bars on the sleeves of the pulpit robe. It is wonderful that we all feel comfortable with him.

What is twenty years? 1973-1993. Watergate. Nixon, Ford, Carter, Reagan, Bush, Clinton. Through these twenty years, faithful people in this congregation have worked with Bruce to be a blessing to this community.

In our congregational church, part of the United Church of Christ, there are only two sacraments, The Lord's Supper and Baptism. In his first twenty years with us, Bruce has presided at more that 200 communion services.

"This is my body which is broken for you"

"This cup is the new covenant in my blood."

He has baptized 411 individuals, mostly infants and children, and he made every one of the 200 services which included baptism, a special service by relating the lectionary text to the sacramental act in which those being baptized, their sponsors, and the congregation were participating.

Through the years, faithful people like Grace, Margaret Jacobson, Barbara Palmer, and Lucille Morse, have given the children a church school experience, using whatever facilities were available. Now, using much improved facilities, a group of dedicated teachers led by Barbara Namm, Marilyn Plowman, and Robin Carlson continue the work. Mary Ellen and Jim Hetrick are now the coordinators of youth ministry, continuing the work Mary Ellen took up in 1984 when Lucius Watson was chair of the Board of Christian Education.

For twenty years, Bruce has annually led a group of young people through a careful class preparation for the experience of confirmation as full members of the church.

Bruce has led the congregation in twenty seasons of Advent and Christmas, and twenty seasons of Lent and Easter.

He has preached nearly a thousand sermons, taking the Bible reading from a lectionary and facing the challenge each time of finding in it what might be God's message for us. Except on Communion Sundays, Bruce gives a children's story that is related to the children's real lives and to the theme of the day's sermon. They are real conversations because he knows the children by name and their family situations and listens to their responses.

The 1985-1986 Sunday school year was especially challenging because we no longer had the use of the Church Lane House, which was demolished to make way for the construction of the new Center for Christian Education. So our Nursery-Kindergarten, First Grade, Junior and Senior PF and Adult Bible Study met in the vestry. Grades Two-Six met at the Richard Risley Dance Studio in the building next to the church.

In the October 1986 Church Call, Bobbie Namm, Superintendent, reported, "Although Sunday School doesn't officially start until October 5, the teachers already have contributed much of their time and effort to prepare for this day. They have helped paint the rooms, carry supplies, and sort through boxes saved from the Church Lane House.

October 1986 was also the beginning of Children's Church. On the first Sunday of the month, all the Sunday school classes come into the sanctuary for a brief but complete worship service led by Bruce. As Marilyn Plowman wrote, "Everyone enjoys the opportunity to sing hymns of praise and celebration together and to listen to an enthusiastic and colorful message directed to the youngest children but reaching all, even the high school teens."

The Sunday Schedule then was Sunday school 9:30 –10:30, and worship at 11:00. From December 1991 until May 1992, a trial was made of having a two services Sunday morning schedule, with a service at 9:00 at which the Sunday school children could be present with their parents for the first half hour, and another worship service at 11:00. Bruce was disappointed when the congregation felt this was divisive and not additive and voted to return to a single worship service at 10:15, Sunday school to be 9:00 to 9:50 with Children's Church on the first Sunday. The challenge remains to provide some kind or worship opportunity for parents who drop off their children for Sunday school and neither stay nor come back for the regular service.

For the 350 weddings Bruce has performed in these twenty years, he has always endeavored to provide as much premarital counseling as possible and to highlight the spiritual significance of the occasion.

For the 316 funerals he has conducted, he has always met with the bereaved and tried to have it be a healing experience for all.

In these twenty years, Bruce has taken part in over 200 regular monthly meetings of the Church Council, and in twenty regular annual meetings of the congregation, and in many special meetings.

He has written over 200 letters for the monthly newsletter, the Church Call, to go with its other reports of church activities. He has written twenty annual reports to go with the annual reports of the staff, boards, and committees.

These provide an extraordinarily complete history of the congregation's activities.

June 15, 1973, Bruce was ordained to the Christian ministry by the New Haven East Consocation of the Connecticut Conference of the United Church of Christ. In his June 1988 letter in the Church Call, he wrote, "That ordination took place at the First Congregational Church in Branford, and among the dignitaries who took part in the 'laying on of hands' was the chair of the Search Committee for First Church, Coventry, Len Gillon. Not long after the service, Herb Crickmore and Frank Kristoff drove a U-Haul truck to New Haven's Yale Divinity School for moving our couch, chair, rockers, one mattress (no bed…just mattress), one rug, and a few other domestic items to your parsonage in anticipation and preparation for our coming to Coventry, me as the pastor of our church. I am still very proud and glad that Len participated in my ordination, and every time I think of Herb and Frank and that big truck and our few possessions, I chuckle."

Now, twenty years later, we are grateful to that Search Committee, which also included Doris LeDoyt, Herb Crickmore, Harriet Eaton, Margaret Jacobson and Kenny Gillon, and to the congregation who committed themselves to grow with their new young pastor.

Inspired by Bruce's example, four of our people were called to ordained ministry.

Leslie Kennard attended Yale Divinity School and was ordained here on March 13, 1983. Since October 8, 1989, she has been our Associate Pastor.

Susan Prichard attended Bangor Theological Seminary and was ordained here on March 13, 1988. Susan has had special training and experience as an interim minister.

Tom Adil had graduated from Drew University. He resumed studying there, receiving his Master of Divinity degree on May 20, 1989. He was ordained June 9, 1989, in the Newent Congregational Church where he was serving as a Licensed Minister. He is now the minister of a church in Quakertown, PA, near Philadelphia.

Marie Ford completed her undergraduate work at St. Joseph's College and graduated from Andover Newton Theological Seminary. She was ordained here on June 3, 1990, and is now the minister of the Thompson Congregational Church.

Hymns are poems set to music. They can be prayers or affirmations. They help us all, young and old, to experience the Christian message. The congregation and the choirs, Senior, Youth, Cherub, all benefit from the work of Margo Lazzerini, our Director of Music, since January 1986.

After Pauline Little retired from active duty as Church Clerk, Barbara Brand was elected in her place, February 12, 1984. In her summary of the 1988 Annual Meeting appears:

Bruce explained that Chuck Waugh would sell to the church an IBM AT computer for the church office at a cost of $1,500, which is $500 less than the retail value. Bruce stated that if anyone would like to make a donation toward the purchase of this computer, they could speak to him after the meeting. (Someone did approach Bruce and purchased the IBM AT computer for the church office, and both Bruce and I agree it has made working in the office easier, faster, and more efficient. The computer and its software are compatible with what Bruce has at home and with the one Paul Watson uses in his office, which is very helpful.)

The Christian spirit, the kindness, the confidentiality of the church office remain the same. The tools and the skills to use them change.

Today our congregation owns the church building with its beautiful and functional Center for Christian Education, a large parking lot, and two houses holding six residential apartments, and the offices of HUGS, Inc. We also owe a $400,000 mortgage and a $19,000 sewer assessment.

This didn't happen by chance, but by the generosity, hard work, and faithfulness of the entire congregation led by two committees.

Church School Building Committee

Garland Reedy, Chair
Lucius Watson, Orin Miles, Susan Prusack, Roy Palmer, David Caldwell, Ken Gibbs, Dudley Brand, Theresa Crickmore, Ruth Spink, Tom Kolodziej, Ethel Harris, (alt.), Emily Miles, (alt)

Church School Financial Committee
and Task Group Chair

Rev. Bruce Johnson, Minister
Rev. Richard Whitney, Director
    Peter Sturrock, General Chair
    Scott Rhoades, Brochure
    Ruth Spink, Publicity   Larry Naviaux, Visitor
                                   Recruitment

F. Pauline Little, Visitor Recruitment   Mark Spink, Policy Forms
    Lucius Watson, Group Meetings
    Ethel Harris, Clerical
    Susan Prusack, Auditing
    Joan Kristoff, Follow-Up

December 2, 1984–Celebration Sunday climaxed a successful campaign by mail and personal visits to secure pledges for three years for a building fund. We had fine local leadership and were materially helped by the professional experience of the Rev. Richard Whitney of the Church Finance Advisory Service of the United Church Board of Homeland Missions.

In the meantime, the Building Committee had some preliminary drawings by David Caldwell, and had chosen Dziki and Associates as architect.

September 23, 1984–Voted to purchase the Smith property, a big, red, four apartment house then right next to the church. This purchase was aided by the bequest of Alfred G. Crickmore, our oldest and longest member, who died June 21, 1984. In November 1985, the Smith building was moved to be behind the church, thus clearing the land for parking.

June 23, 1985–Annual meeting authorized trustees to seek a $412,000 construction loan for the whole church facility, not only the new building. There was a Groundbreaking Ceremony after the meeting.

July 1985–Church Lane House razed, to make way for a new building.

September 29, 1985–The bids from general contractors were too high, so it was voted that the church, through its Building Committee, should be the general contractor, and to employ Kart Construction Services, Inc. with Arthur England as Superintendent and with Garland Reedy and Dudley Brand to be the church's authorized representatives.

November 1985–Foundations had been poured for the Center for Christian Education and for the relocation of the Smith Building.

By May 1986, the building was up and a lot of painting and finishing was being done by volunteers. There was an informal open house on December 7, 1986, but the formal dedication was postponed to July 12, 1987 to coincide with Coventry's 275 Anniversary Celebration.

REPORT OF THE TREASURER REGARDING THE FINANCING OF THE CENTER FOR CHRISTIAN EDUCATION

Fellow members:
On May 23, 1986, we finally had a closing for our construction mortgage at the Savings Bank of Manchester. The financial has indeed been troublesome. The bank required the rental properties to be separately conveyable; therefore, we needed additional surveying work. We were resolving difficulties with the surveyor, so the request was temporarily postponed. When the additional work was completed, we discovered a part of the property was in a flood zone therefore; we

needed flood insurance. In order to obtain flood insurance, we needed elevation certificates and had to go again go back to the surveyor. When the certificates were received, Laura Barrette sent them express mail to the insurance agent. Once we got the flood insurance, we found that the bank appraiser had not completed his work. I personally escorted him around the properties and gave him my copy of the plans so he could rush his report. The attorneys then had to prepare and review all the paperwork. At the closing, Dave Rappe's file must have been two inches thick with various documents to be signed.

I would like to publicly thank Roger Somerville, Commercial Loan Officer at the Savings Bank of Manchester, for working with the church during our complications. He had advanced $150,000 to us unsecured and with no personal guarantees. Without his help, the project would have been shut down in early March.

At present, we have spent approximately $259,000 for the project, plus paid off two mortgages amounting to about $95,000. We have borrowed $230,000, of which around $30,000 is being held to pay outstanding bills. Our financial situation is back in line with the original plan. Our only concerns now are that we not exceed the budget and that pledges are paid in a timely manner.

Respectfully submitted,
Paul L. Watson, Treasurer

Paul Watson's status report of September 19, 1986, showed for twenty-eight lines the costs to date, the estimated costs to complete, and the total estimated costs. The total estimated cost for the education wing was $472,899.52, and for the total facility $621,588.21. The congregation voted October 19, 1986 to liquidate the building stock portfolio, appropriate $14,000 from the operating fund surplus, and secure an additional line of credit not to exceed $75,000.

Clearly, it was a tremendous effort. The original building fund pledges were for 1985, 1986 and 1987. Then we were asked to continue them for two more years, 1988, 1989. Since then, the support of the entire facility is part of our regular budget, with both the income from the apartments, and from other uses of our facilities, and the taxes and costs being included.

We are indeed indebted to Barbara Caldwell, Betsy Sturrock, Gordon Smith and all who have served on the Board of Finance in conducting the annual pledge drive every spring.

In this review of Bruce's first twenty years as our pastor, there are hundreds of things I have not mentioned. Bruce is intimately involved in all of them and brings a blessing to them. Bible study groups, bereavement groups, interfaith relations with our Jewish and Catholic neighbors, are examples.

Let me end with Bruce's words from his June 1993 annual report.

> Finally, and in closing, I want to thank the staff for their dedication and hard work. Leslie's illness, of course, has been a source of great concern to us all but we will continue to be vigilant in our prayers for her full recovery and her return to her pastoral ministry among us. As always, Barbara, Margo, Herb, Jim and Mary Ellen have given themselves unselfishly so that our church could be the lively, vital and faithful community that it has become. Paul, Mark, Kris and Marcia handled the business and financial affairs of the church with remarkable competence. I remain in their debt and look forward to another year of being their colleague in ministry.

As we begin our third decade together, may Jesus Christ be praised!

****

APPENDIX #4

DEDICATIONS

The story of a congregation can be told from many perspectives. As I look back over the past thirty-seven years, however, and reflect on our successes and failures, our high and low moments, I am moved by the realization that no viewpoint would be more appropriate and therefore, significant, than what I am calling the "Dedication and Dedications" perspective. Because of the dedication of one generation upon another, our congregation has gathered often for "services of dedication," carefully and creatively crafted to honor our fathers and mothers, sons and daughters, brothers and sisters and friends for their faithfulness, commitment, and generosity. *To the glory of God* and *In Memory of ...* have been mantras of gratitude and recognition that we have repeatedly sung. Indeed, when future generations want to know who we were and what we were about in this time and place, one way for them to access the information will be to read through all the dedicatory services that have been conducted over these few decades. They include names and life stories and lasting legacies, which, when preserved, especially in print, establish a living testimony to the dedication and accomplishments of this congregation. In addition, while they pay tribute to the memory of lives and love already given to the Lord, they offer at the same time the unique opportunity for the present generation to rededicate itself to the faith and well-being of the next. This has clearly and nobly been the case at First Church.

Whenever we sing that wonderful hymn "I Sing a Song of the Saints of God" I first look for Joan Kristoff in the congregation and smile because it is one of her favorites. Then, I think not only of all those who have preceded us, 'the saints of God,' the people just like you and me who have kept the faith so that we could bequeath it to the next generation, but also those presently involved in our various ministries. The story of a congregation is about the 'saints of God' past and present, people who 'dedicate' acquisitions and projects that enhance worship, beautify our sanctuary, our Center for Christian Education, and our grounds as a way of honoring others while they rededicate themselves.

I include in this Appendix the various 'Services of Dedications' as a way of re-telling the story of our congregation over these past thirty-seven years.

I. CHANCEL PROJECT

The first project and then its Service of Dedication of my pastorate involved the redesign and reconstruction of our sanctuary chancel. Years of small installments of neglect had taken their toll. For many years, the church held fast to its hopes for a renovation of the chancel. Jack Westland had submitted sketches of a possible redesign many years prior to the actual commencement of the project. Absent the necessary courage, consensus and resources, however, nothing had been done. Upon my arrival and armed with what turned out to be forgivable inexperience and youthful enthusiasm, we pressed forward, using donated labor for the destruction part of the project and the skilled carpentry work of Mr. Robert Flint for its reconstruction. The present chancel results from our perseverance, and to this day, it enhances worship, always *To the Glory of God and In Memory of … John W. Rose, son of Herbert and Carol Rose, Bertha G. Flint, (Bob's mother) and Herbert W. Couch,* the longtime member and chairman of our Stewardship Committee.

FIRST CONGREGATIONAL CHURCH OF COVENTRY, CT
Organized in 1712

WORSHIP SERVICE

June 13, 1976   11 a.m.

PEOPLE'S MEDITATION: *God is not to be worshipped with sacrifices and blood; for what pleasure can He have in the slaughter of the innocent? But, with a pure mind, a good and honest purpose. Temples are not to be built for him with stones piled high; God is to be consecrated in the breast of each.* (Seneca)

I - THE GATHERING OF GOD'S PEOPLE

ORGAN PRELUDE   "Air" J. S. Bach
*PROCESSIONAL HYMN "The Church's One Foundation"   #260
CALL TO WORSHIP

Leader:	Good morning. Today we sing a Song of the Saints of God who were patient, brave and true.
Response:	Good morning. We remember those who toiled and fought and lived and died for the Lord they loved and knew.
Leader:	But they lived not only in ages past. There are many more living still.
Response:	The world is bright with the joyous saints who loved to do Jesus's will.
Leader:	So, let us gather to recite this song and revere our past and rejoice in our future. Let us pray.

PRAYER OF INVOCATION (In Unison)

Our heavenly Father, through all the ages you have been at work in our lives with your heavenly grace, granting us your guidance, comfort and support. We ask you now to grant us the awareness of your Holy Spirit. Enable this hour to be one of meaning and promise. We humbly pray that as we gather to worship and glorify your name, we may be blessed and allowed to recommit our lives to you. Through Jesus Christ our Lord. Amen.

THE LORD'S PRAYER

UNISON READING: Statement of Faith for the UCC
*THE GLORIA PATRI
THE ACTS OF THE CHURCH and MOMENT OF CONCERN

II - THE MINISTRY OF THE WORD

THE OLD TESTAMENT LESSON   Isaiah 6:1-8
THE NEW TESTAMENT LESSON   Romans 8:12-17
THE CALL TO PRAYER

Leader:	The Lord be with you.
People:	And with thy Spirit.
Leader:	Let us pray. O Lord, show Thy mercy upon us.
People:	And grant us Thy salvation.
Leader:	O God, make clean our hearts within us.
People:	And take not thy holy spirit from us.

A time for silence, pastoral prayer, and choral response
Pastoral Prayer:

THE CHILDREN'S STORY "Signs of Forgiveness"
THE SERVICE OF CONSECRATION
        Offering & Offertory
        *Doxology & Dedication of Gifts
*HYMN   "Faith of Our Fathers" #365

III - THE SERVICE OF DEDICATION

SERMON: "Sent from God"

ANTHEM "   Let Us Now Praise Famous Men" R. Van Williams

THE ACT OF REMEMBRANCE

John W. Rose
Bertha G. Flint
Herbert W. Couch

PRAYER OF DEDICATION
*RECESSIONAL HYMN   "For All the Saints"   #306
BENEDICTION
ORGAN POSTLUDE: "Menuetto"   Mozart

Minister   Bruce J. Johnson
Organist & Choir Director   Frank B. Cookson
Greeters   John & Frances Macyko
Guest Organist & Choir Director   Bruce Gale

****

II. CREATURELY COMFORTS

My early visits to parish members revealed their views of our congregation's strengths and weaknesses. They also served me as a way to stay informed on matters such as what brought people to church and what often kept them away. Whenever I would visit with Alfred Crickmore at his home in Columbia, I would hear both a complaint about the discomfort caused by our un-cushioned pews and the promise to do something about it someday. In March 1977, that day arrived. Because of his generosity, we could purchase red velvet cushions from the Ridges Fabric Outlet in Willimantic, Connecticut, and on March 13th, we formally acknowledged his gift and honored the memory of his beloved wife, Dorothy, three of his sons, David, Arthur and Leonard, and one of his daughters, Gladys Salcedo who had just recently died after a difficult battle with cancer. The Crickmore cushions still provide some measure of creaturely comfort to congregants to this day.

FIRST CONGREGATIONAL CHURCH
COVENTRY, CONN
Organized in 1712

Welcome to this service of worship. Please participate to whatever degree and in whatever way you may feel comfortable.

WORSHIP SERVICE

March 13, 1977   11 a.m.

PEOPLE'S MEDITATION: "To repent is to alter one's way of looking at life; it is to take God's point of view instead of one's own."

I - THE GATHERING OF GOD'S PEOPLE

ORGAN PRELUDE
*PROCESSIONAL HYMN   "A Mighty Fortress"   #363

THE CALL TO WORSHIP
INVOCATION
THE LORD'S PRAYER
THE RESPONSIVE READING: Selection 75, Pg. 520-21

*THE GLORIA PATRI

A SERVICE OF RECOGNITION Rev. Bruce Johnson

I would like to take a few moments to acknowledge the gift of the cushions upon which you now sit comfortably. We are indebted to the generosity, and most would say, the compassion of Mr. Alfred Crickmore - a member of this church for the past sixty-two years. While he has asked me to say very little and what is said should be short and to the point, I would like to share with you the spirit of this gift.

First, he gives them as a memorial gift in loving memory of his loved ones whom he has survived:

His beloved wife, Mrs. Dorothy Crickmore

His beloved sons, David, Arthur and Leonard

His beloved daughter, Gladys Salcedo

Second, and just as important, he makes this gift to and indeed, for the members of his family, who continue to care for him, share their lives with him and allow him to remain at the head of this remarkable family.

It is his prayer that these cushions will grace this sanctuary by adding to its elegance and beauty, adding comfort to worship and spiritually, remind us of all that is good and wholesome in Christian families.

Acceptance: On behalf of the members and friends of First Church and those who will enjoy these cushions, I would like to express our appreciation and accept them in the spirit in which they were given.

Let us pray: Most loving God, thankfully we accept the gift which now graces this house of worship. We ask for your full and free dedication, that all might share in the spirit and purpose of this act of generosity. Grant that as a congregation, we may nurture all that is good through what is experienced in worship. May we truly memorialize those in whose name they are given and worthily glorify your name. Through Jesus Christ our Lord. Amen.

THE ACTS OF THE CHURCH and MOMENT OF CONCERN

II - THE MINISTRY OF SCRIPTURE & PRAYER

THE OLD TESTAMENT LESSON   Exodus 3:1-8
THE NEW TESTAMENT LESSON   Luke 13:1-9

ANTHEM: "O Jesus, Crowned with all Renown"   Oberle

THE CALL TO PRAYER
A time for silence, pastoral prayer, and choral response

THE SACRAMENT OF BAPTISM

III - THE MINISTRY OF THE WORD

THE CHILDREN'S STORY: "The Gardener"

THE SERVICE OF CONSECRATION
*HYMN: "Nearer My God to Thee"   #351
SERMON: "The Call to Repentance"
*RECESSIONAL HYMN   "Crown Him"   #199
BENEDICTION with Choral Response
ORGAN POSTLUDE

****

III. DO YOU HEAR WHAT I HEAR?

In 1975, when Dr. Frank B. Cookson, the Dean of the School of Fine Arts at the University of Connecticut, responded to a newspaper advertisement concerning our vacant organist/choir director position, the music program entered a period of extraordinary achievement. His impact was immediate and transformational. His charm and professional expertise created a legacy that has endured long beyond his tenure as our Director of Music, which, sadly, ended prematurely with his death on February 2, 1977 at the age of 64.

Although his time with us was short, it was significant. The standards he set for himself as our organist and the choir, as its director, were high, but together they strived for excellence and indeed, thrived on the challenge. One project that came to fruition shortly after Dr. Cookson died was the installation of a set of speakers just for the choir, positioned so that there would be no delay in hearing the notes from the organ speakers, which we located in the back of the sanctuary. To no one's surprise, when the time came for these speakers to be dedicated, both his memory and the contribution he made to the music program of the church and that of Mrs. Elizabeth King were to be gratefully acknowledged. The service that follows represents what we did and said on that day.

THE FIRST CONGREGATIONAL CHURCH, COVENTRY, CT
Organized in 1712

Welcome to this service of worship. You are invited to participate to whatever degree and in whatever way you may feel comfortable.

WORSHIP SERVICE
DEDICATION SUNDAY

FEBRUARY 5, 1978   11 a.m.

PEOPLE'S MEDITATION: "The church lives by its memory and its hope...The church finds the source of its inspiration in the memory of God's acts in which He has communicated His presence, His saving power and His love."

I - THE GATHERING OF GOD'S PEOPLE

ORGAN PRELUDE: "Benedictus"   Reger
"Adagio from Duet for violin and viola" Ludwig Spohr

*PROCESSIONAL HYMN: "Holy, Holy, Holy" #251

THE CALL TO WORSHIP
INVOCATION (in unison)
THE RESPONSIVE READING: Selection 106, Psalm 139
*THE GLORIA PATRI

THE SERVICE OF DEDICATION with Special Anthem

"By the Waters of Babylon"
-Dr. Frank B Cookson

Monitor Speakers
Given in Loving Memory of
Elizabeth K. King
Frank B. Cookson
By Family and Friends
Dedicated February 5, 1978

Music enjoys a special place in all our lives. It provides rare moments of insight and private experiences of truth that cannot be expressed in language or taught. They come only through the mystical expression of music. There is a charm and mental movement that only music can provide.

For others, music provides an occasion for pure entertainment during which we can respect a musician's gift and be lifted by our emotional and spiritual experience of a performance.

Within the context of worship and the life of the church, music finds its most significant meaning in the message it proclaims and the associations it nurtures. It brings us together as a family of faith around familiar hymns. We feast on the sounds in an anthem by the choir; the pure pulse of a well-played organ and the full-throated congregational singing, which is sometimes on key and sometimes off.

Today, we dedicate our new monitor speakers to the memory of two people who loved music for all three reasons.

Elizabeth K. King died on January 1, 1977, at the age of eighty. As a Kingsbury, she was certainly no stranger to this congregation, nor was she as a King. A tiny woman in stature, she was oversized in spirit. Her family was her greatest love, but life itself followed not far behind. She was a feisty little lady whom I felt was as stubborn and vocally resistant to change in her church as she was about giving up on life and submitting to illness. I think she was proud of her heritage, respected time-tested traditions and preferred simplicity.

We now dedicate this speaker system in her name, that it may always breathe life into the fellowships gathered here and remain as a testimony to her life and to her faith.

Dr. Frank B. Cookson was our organist and choir director from August 1975 to his death on February 2, 1977. He was a kind and gentle man whose talents and abilities were recognized frequently. He was a man of few words, but what spoke for him was a spirituality that emanated from his being and was clearly present in his music. His spirituality was graceful and the sense of community he helped create was inclusive. Our congregational indebtedness to him cannot be measured, but our choosing to dedicate these speakers in his name should memorialize for years to come the legacy he leaves among us. With affection and gratitude, we now dedicate these monitors to the glory of the God he served.

PRAYER OF DEDICATION

THE ACTS OF THE CHURCH and MOMENT OF CONCERN

II. THE MINISTRY OF THE WORD

THE SCRIPTURE LESSONS   Numbers 13:1, 14:4
                                         Psalm 137

THE CALL TO PRAYER
A Time for silence, pastoral prayer and choral response

THE SERVICE OF CONSECRATION
Offering and Offertory "Ah, Jesus Lord, Thy Love To Me" Johnson
*Doxology and Dedication of Gifts
*HYMN   "Spirit Of God"   #232
Communion Meditation: "Memory and Hope"

III - THE COMMUNION OF THE UPPER ROOM

THE INVITATION
*COMMUNION HYMN   "Come, Risen Lord" #286
THE EUCHARISTIC PRAYER
PRAYER OF THANKSGIVING
THE LORD'S SUPPER

*RECESSIONAL HYMN   "Blessed Be The Tide" #272

BENEDICTION with Choral Response
ORGAN POSTLUDE "Grand Jesu"   DuMage

Minister	Bruce J. Johnson
Organist & Choir Director	Cheryl Wadsworth
Greeters	Joan Kristoff & Peter Kristoff
Ushers	Lucy Smith, Orin Miles, Jr.
	Crystal Snow and Bruce Baldwin

****

IV. ACCESSIBILITY

THE FIRST CONGREGATIONAL
CHURCH OF COVENTRY, CT
Organized in 1712

SERVICE OF DEDICATION
OCTOBER 7, 1979

INTRODUCTION   Rev. Bruce J. Johnson

We dedicate these ramps and the new sign that so gracefully enhance the appearance of our church to the Glory of God, as a witness of faith and as a tribute to the faithful and hardworking men, women and children who made the completion of this project possible.

These ramps and the sign were born of the vision of a few but were crafted as the living commitment of the many.

We come to this dedication with immense gratitude for the many hands and hearts, without whose generosity these symbols of faith would not have been completed. We come with a deep sense of our responsibility as Christians and a keen awareness of our commitment to one another. Thus, as we dedicate them, we think not just of ourselves but also of others, the countless numbers who will now have access to worship and whose lives the God who inspires and sustains us will profoundly touch. May the sign be as a beacon to all who are looking for faith and meaning in life, and may these ramps lead them to discoveries of the love of God which abides in all our hearts, and which fulfills our most cherished and fervent hopes and dreams. Let us pray...

PRAYER OF DEDICATION   Charlie Thomas

Almighty and most merciful God, with the dedication of this new sign and the walkways that lead to our beautiful and historic sanctuary, we celebrate the completion of our labors and how they bring the body of Christ together. We ask you to dedicate this project as a living symbol of our faith and as a lasting reminder for generations that your will is for all your children to be one in the Lord. Provide the blessing of your Spirit so that we, in genuine humility, may not look back with complacency on what we have done, but look ahead with vision and commitment to challenges lie ahead. In Christ's name we pray. AMEN.

BENEDICTION
CHORAL RESPONSE by THE CHOIR

****

V. CHANCEL PIANO

April 8, 1984   WORSHIP SERVICE   11 a.m.

Welcome to this service of worship. We trust you will experience God's presence. Should you need the assistance of an earphone hearing aid, you will find one in each of the pews marked with a brass cross. Following the service, please join us in the vestry for our coffee hour.

PEOPLE'S MEDITATION:

> *For the Lord has ransomed Jacob and has redeemed him from hands too strong for him. Then shall the young women rejoice in the dance, and the young men and the old shall be merry. I will turn their mourning into joy.*
>
> (Jeremiah 31:11, 13, NSRV)

I- THE GATHERING OF GOD'S FAMILIES

PIANO PRELUDE ON OUR CHANCEL PIANO:
Prelude in C major - J.S. Bach
Allegro from Sonata K.545 - W.A. Mozart
Adagio from Sonata Op.2 No.3 - L.V Beethoven

Our Chancel Piano is being dedicated today to the loving memory of Michelle Dawn McKinney and Carol Bissett Carpenter, and our Director of Music, Mrs. Cheryl Wadsworth, in their honor and memory is performing the musical selections.

*PROCESSIONAL HYMN: "O Worship the King…." #6

CALL TO WORSHIP:

Minister:	Good morning. Come, let us sing aloud about the goodness of God.
Response:	Good morning. Although death brings sadness, faith brings a promise of new life.
Minister:	Indeed, sorrow gives way to gladness and mourning is turned into joy.
Response:	Let us pray we may be satisfied with God's goodness and grace.
Minister:	Let us pray.
People:	And take not thy holy spirit from us.

INVOCATION (in unison)

Gracious and loving God, we gather to praise you for the comfort and hope you have provided us in times of death and distress. Sustained by the memories of all loved ones with whom we have shared our lives, we seek to honor their memory by living well today. During this hour of worship, we ask for the blessing of your Holy Spirit so that Jesus, the Christ, may be revealed as Lord and Savior. And with His call and claim may we discover the courage to affirm your life and live as your people. In His name, we pray.

THE LORD'S PRAYER (using debts)
THE RESPONSIVE READING: Selection 71 pp. 518-19
*GLORIA PATRI
THE ACTS OF THE CHURCH AND A MOMENT FOR SHARING
JOYS AND CONCERNS

II - THE MINISTRY OF SCRIPTURE

THE OLD TESTAMENT LESSON Jeremiah 31:10-17 p. 845
THE NEW TESTAMENT LESSON John 14:25-31 p. 146

III - THE SERVICE OF DEDICATION

"Remembering"   Michelle Dawn McKinney
                       Carol Bissett Carpenter
DEDICATION ANTHEM   "Sing Ye Joyfully" D. Besig
A moment of silence with prayer of dedication

IV - THE MINISTRY OF PREACHING WITH RESPONSE

THE CHILDREN'S STORY "To Whom Do You Sing?"

THE SERVICE OF CONSECRATION
Offering and Offertory   "All in the April Evening" H. Robertson
*Doxology and Dedication of Gifts
*HYMN   "In Heavenly Love Abiding" #343

SERMON   "O Sing to the Lord"

*RECESSIONAL HYMN "In the Cross of Christ…" #157
BENEDICTION WITH CHORAL RESPONSE
ORGAN POSTLUDE   "O Sacred Head Now Wounded" J. Brahms

*Congregation Standing

Minister   Bruce Johnson
Director of Music   Cheryl Wadsworth, CAGO
Interim Dir. of Jr. Music Program.   Tory Owen
Accompanist for Cherub Choir   Arthur Haloberdo
Parish Associates   Marie Ford
                  Susan Vannais
Coordinator of Youth Activities   Mike Mansfield
Ushers   Bruce Baldwin. Scott Rhoades
                Lucy Smith. Sherri Rhoades
Acolytes   Delyn Hall, Summer Rhoades

For parents of children who would prefer not to remain in the sanctuary
during any part of the worship service, there have been two speakers
installed in the vestry for your listening convenience. In addition, sermons
are now being taped.

****

VI. CARILLON DEDICATION

3 November 1985

In Loving Memory of

Alfred G. Crickmore, April 6, 1892, to June 21, 1984
Nathan C. W. Jacobson, February 19, 1911, to Jan. 10, 1983
Rev. William V. North, February 20, 1916, to May 23, 1982

By Family and Friends

Webster's Dictionary defines a Carillon as a set of bells, each producing one tone of chromatic scale… sounded by means of a keyboard. As one might expect, today's bells are electronic… struck not by keyboard but by computers. We own just such a Carillon, and this morning we assemble here to dedicate it in memory of three good, faithful men.

But before we do, however, let us be clear on its purpose and how it functions in the life and ministry of First Church. High aloft in the belfry are the speakers which broadcast the chromatic tones of our electronic bells, which, when put together are the much beloved and easily recognized melodies of hymns that tell the story of God's love in Christ and God's prayer for us, that we be reconciled to God and live in peace. I am reminded of Longfellow's poem that brings to heart and mind both the bells and the message: This as a time of special meaning:

I Heard the Bells on Christmas Day

I heard the bells on Christmas Day
Their old, familiar carols play,
And wild and sweet the words repeat
Of peace on earth, good will to men.

I thought how, as the day had come,
The belfries of all Christendom
Had rolled along the unbroken song
Of peace on earth, good will to men.

And in despair I bowed my head:
"There is no peace on earth," I said,
"For hate is strong, and mocks the song,
Of peace on earth, good will to men."

Then pealed the bells more loud and deep:
"God is not dead, nor doth he sleep;
The wrong shall fail, the right prevail,
With peace on earth, good will to men."

Till, ringing, singing on its way,
The world revolved from night to day,
A voice, a chime, a chant sublime,
Of peace on earth, good will to men!

Henry Wadsworth Longfellow

Our commitment for today is to let the bells be heard…both loud and deep… For God is not dead nor doth He sleep. The wrong shall fail…the right prevail, and people's hearts will be touched, people's wills strengthened, and together we shall be known by our peace on earth and goodwill toward one another.

The men in whose memory we dedicate this Carillon would want it that way.

Alfred G. Crickmore, Ethel's and Herb's father… born on the fourth day of April 1892 and who died just last year, June 21, 1984… a member of this church since September 9, 1915. His generosity to this congregation will be felt for years to come. He provided the cushions upon which you sit, and it is, as most of you know, his bequest that makes the purchase and relocation of the Smith Building possible. The long-range effect of that gift is enormous. This congregation will remain eternally in his debt.

Nathan C. W. Jacobson… Margaret's brother… born on February 19, 1911, and died on January 10, 1983. A member of this church since 1927 and a significant contributor to the character of this town and church for so many years, he loved this church. He loved this town; he loved his farm on Cooper Lane. I can just imagine the level of pleasure he would get from hearing these bells when the wind is just right.

Reverend William V. North… Betty's husband and the father of one very fine organist, Fred. Born five years and one day after Nathan, and died suddenly on May 23, 1982. Bill was a minister of the gospel in the United Church of Christ… a powerful preacher and a man of great compassion and commitment to truth and justice and peace. He and Bet built Coral Isles Church in Plantation Key, Florida, and the gates to its sanctuary were called the Everlasting Doors. Carved into the doors were symbols of the Christian Church, but none were more important than the doors themselves, opening to let people in for worship, opening to let people out for service. We are both privileged and proud to honor him. May the bells not only tell the old, old story but also call people to worship and empower people to serve.

Now let us listen to our Carillon proclaim the gospel.

"Christ The Lord Is Risen Today"

Prayer of dedication.

O gracious God, just as the spire of this church reaches gracefully to the heavens, so may the sound of bells be telling the story of Jesus and his love. Just as the bell in our belfry has, for generations, called the faithful to worship and service, so may the Carillon now make known to all who hear it that here is a congregation that is alive in the faith and empowered to meet the challenge of our Lord to do justice, love mercy and walk humbly with our God. We ask for your blessing upon it, that as we dedicate this Carillon in loving memory of Alfred G. Crickmore, Nathan C. W. Jacobson, and Reverend William V. North, it will, from this point on, truly be a musical beacon, set not upon a hill but here in a valley, broadcasting the testimony of faith. In Christ, light expels darkness, joy replaces sorrow, and death has no victory or sting, for He is our light and salvation. All who believe shall not die but have eternal life. May the bells ring out the songs, and may they be sung aloud in gladness and proclaim with praise that the Lord has saved his people. In Jesus's name, we pray. Amen.

****

VII. DEDICATION OF PLAQUES

*OPENING HYMN   "For All Saints"   #306

INVOCATION (in unison)

O Lord, our God, we have set aside these few moments to recognize those who have preceded us in the faith and in whose memory, much has been done in the life and ministry of this congregation. We are grateful for their proud tradition of faithful service and effective generosity. Lest we forget and their story is lost, we gather this morning to dedicate these enduring reminders of them and their lives. May the words of our mouths and the meditation of our hearts express the full measure of the gratitude we feel. And, as we so honor loved ones who have died in the faith, may we be consecrated in the gospel's truth of our Lord and be empowered to live with renewed faithfulness. In the name of Jesus we pray. Amen.

THE READING OF THE PLAQUES

INTRODUCTION Reverend Bruce Johnson

We are told in the Book of Joshua that when Joshua led the Israelites across the Jordan and into the Promised Land, he appointed twelve men to take from the dry bed of the Jordan twelve stones. They would then be placed be placed where they would lodge that night so that when their children and their children's children would ask what these stones mean, they could tell them the story of how God delivered them from slavery to freedom, from death to life. These stones were to be as an everlasting memorial to God's love and the people's faithfulness.

It is within this same context that we assemble to dedicate these plaques and the donor plates on them. They are being dedicated not so much for us but for future generations. We know the individuals whose names they bear and to whose memory they are given. We know the story of their faithfulness and generosity. But lest we forget and cannot tell our children and our children's children about our fathers and mothers, husbands and wives, brothers and sisters, sons and daughters, nieces and nephews, friends and church members, we use wood and brass and place them throughout this church as an everlasting memorial. May they always remind us that the proud past and the people in it are but prelude to our present and we hold not only a debt to the past but an obligation for the future.

In faith and respect, let us read the inscriptions and remember those memorialized here at First Church.

CARILLON- whose chimes and bells call the community to worship and service, reminding everyone that the church remains at the center of our lives.

CLOCK- whose tick and whose tock times our services but reminds us that all of time belongs to God.

CUSHIONS- because your pastor disregards that tick and tock, this community can at least sit in comfort.

ORGAN LAMP- to remind us of the light that music brings to the life of this congregation.

PARAMENTS- important to the liturgical life of our church, bearing the colors of the season and their spiritual significance.

Sanctuary Plaque:

Donor Plates:

Carillon "Given in Loving Memory of Alfred G. Crickmore, Nathan C. W. Jacobson and The Reverend William V. North" …..Elizabeth North

Clock "Sanctuary Clock Given in Loving Memory of Carleton P. King - 1981 ….Doris LeDoyt

Cushions "Given in Loving Memory of his wife, Dorothy C. Crickmore, his sons, David, Arthur and Leonard Crickmore and his daughter, Gladys C. Salcedo by Alfred G. Crickmore, Dedicated March 13, 1977…..Ethel Harris

Organ Lamp "Given in Loving Memory of William H. Cope - 1987….. Margo Lazzerini

Paraments "Given in Loving Memory of The Albert Sutherland Family - 1970 ………………..Carolyn Olmstead

Kingsbury House:

Donor Plates

'In Appreciation'

"Memorial gifts, given in memory of the following loved ones, were dedicated to the construction and support of this Center of Christian Education."......Garland Reedy

Book Shelves

"The gift of Robert and Natalie Flint Dedicated July 12, 1987"
....
Bruce Johnson

Kitchen Stove

"Given in Loving Memory of Kenneth M. Spencer by his wife, Marion A. Spencer"....Joan Kristoff for her mother, Marion Spencer

Nursery and Piano

"Given in Loving Memory of Donna Lynn Jacobson by her Aunt, Margaret E. Jacobson, Dedicated July 12, 1987"...............................
Margaret E. Jacobson

Bequest Plaque

"The First Congregational Church of Coventry Bequests In Appreciation of Their Generosity and Faith Both in Life and in Death."
Donor Plates: Frank L. and M. Gladys Murray
Richard E. and Helen B. Young
Alfred G. and Dorothy C. Crickmore
....Herbert Crickmore

PRAYER OF DEDICATION (IN UNISON)

Eternal, loving God, we pray you will bless each of these plaques and the donor plates some of them display. May they be for us like the stones which Joshua had the Israelites carry from the Jordan. When people of succeeding generations ask what they mean, may we tell them the story of what You have done for us and how, in response to your goodness and grace, especially in Jesus Christ, we have tried to live out our faith. Although they may appear to be silent upon these sacred walls, may they speak poignantly of our commitment in humility to compassion, charity, and justice. Grant that as often as they are noticed, we might be reminded of our debt to those who have preceded us and our obligation to those that follow. In the name of Jesus we pray. Amen.

*CLOSING HYMN   "I Sing A Song of the Saints of God"   #481

The membership of our church wishes to thank Doris LeDoyt, Margaret Jacobson, John Westland, Nelson Bearce and Garland Reedy for their commitment to completing this very important project. Your commitment of time, attention to detail and physical labor are much appreciated.

****

VIII. THE CENTER FOR CHRISTIAN EDUCATION

The Center for Christian Education has been the most significant building project for First Church. We completed it in 1987, and it has been a reason for celebration for the church and, as is clear in this service, for the community of Coventry as well.)

SERVICE OF CELEBRATION AND DEDICATION
Sunday July 12, 1987 7:00 p.m.

THE GATHERING OF GOD'S PEOPLE

PIANO PRELUDE -   "Concerto For Oboe" Cimarosa   (1749-1802)

*PROCESSIONAL HYMN   "The Church's One Foundation" #260

CALL TO WORSHIP - Rev. David Jarvis, Pastor, Second Congregational Church of Coventry

Leader:	Good evening and a friendly welcome to you for this service of celebration and dedication.
Response:	Good evening. Tonight, we celebrate our past, our present, and our future.
Leader:	The Word became flesh and dwelled among us, full of grace and truth, and we continue to behold its glory.
Response:	We celebrate our response to this grace and truth, and through our lives, the desire that the word might again become flesh.
Leader:	The light that came into the world in Christ is again to be seen in us. As we dedicate this building, let our light shine before all people that we may know who we are and to whom belong.
Response:	In gratefulness for the grace and truth that lead and inspire us, let us pray to the Lord God and praise God for the abundant life.
Leader:	In gratefulness for the gift of love and the fruits of the Spirit, let us rededicate ourselves to the mission and ministry of Christ's church.
Response:	Let us pray.

INVOCATION (IN UNISON)

Almighty and Eternal God, whose power is always experienced in a forgiving love that is without limit, we rejoice tonight in our calling as your people and receive anew the charge to do justice, to love mercy and to walk humbly in your presence. We assemble to praise you for the abundant blessings you have bestowed upon us and give thanks for the generations of faithful Christians who, as members and friends of this church family, have worshiped and worked together that your Kingdom might come on earth as it is in heaven. Grant us your grace that we may sense your presence and be empowered by the promise of past, present, and future. May our words of dedication be heard as a declaration of faith. May our act of re-dedication send us forth with vigor and vision to address the concerns and issues of both church and society. In Jesus's name we pray. Amen.

THE LORD'S PRAYER (USING DEBTS)
*GLORIA PATRI

A WORD OF WELCOME AND APPRECIATION
Mr. Garland Reedy and Mr. Thomas Adil

THE MINISTRY OF THE WORD

THE OLD TESTAMENT LESSON Ezekiel 40:1-16
       Rev. Jim Williamson, St. Mary's Catholic Church, Coventry
THE NEW TESTAMENT LESSON Revelations 2:1-7
       Rev. Jim Williamson

ANTHEM: "Build the More Stately Mansion"   Andrews

SERMON: "A LIVELY VISION"
       Rev. Dr. Kenneth Taylor, Associate Conference Minister, Connecticut Conference

*HYMN   "We Would Be Building" #494

SERVICES OF DEDICATION

DEDICATION OF THE CENTER OF CHRISTIAN EDUCATION
       Rev. Bruce Johnson

Pastor: Blessed be the Lord God, who has done wonderful things for us, and now, through what we have built And how we live, desires that all may know of the power of divine love and find peace and joy in life!

People: Blessed by the Lord God who has enabled us to construct this facility and bring us from our private separateness to celebrate a public unity of purpose!

Pastor: May we proceed to set it apart to its proper and sacred uses, trusting that the words of our mouths may express the love in our hearts, not only for our Lord but also for each other.

People: We do now with joy and gratitude dedicate this Center of Christian Education.

Pastor: To the glory of God, as a testimony of faith and as a symbol of commitment both to church and society.

People: We dedicate this building.

Pastor: For the purpose and promise of Christian Education; For the mission and ministry of those who teach; For the growth and development of those who learn; For those, who because of their learning, live and love as Christ would have them.

People: We dedicate our classrooms and fellowship hall.

Pastor: For the study of scripture and the spiritual enrichment of life as it unfolds; for the description and development of Christian character and the clarification of values; for the affirmation of all persons and their inclusion in the community of faith; for the celebration of our unity in Christ.

People: We dedicate this Center.

Pastor: To the service of young people and the purpose of their fellowship; To wholesome recreation and fun; To joyous Christian sociability and responsible Christian service.

People: We dedicate this building.

Pastor: That all who enter and make use of this facility may find a Christian welcome; That all who meet here be guided by the Spirit of God in Christ and themselves; That all who are sent forth from here may be empowered by God's love to love and serve others gladly.

People: We dedicate this addition.

Pastor: In grateful remembrance of those who have gone before us, upon whose inspirational labor and generosity we relied. Thankful for their fellowship in worship and work, allowing dreams and visions to come true.

People: We dedicate this Center for Christian Education.

In Unison: We, the members and friends of this church and community, mindful of the inheritances into which we have entered, and the glorious company seen and unseen, whose commitment we would not have been able to build the building, do covenant together in this act of Dedication, offering ourselves anew to the worship and work of our God, through our Lord Jesus Christ.

*DOXOLOGY

DEDICATION OF THE MINISTER'S OFFICE
Mrs. Elizabeth North

A Brief Biographical Sketch of Reverend William V. North

Mrs. North: To the glory of God, and in loving memory of the Reverend William V. North, who served his Lord as an ordained minister of the gospel for forty years.

People: We dedicate this office.

Mrs. North: That it may be a place where persons can explore their faith and celebrate their freedom, can express their individuality and experience community, can find inspiration and insight, counsel, comfort, humility and humor, and can be affirmed in the gospel's hope.

People: We dedicate this office.

DEDICATION OF THE SECRETARY'S OFFICE
Mrs. Doris LeDoyt

A Brief Biographical Sketch of Ernest G. LeDoyt

Doris LeDoyt: To the glory of God, and in loving memory of Ernest G. LeDoyt who loved with his heart and served this church with his hands.

People: We dedicate this office.

Doris LeDoyt: In gratitude for his virtue as husband, father, and grandfather. In recognition of his deep faith, and generous spirit. For the enabling of honest labor and the enhancement of time spent at leisure. That the members of this church might be reminded of the sacredness of their covenant and inspired to enrich it.

People: We dedicate this office.

DEDICATION OF THE NURSERY AND MEMORIAL PIANO
Ms. Margaret Jacobson

A Brief Biographical Sketch of Donna Lynne Jacobson

Ms. Jacobson: To the glory of God, to honor Christ, to the praise of the Holy Spirit and in loving memory of Donna Lynne Jacobson.

People: We dedicate both the Nursery and the Memorial Piano.

Ms. Jacobson: That our nursery may be a place where children may: Sleep securely, play safely and grow in the awareness of their being loved by family and by this church.

People: We dedicate the Nursery.

Ms. Jacobson: For the ministry of music to those who perform and to those who listen; that we may be lifted and inspired by giftedness of both instrument and voice. For the worship and glorification of God through music and that this church might be noted for its musical expression of faith and joy in the Lord Jesus Christ.

People: We dedicate this Memorial Piano.

ANTHEM: "Psalm 95"   Clatterbuck

PRAYER OF DEDICATION AND RE-DEDICATION (IN UNISON)
JoAnn Watson

O Lord, our God, we, the members and friends of First Church, gather on this 275th Anniversary Sunday to celebrate our heritage, dedicating this Center for Christian Education and rededicating ourselves to the ministry and mission of Christ. Grant us your grace that we may recognize and rejoice in your abiding presence. We give you thanks for the faithful witness of generations and the proud traditions of this church family that give us a sense of our roots and inspire us to adventure forth in the land and time of promise. We give you thanks as well for sustaining the dream of some concerning the construction of this facility and the will of those present here, which helped transform the dream into a reality. Aware that its proper use is important, we pray you confirm for us that what we have built by the faith, generosity and labor of many will be a place of peace and pleasure, contemplation and instruction. Finally, help us renew our pledge of faith that in worship and service, in work and play, as individuals and as family, we will bring to our life together all that is true and just, pure and lovely, full of promise and worthy of praise. As we face the challenges of the future, we ask for your guidance and strength, so that with renewed vigor and inspired by the vision of who we are and what we can become, we may live faithful and loving lives. Through Jesus Christ our Lord. Amen.

*RECESSIONAL HYMN: "Joyful, Joyful, We Adore Thee" #8
BENEDICTION WITH RESPONSE: "Hosanna! I Build A House"
Edwards
PIANO POSTLUDE
Participating in the Service:

> Kenneth Taylor, D. MN - Associate Conference Minister, CT. Conf., UCC
> Bruce J. Johnson -Minister, First Congregational Church of Coventry
> David Jarvis -Minister, Second Congregational Church of Coventry
> Father James Williamson -St. Mary's Catholic Church, Coventry
> Margo Lazzerini - Director of Music, First Congregational Church of Coventry
> The Choir, First Congregational Church of Coventry
> Garland Reedy - Chair, Building Committee
> JoAnn Watson - Vice-Chair of the Diaconate
> Thomas Adil - Chair, Board of Christian Education
> Mrs. Elizabeth North - Representing the North Family
> Mrs. Doris LeDoyt - Representing the LeDoyt Family
> Ms. Margaret Jacobson - Representing the Jacobson Family

CHURCH SCHOOL BUILDING COMMITTEE

Garland Reedy, Chair
David Caldwell, Orin Miles Jr., Dudley Brand, Roy Palmer,   Theresa Crickmore, Ken Gibbs, Tom Kolodziej, Jay Gorden, Emily Miles, Ruth Spink, Ethel Harris, Lucius Watson, Elizabeth North, Susan Prusack

CHURCH SCHOOL FINANCE COMMITTEE
AND TASK GROUP CHAIRPERSONS

Rev. Richard Whitney, Director
Lucius Watson
Rev. Bruce Johnson

Susan Prusack
Peter Sturrock
Scott Rhoades
Mark and Ruth Spink
F. Pauline Little
Ethel Harris
Larry Naviaux
Joan Kristoff

CLERK OF THE WORKS
Superintendent and Clerk of the Works
Mr. Arthur England
Architect
Mr. Frank Dziki of Dziki and Associates

Special thanks are extended to all of tonight's participants, especially those who have worked to hard on floral arrangements and hospitality. Therefore, the Flower and the Hospitality Committees deserve special recognition. Following the Service of Celebration and Dedication, everyone is invited to attend a reception in this fellowship hall.

****

IX. A SIGN OF HOSPITALITY

The members and friends of the First Congregational Church of Coventry welcome you to this service of worship. We invite you to participate to whatever degree and in whatever way you may feel comfortable. For those of you with small children of first grade age and younger, we provide nursery care. Following the worship service, there will be a coffee hour in our fellowship hall, and we hope everyone will attend.

A PRAYER FOR MEDITATION:

Lord God, you have filled the world with an abundance of blessings. We see them in and throughout the created order. We experience them in people, especially where and when families gather to acknowledge and celebrate the various stages of the life cycle. Their presence brings joy to our hearts and a sense of fulfillment to our lives. Open our eyes to the wonder of it all, and may we translate our gratitude into service. Amen.

I. THE GATHERING OF GOD'S PEOPLE

ORGAN PRELUDE: "Prayer of Thanksgiving"   Oberg
*PROCESSIONAL HYMN: "Come, Ye Thankful…"   #461

CALL TO WORSHIP:

Leader:	Good morning. In a spirit of thanksgiving, let us come together to worship God.
Response:	Good morning. It is right and good to give thanks, for God has surely blessed us abundantly.
Leader:	We have been blessed with deep faith, loving families, and good friends.
Response:	We are grateful for full harvests from the land, from the sea and indeed from the heart.
Leader:	It is God who provides and sustains. Let us rejoice and be glad.
Response:	Let us pray.

PRAYER OF INVOCATION (IN UNISON)

Gracious God, by whose generosity we live and work and share in community, and from whose hand we receive all things we need, gift upon gift, all freely given, we praise you and give you thanks for the harvest of your goodness which fills our lives with good things. In love you have spread before us a table of blessings, which enables us all to be satisfied. At this table, you speak to us with words of assurance that remind us that nothing can ever separate us from this love. Grant us your grace that in the festive spirit of Thanksgiving we may not only express our gratitude for the abundance of creation but discover in a fresh way the presence of the Creator. Through Jesus Christ our Lord. Amen.

THE LORD'S PRAYER (USING DEBTS)
THE UNISON READING: THE UCC STATEMENT OF FAITH
*GLORIA PATRI

THE ACTS OF THE CHURCH AND A MOMENT FOR SHARING
JOYS AND CONCERNS

THE DEDICATION OF THE TEA SERVICE..."In memory of Jay
Earl Gorden"

It is now my privilege to preside over the Dedication of two Tea
Services... both given in memory of Jay E. Gordon Sr., one by the
Diaconate... the other by the Friendly Circle. This pastoral duty is a
privilege because of who Jay was as a member of this church and because
of the symbolism of the Services themselves.

At his memorial service, which was held here in this sanctuary a
few days after his death on July 19, 1987, I mentioned that "Things just
wouldn't be the same around here without Jay Gordon." I believed that
then and I know it now because he was the consummate 'churchman,' a
member of this church for almost thirty years. He loved the church and
churches, church meetings and church suppers, church music and church
mice, church plants and church people. You may say that is weird, but that
was Jay. His death created a loss for us and a void not easily filled. Today
we set aside a moment in this service, one that he would have thoroughly
enjoyed with all the wonderful things happening in it, for the Dedication
of two Tea Services... so that we may have a shining reminder among us
of him and his commitment to the church and its people. That they are
Tea Services is particularly meaningful. For those who give them in loving
memory of Jay, they are the symbols of hospitality...signs of congeniality...
invitations to community. May they serve us well for years to come, and
always in loving memory of Jay Earl Gordon, Sr.

Prayer of Dedication:

O Lord, our God, we pray that You honor the memory of your faithful
servant Jay Earl Gordon, Sr., by being present to the dedication of these
Tea Services. More valued than the precious metal from which they have

been crafted is the memory of the one in whose name they are given and the uses to which they are now being offered. Grant that your spirit may set them aside for their appointed purposes. As often as they are taken from the cupboard, may they glisten with the goodness of the human spirit and shine with the light of your love that we help make evident when we serve one another. As often as we use them, may they be seen as symbols of hospitality to all to be a part of our community of faith. In Jesus's name, we pray. Amen.

THE HEBREW BIBLE LESSON   EXODUS 22:21-27 p. 67
THE CHRISTIAN BIBLE LESSON MATTHEW 22:34-40 p. 23

YOUTH CHOIR ANTHEM "All Good Gifts"   Sleeth
THE CALL TO PRAYER

> Minister: The Lord be with you.
>
> People: And with thy spirit.
>
> Minister: Let us pray. O Lord show thy mercy upon us.
>
> People: And grant us thy salvation.
>
> Minister: O God, make clean our hearts within us.
>
> People   And take not thy holy spirit from us.

A TIME FOR SILENCE, PASTORAL PRAYER AND CHORAL RESPONSE
THE SACRAMENT OF BAPTISM

CHERUB CHOIR ANTHEM: "God Hears My Prayers" Old French Melody
THE CHILDREN'S STORY: "Is There An Answer?"

THE SERVICE OF CONSECRATION
  Offering and Offertory – The Youth Choir will sing "It's A Wonderful Thing To Sing" Arr. Coates, Jr.
*Doxology and Dedication of Gifts

*HYMN: "We Gather Together" #21
SERMON   "On Owning the Covenant"
The Acceptance of New Members

*RECESSIONAL HYMN "We Plow the Fields…" #460

BENEDICTION WITH RESPONSE
ORGAN POSTLUDE: Gavotte
*Congregation Standing

Minister	Rev. Bruce J. Johnson
Minister of Visitation	Rev. Frank Duggan
Director of Music	Margo C. Lazzerini

****

X. A NEW ORGAN

"ORGAN DEDICATION SERVICE"
JANUARY 4, 1998

The members and friends of the First Congregational Church of Coventry welcome you to this Dedication Service for our new MDS-51S ALLEN ORGAN. We hope you will feel comfortable among us and share in our excitement and sense of accomplishment. When we consecrate this organ, we do so to the glory of God and in grateful appreciation of the dedication and generosity of our members and friends who shared in our vision and supported the project.

Following the service, there will be a reception in our Social Hall. Both the Board of Music and the Diaconate invite everyone.

PROCESSIONAL HYMN: *"Christ Is Made Sure"*   #263

INSTRUMENTAL SELECTION:

"A Meditation on 'Brother James Air'----Darke

CALL TO WORSHIP:
LEADER: Good afternoon. O come, let us sing to the Lord; let us make a joyful noise to the rock of our salvation!
PEOPLE: Good afternoon. Let us come into God's presence with thanksgiving; let us make a joyful noise with songs of praise.

LEADER: With organ and flute, the sound of trumpets and horns, with joyous songs of testimony, let us show we rejoice in our faith.

PEOPLE: The Lord is good because God's love in Jesus Christ has endured for generations. We are here as living memorials to the life we found in Him.

LEADER: As we dedicate our new organ, may the spirit draw us together so that we soar as if on eagle's wings to the music of heaven and earth. This service is truly a joyous occasion, and may all praise be given to God!

INVOCATION: (IN UNISON)

Creator God and Eternal Spirit, we pray you will bless our worship with the gift of your Holy Spirit. Fill us, we pray, with the fruit of the Spirit. May the time we spend together be marked by love and joy, peace and patience, kindness, goodness and faithfulness. During worship, awaken within us a deep and abiding faith. Touch our hearts with your amazing grace and bring forth new life. To the sound of melodies as ancient as psalms sung to the harp and lyre and as new as the electronic sounds of our magnificent organ, may we come alive to your presence and power in our lives. We pray in the name of Jesus, our Christ. AMEN.

THE LORD'S PRAYER (P.513) (USING DEBTS)

LITANY OF DEDICATION

LEADER: For the worship of God, in support of prayer and preaching, the celebration of the sacraments and the accompaniment of the choirs.

PEOPLE: We dedicate this organ.

LEADER: For the comfort of those who mourn, for the help of those who are perplexed, for the hope of those who despair, for the inspiration of those who are discouraged and for the joy of those who know no reason to rejoice,

PEOPLE: For the nurture of families, for the inclusion of children in worship and for the building up and for the unity of the community of the community of faith through our ministry of music,

LEADER: For the musical education and appreciation of all who may worship in this historic Meeting House, for the inspiration of those who may aspire to be musicians, and for those who simply desire to be blessed by its music and message,

PEOPLE: We dedicate this organ.

LEADER: For its place in God's plan to consecrate us all to lives of testimony and service, and in grateful remembrance of those who have gone on before us and in gratitude for our life together in this church and in history, and as a sign of commitment to future generations of the faithful,

PEOPLE: We dedicate this organ
> to the glory of God
> to the honor of Jesus Christ, our Lord and Savior,
> and to the praise of the Holy Spirit.

ALL: THANKS BE TO GOD!

*GLORIA PATRI (513)

WELCOME AND ANNOUNCEMENTS

II. DEDICATION SERVICE

THE HEBREW BIBLE LESSON   Isaiah 55: 6-13
THE CHRISTIAN SCRIPTURE LESSON   Colossians 3: 12-17

ANTHEM: "Jesu, Joy of Man's Desiring---Bach
                   (Ms. Sarah Eddy - Flutist)

PROGRAM: Introduction

INSTRUMENTAL SELECTION:
    "Praeludium and Fuge in C-Dur" ---Bach

    A Brief History of the Organ in Worship

INSTRUMENTAL SELECTION: "My Heart Ever Faithful" --- Bach

    (Piano and organ Duet with Christine Collins)

A Brief History of our Organ

*HYMN: "I Sing the Mighty Power of God" #68

The Joy of our Music Ministry

PRAYER OF DEDICATION

*RECESSIONAL HYMN: "God of Our Father's..." #433
BENEDICTION WITH CHORAL RESPONSE
ORGAN POSTLUDE: "Trumpet Tune"---Johnson
                (Please remain seated for the entire Postlude)
(*Those who are able should stand)

We are grateful for the dreams of previous organists such as Donald Hand, Dr. Frank Cookson, Cheryl Wadsworth, Bruce Gale, and Margo Lazzerini and respective Boards of Music, without whose support this project would not have been possible. Special thanks to Donn Federowicz, Jill Hackett, Herb Crickmore, George Jacobi, Irene Gale, and members of this year's board, Janice Page (Chair), Sherry D'Alessandro, Leonard Gillon, David Christiansen, Cathy Salinsky and Diane Laneri.

Also, we extend our deepest thanks to the Organ Committee for its hours of research, travel and discussion. They have completed a difficult task in an exemplary manner, and we are truly grateful. Committee members are Herb Crickmore (Chair), Janice Page, Fred North, Reverend Elizabeth Kennard, Peter Olson, Margo Lazzerini and Bruce Gale.

****

XI. SANCTUARY RENOVATION, 2000

WORSHIP
November. 26, 2000 Twenty-fourth Sunday After Pentecost 10:30 a.m.

The members and friends of the First Congregational Church of Coventry welcome you to this special *Dedication Service*. We hope that you will feel comfortable among us. Although we aspire to be friendly and spirited, we also reserve these first few minutes before and during the Prelude for quiet, prayerful preparation.

Infant care is provided for children during the service on the first floor of our Center for Christian Education. Children are invited to take part in worship, but parents should make use of our childcare program at any point during the service.

At the conclusion of the service, everyone is cordially invited to our Social Hall for a luncheon that is being hosted by the Diaconate.

Again, welcome and thank you for worshipping with us.

Thought for Meditation:

> *Love, the highest principle, is the virtue of virtues, from whence they flow forth. Love, being the greatest majesty, is the power of all powers, from whence they severally operate.*
>
> Jakob Boehme

> *He who loves brings God and the world together.*
>
> Martin Buber

ORGAN PRELUDE:
YOUTH CHOIR INTROIT: "Morning Has Broken"

PROCESSIONAL HYMN: "We Gather Together" #21

CALL TO WORSHIP:

LEADER:	We come to this time of worship filled with a feeling of gratitude for the blessings of harvest and heart.
PEOPLE:	Truth, tradition and the living faith of countless generations surround us.
LEADER:	We come to this time of worship filled with the feeling of gratitude for the blessings of family and friendship, church and community.

PEOPLE:	It is in the cross of Christ that we glory. We live in the light of God's love and this light shines forth is us.
LEADER:	We gather in faith and fellowship filled with the feeling of gratitude for the gift of life, the lessons of love, our horizons of hope and the promise of faith.
PEOPLE:	The seeds have been sown. We have heard the Good News of God's love in Jesus Christ. Let us rejoice and be glad and honor the memory of loved ones while we rededicate ourselves to His mission in the world.
LEADER:	Let us pray.

PRAYER OF INVOCATION (in unison)

O God, Creator God, Lord of all harvests, we give you thanks for all the blessings of this day. We are gathered to rejoice in our faith, a faith that has been kept by those who have preceded us, a faith that is lived by those assembled here and a faith that will be passed on to the next generation as our legacy. Today in our worship, we honor the memory of loved ones by affirming and embracing the truths and joys that made their lives so meaningful and their relationships so loving. Bless us with your Spirit that, as we give thanks for your blessings, we may bring gifts of our own. We ask this in the name of Jesus, our Christ. Amen.

THE LORD'S PRAYER (p. 513, using debts)
GLORIA PATRI (#513)

The Cherub Choir: "Lord, I Want to be a Christian…"
The Children's Story: "Let's Do a Hand Count!"

ANNOUNCEMENTS

CHORAL SOLO "You'll Never Walk Alone," **Ms. Gail Spink**

INTRODUCTORY REMARKS Rev. Dr. Bruce Johnson
In Memoriam: Rupert and Bertha Hodgkins
Scripture: 1 Corinthians 1: 10-24 p. 156.

Cross
Given in Loving Memory of
Rupert and Bertha Hodgkins
by
Clayton and Carol Hodgkins, Gerald, Lydia,
Rhonda and Gerald Hodgkins, Jr.
Ronald, Linda Heather, Heidi and Lindsey Hodgkins
Family and Friends

Prayer of Dedication:
Anthem: " Lift High the Cross"

In Memoriam: Ruth E. Spink
Scripture: 2 Corinthians 4: 1-12 p.170.
Chandelier
Given in Loving Memory of
Ruth E. Spink
by Mark M. Spink and Family

Prayer of Dedication
Hymn: "O Love That Wilt Not Let Me Go" #399

In Memoriam: William and Elizabeth North
Scripture: Matthew 13: 1-9; 18-23
Hearing Assistance System
Given in Loving Memory of
The Reverend William and Elizabeth North
By
Frederick, II and the Reverend Carol North and Family

Prayer of Dedication
Anthem: (Something with Fred and Chris?)

In Memoriam: "Loved Ones"
Scripture: Psalm 100
Redecoration of the Sanctuary
Done in Memory of Loved Ones
By Family and Friends

Prayer of Dedication
Hymn: "God, You Have Set Us" NCH #372

CLOSING REMARKS

THE SERVICE OF CONSECRATION
THE OFFERING AND OFFERATORY
"To Christ Be the Glory"
*DOXOLOGY (#515) AND DEDICATION OF GIFTS

* RECESSIONAL HYMN: "Take My Gifts" NCH #   362 (see insert)
BENEDICTION WITH CHORAL RESPONSE:
ORGAN POSTLUDE:

(* Those who wish may stand.)

****

XII. DEDICATION OF GARDEN STEPS
(An Eagle Scout Project- Timothy Wicks)
2007

Opening remarks: Reverend Dr. Bruce Johnson

We are pleased to gather for these few minutes to acknowledge the successful completion of the Eagle Scout Project for Timothy Wicks.

Every time I attend an Eagle Scout Award ceremony, I am impressed by the lighting of the candles- each representing a different aspect of the spirit of scouting- a spirit that burns in the heart of each scout.

Tim took on quite a project on behalf of the church, embodying the twelfth candle- reverence- which includes being faithful in his religious duties. As you can see, we are now truly blessed by his work. I had the pleasure of watching the project unfold and develop, the fun that was had, the hard work that was done and the significant contribution it has made to these historic and beloved grounds, now beautifully landscaped.

Here are a few statistics that were provided by Tim.

"I chose my project because it was clearly in need of being done. I had said to myself and others many times that something needed to be done with the stairs, and I decided that perhaps the best way to deal with the problem was to take it on myself."

Surveying for the project began in 2005. Fundraising was done in August 2005, and after obtaining all the necessary permits and municipal approvals, ground was broken in August 2006 with the removal of the old stairs.

In order to complete the project, several steps (no pun intended) had to be taken. First, surveying and planning were required to apply for a building permit and obtain the approval of the church's Board of Trustees. Fundraising was required to pay for materials for the project. The old stairs had to be removed, then new ones had to be installed. The cement sidewalk at the top of the stairs had to be poured, and finally, new railings had to be installed and painted and the area around the construction site had to be created and replanted.

The total budget for the project was $1954.79, all of which was raised through fundraising by volunteers.

The project required 584 hours of work by twenty-two volunteers, as well as over thirty (30) hours of planning and 138 hours of work by me, for a grand total of about 752 hours of time donated to the project's completion.

The project was officially finished on April 7, 2007.

So, today we gather to dedicate these steps to the glory of God, as a tribute to Tim's faith and hard work and that as well of all those who assisted him. We thank him for their landscaping beauty, their functionary strength, and their usefulness- as people will use them to enter and exit the life and ministry of this church.

LET US PRAY:

O Lord, our God, we ask for your blessing upon Tim, his family, all of his friends who assisted him and upon scouting itself an integral factor in raising young men to be patriotic and practical, virtuous and persons of character. Just as the Good Book admires the eagle as it soars to new heights, we admire Tim's eagle project and what these steps will mean to the life and ministry of the First Church. We gather to dedicate these steps as a sign of faithfulness, friendliness, and commitment. Although Tim will soon be honored and receive his award for his work, these Steps will stand for generations offering a safe and welcoming access into the life of our church for countless worshippers and educators, youth groups and outreach workers. It is to your glory, O God, and for their safe serviceability that we now dedicate this project. Bestow your spirit of grace upon each step and the spirit of gratitude upon all who use them. We ask this in Christ's name. AMEN.

Printed in the United States
by Baker & Taylor Publisher Services